THE BEST PLACES

The Gourmet Notebook Guide
To the Pacific Northwest

The Best Places

THE GOURMET NOTEBOOK GUIDE TO THE PACIFIC NORTHWEST

Edited by David Brewster

MADRONA PUBLISHERS, INC.

ARGUS PUBLISHING COMPANY

SEATTLE

Copyright © 1975 by Argus Publishing Co.

Manufactured in the United States of America

First printing, November, 1975

Published simultaneously in Canada by J. J. Douglas Ltd.

Library of Congress Cataloging in Publication Data

Brewster, David, 1939-
  The best places

  Includes index.
  1. Restaurants, lunch rooms, etc. — Northwest, Pacific — Directories. 2. Hotels, taverns, etc. — Northwest, Pacific — Directories. 3. Motels — Northwest, Pacific — Directories. 4. Northwest, Pacific — Description and travel — 1951- — Guide-books.

I. Title		
TX907.B73	647'.94795	75-31981
ISBN 0-914842-07-2		
(USA)		
0-88894-101-3		
(Canada)		

Distributed in USA by
Madrona Publishers, Inc.
113 Madrona Place East
Seattle, Washington 98112

Distributed in Canada by
J. J. Douglas Ltd.
1875 Welch Street
North Vancouver, B.C.

Drawings by Ann Downs; cover photograph by Bob Peterson.

Introduction

As editor for the past three years of a monthly guide to restaurants and food in the Pacific Northwest, I have been constantly getting telephone calls from friends, friends of friends, subscribers, and friends of friends of subscribers. These frequent calls for information about where to eat, where to stay, and what to do in such and such a city all underscore the need for a reliable guidebook to this intriguing region. Guidebooks of course exist, here as in the rest of America and Canada. But they nearly all suffer from the same mistake of aiming at the common denominator of travelers. Truly distinctive places are submerged in a welter of listings, if they are found at all. One might find thirty-five mediocre motels listed for a given city—but my telephoners shut me up after I describe the first few best places. Ordinary guidebooks, if followed, treat tourists like a species of humanity to be quarantined from the natives and confined to their own peculiar quarters. Being dedicated to stimulating travel or the purchase of more gasoline, these guides typically overpraise, overinclude, and overstress the value of places aimed primarily at tourists.

Our desire to do a different kind of a guide to this region is derived from four distinct goals.

First, we wanted to do a book that made clear to anyone who read it what exceptional range and quality of experiences for serious tourists the Northwest actually possesses. Being an area relatively unexploited for tourism so far, this region has not developed tourist ghettoes. The visitor and resident are therefore in a relatively unspoiled and uncharted land, where formula restaurants and conglomerate resorts have not taken such a chilling hold as they have elsewhere in the country. Conversely, individuality and character still survive.

The Northwest, we discovered, has some peculiar advantages. Its remarkable variety is reinforced by varied topography, which ranges from rain-forest coasts to English countryside valleys, to Swiss-style mountains, to cataclysmic, moonscape plateaus. Also, there is no single dominant city in the Pacific Northwest. Instead, there are three metropolitan areas, each nicely proportioned at about one million persons, reflecting the different spirits of two states and a Canadian province. The combined population of about 7,500,000 is big enough to support quality, but not concentrated enough to encourage the chains and the fads to colonize us. The rainy winter weather has helped, too, by keeping tourism in proper proportion to the rest of the economy. Restaurants and shops that must rely primarily on the local trade, the repeat business, will pay far greater attention to quality than those that do not.

This leads to our second goal. Having found places that show a commitment to quality and individuality, we wanted to put them in high profile. This meant finding these places, many of which emerged only after we would insist to our local informants, "I know where you think *tourists* should eat. What I want to know is where *you* eat when you want a good meal." "Ah, well," would come the timid answer, and we would be on the trail of an honest steak house or a little cafe that has never heard of pre-cooked, frozen "convenience" foods. We want to honor such places by featuring them in the book, and taking some space to say what it is we like. A guidebook devoted only to the best will help such places to do a better business and (we hope) their standards to be emulated by others. Much of tourism's economics depends on captive markets: the breakfasts or the bars at the major downtown hotels, for instance. We want our book to praise places that serve captive markets well, but in addition, to direct people and money to the disciples of quality off the beaten track.

Our third goal in doing this guidebook was to express forcefully a set of standards about travel that is now emerging from a long era of neglect. The travel industry, and in this it is largely supported by the existing guidebooks, has been stressing reliability, consistency, and uniformity. When you walk into an American airport these days, you are supposed to be comforted and speeded along by its similarity to all others. If one is in a hurry, he does not want complexity or individuality. It is the same with food. Chain restaurants don't hire cooks so much nowadays as they hire thawers, since much of the food is pre-cooked and frozen, as on the airlines. This "rationalizing" of business and keeping down labor costs might be all right if it were confined to the tourist traps, but it is a spreading disease. Our hams are now injected with liquid smoke, our fruit and vegetables and poultry are bred to sacrifice flavor in order to resist mishandling, and fresh fish grows increasingly rare. An article in the *Wall Street Journal* recently reported that a tasting panel rejected real orange juice because it tasted strange.

It may be true in part, as England's *Good Food Guide* complains, that "the rising generation swallows chain-restaurant sludge with affectedly proletarian docility, and is deeply suspicious of the natural concern for good faith and good materials which it confuses with bourgeois connoisseurship." But it seems to us that many in the rising generation are joining with those in previously risen generations who remember "good faith and good materials." Good cooking at home, often with Julia Child's principles in mind, has become an important national trend. Young people have gone into the restaurant business with a commitment to good, natural foods and unconventional, personalized decor. The discovery of dozens of idiosyncratic restaurants scattered around the Northwest, sometimes hip, sometimes just inspired amateur cooking, was one of our most pleasant surprises. And we encountered many examples of people who have glimpsed the fast-food and other computer-assisted revolutions, and rebelled to start simpler places with classic standards of quality and individual attention. It seemed to us that the guidebooks we know have trailed behind these developments.

Our fourth objective is to describe the way our Northwest society enjoys its own leisure, and to make this information accessible to tourists and residents alike. When I travel, I want to do the things the local people do, not be treated like some child confined to a special playroom apart from the adults. This need is the keener because the allure of the Northwest lies more in its agreeable overall lifestyle than in any dominant attraction like balmy weather, a well-preserved history, or a first-class metropolitan culture (though it has some of these elements too). Thus we have stressed things like Saturday shopping in Vancouver (followed by a pastry and coffee at Szasz), or leaving a Sonics' basketball game early in order to get a spot at Jake's bar, or heading for the ocean from Portland with a stop for picnic items at Anderson's Delicatessen.

HOW TO USE THIS BOOK

In compiling the listings for *The Best Places*, we relied on personal visits and confirmatory reports for all of the places listed. Our investigative teams traveled under complete anonymity, paid their own way, and subjected many restaurants to multiple visits on different occasions.

The rating system follows this code:

☆ ☆ ☆ ☆ *Of international class.*
☆ ☆ ☆ *Thoroughly distinguished.*
☆ ☆ *Some remarkably good features.*
☆ *A good place.*
No stars. Worth knowing about, if you are nearby.

To a small degree, we have adjusted our standards to conform with the regions; a two-star restaurant in Vancouver is slightly better than one in Bend, for instance. In addition, it should be understood that an establishment that is not listed is quite possibly worthy of listing; it may be we have examined it and rejected it for inclusion, or we simply may not know about it. The principle of the guidebook is simple: if it's in the book, you can be sure it is good.

Under each listing, where it pertains, we have indicated whether a place is "expensive," "moderate," or "inexpensive." Such ratings are based on current prices for a typical room for two in a hotel or motel, and for a typical dinner (with wine or some drinks) at the restaurant.

> *Expensive:*   *Means the room for two costs more than $25 a night; a dinner is more than $15, per person.*
>
> *Moderate:*   *Falling between expensive and inexpensive.*
>
> *Inexpensive:*   *The room for two is less than $15, and the dinner is less than $5 per person.*

Credit card symbols are probably self-explanatory: AE is American Express; BA is BankAmericard in the U.S., which corresponds in Canada to Chargex; CB is Carte Blanche; DC is Diners' Club; and MC is MasterCharge.

We have designed the book to be used wherever you are in the Pacific Northwest. At the start of each of the three major sections is a map of the state or province. Any town whose name appears on the map has at least one listing.

Finally, it is our hope that this guidebook, with its rigorous standards, will become a force for quality throughout the region. The *Guide Michelin* advises its users to carry the red guide prominently when walking into a hotel or sitting down for dinner. We hope that our demanding readers will likewise raise standards and profits at deserving places. We shall of course be doing our own further examinations of places listed and unlisted. At the back of the book are some forms that you can fill out to improve future editions. We will welcome new nominees, as well as reports of places that have changed or which you feel we have undervalued or overpraised.

DAVID BREWSTER

Contents

British
Columbia

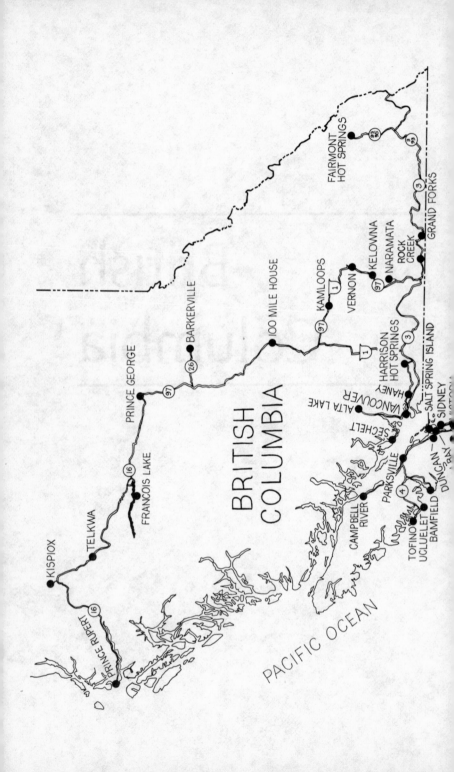

Greater Vancouver

VANCOUVER

RESTAURANTS

William Tell ☆ ☆ ☆ ☆

This walk-up Swiss restaurant suffers from an average wine list (a fact of life imposed on all B.C. restaurants by provincial regulations) but is otherwise nearly perfect. The room is smallish—and a bit noisy—decorated in heraldic style. From the very first you are placed in the hands of a corps of waiters truly extraordinary in courtesy, dispatch, and knowledge. So far as we know, the restaurant never has a bad night, so if you are willing to part with about $30 a person, you can be assured of superb food and soul-restoring pampering.

Nearly everyone on first visit has the famous fondue Bourguignonne, in a version that rescues this dish from its novelty status with a half-dozen excellent dipping sauces. We recommend being more adventurous. Superb smoked salmon is offered, either cold with onions and capers or encased in a splendid crepe and robed in a luscious swiss cheese sauce. The trout are taken live from a tank on the premises and prepared *au bleu* if you wish. The presentation of the beef dishes is excelled only by their goodness. An order of filet mignon with morels, for instance, comes in a copper dish which keeps half the serving warm while you eat the first filet in a fragrant sauce of morels and bacon, the first bit of braised romaine, the first two peerless duchess potatoes.

3

The fine selection of cheese is a marvelous way to stretch out such a meal, and—acid test—the creme caramel is exactly as it should be.

The menu benefits from being relatively limited, but you can still find veal in various excellent preparations, a pheasant stew, and a range of steaks and grills. With advance word, the chef will also do some dishes with different sauces during weekdays. Ernest Doebeli is the owner and the recipes are all his; but the great distinction of the William Tell comes from his past experience as a head waiter. As a result, you get a dinner served with all of the skill of New York waiters with none of their condescension.

722 Richards Street, at Georgia, Vancouver
Dinner only, 6-11 p.m.; closed Sunday
Reservations: 683-8810
Expensive
Credit Cards: AE, BA, DC
Full Bar

Umberto ☆ ☆ ☆

Umberto Menghi, a Florentine gentleman, has created a lovely restaurant in a small house tucked under the Burrard bridge. It is very cheering, very elegant—the bright yellow exterior mellowing into a soft cream inside; the subdued Tuscan etchings on the walls; the illuminated garden in the rear, glimpsed from one of the two dining rooms; the little room upstairs where you sip vermouth while awaiting a table; the dashing waiters; and the voluble clientele dressed more beautifully than anywhere else in town.

After such a feast for the eyes, the food may be slightly disappointing, but it is still far and away the best Italian cooking you'll find in the Northwest. It starts slow with merely decent antipasti and soups. The pastas are good, but not pure examples of the way this most misunderstood of delicacies is handled in Italy: they are slightly overcooked by Italian standards, and perhaps a little shy on fresh herbs in the sauces. The entrees are splendid: chicken cooked with dried laurel and fresh lemon, a rack of lamb in a vermouth sauce prepared at the tableside, and a capon in a luxurious cream sauce with brandy and port; and they come with lovely vegetables. The richer and more Frenchified the dishes the better, we have found; simple veal dishes that require the most exact cooking and superior ingredients suffer a bit in comparison. The wine list is not bad, and the desserts can be fine. Umberto is also a dandy place for lunch.

1380 Hornby Street, Vancouver
Weekday lunches, noon-2; dinners, 6-11:30; closed Sunday
Reservations: 687-6316
Expensive
Credit Cards: AE, BA
Full Bar

La Brochette ☆ ☆ ☆

The owners of the excellent La Creperie opened a new place a year ago, also in Gastown, that extends the range of French cooking in a delicious fashion. A large open grill, complete with a two-hundred-year-old rotating spit turned by counterweights, is the star attraction of the rustic room. Each day La Brochette puts a different specialty on that spit: beef on Monday, pork on Tuesday, duck on Wednesday (a top item), veal on Thursday, live lobsters from New Brunswick on Friday (they are split and grilled with herbs), and a whole beef filet on Saturday (glorious). The meats partake of the aromatic smoke from hardwood hickory charcoal and other woods in the fire. They are served with fresh vegetables in a Bearnaise sauce.

In addition to the daily spit-roasted meat, the restaurant has on the regular menu a very popular rack of lamb — very young lamb from New Zealand — nicely coated with a mustardy sauce, a stuffed Cornish hen, grills, steaks — and brochettes. You can start with good coquilles and end with home-made fruit tarts or a souffle. All very simple, all very nice.

> 52 Alexander Street, Vancouver
> Dinners only, 6-12 p.m.; closed Sunday
> Reservations: 684-0631
> Moderate
> Credit Cards: AE, BA, MC
> Full Bar

Pasparos Taverna ☆ ☆ ☆

Maybe it's the rain all winter long that prompts many diners to seek relief in sun-splashed Greek restaurants; at any rate, this city has many good ones of which this is the best. Pasparos is gaily decorated like a country inn inside; outside is a patio covered by a striped awning and boasting a view back over Burrard Inlet to the romantic evening skyline of Vancouver. Such a steady stream of customers comes to this eatery in North Vancouver that seating in the patio cannot be guaranteed. No matter: the food is just as delicious inside.

The menu is extensive, with many dishes carefully prepared and boldly spiced. The lamb is particularly good, as are the lightly broiled fish, the prawns, and the usual kebabs, dolmathes, and keftedes. A fricasse of lamb, artichokes, and beans may sound like leftovers, but it becomes a superior dish here. The more exotic items, like a casserole of stuffed squid, are also extremely good. The wine list is well selected, and you'll end with a selection of delicious sweets. Not many Greeks eat here, but you'd think you had found Greece.

> 132 West Third Street, North Vancouver
> Daily, 5-12 p.m.; Sunday, 5-10:30 p.m.
> Reservations: 980-0331
> Moderate
> Credit Cards: AE, BA, MC
> Full Bar

Toulouse Lautrec ☆ ☆ ☆

The problem with Vancouver French restaurants, in addition to their lack of fine wines, has been the sameness of their menus. Toulouse Lautrec, located in a prettily redecorated house resembling most of the other French restaurants in town, marks a definite departure from this narrow round of canards a l'orange and escargots. Here one can enjoy, for instance, a marvelously subtle cassoulet, complexly flavored with beef, sausage, veal, duck, and beans, or a mousseline of pike that is robed with a sauce made from fresh lobsters, or crab in that same sauce and baked in a brioche. Other fine touches abound. The avocado is beautifully presented — a perfect one in an exquisite creamed vinaigrette. The terrine has just the right crust. The chicken comes with a green peppercorn stuffing that is both different and delicious. The lamb is cooked with a ratatouille that is a different but not convincing combination. A classic lemon tart finishes the meal.

There were some demerits to be counted during the opening months: not very friendly service, tables too close together in the small rooms, the usual Saturday night breakdowns, ordinary bread. But Toulouse Lautrec shows great promise, thanks to an imaginative chef from Lyons and an owner, Jean-Paul Paterline (who also owns the small, good L'Escargot across the street), descended from a Grenoble restaurant family that claims a Michelin two-star as its proudest family treasure.

1427 Howe Street, Vancouver
Weekday lunches, 12-2; dinner 6-11; closed Sunday
Reservations: 685-7731
Expensive
Credit Cards: AE, BA
Full Bar

Notte's Bon Ton Bakery ☆ ☆ ☆

Vancouver is notable for its fine bakeries scattered throughout the neighborhoods. Our particular favorite is this Northern Italian one located on Granville Mall, hence an easy walk from the downtown hotels if you crave a proper breakfast of coffee and croissants or a delicious afternoon tea. The baked goods are simply wonderful, delicate in size and decoration but gloriously rich.

The style of baking is French, but the shop looks right out of Milan, with dark wood counters and the small cakes glowing with deep colors set in intricate designs. Here is a bakeshop whose appeal to your eye is almost as great as the pleasure to your tastebuds. The pretty, five-inch-diameter, small cakes make a splendid item to take back to the hotel or across the border; there are also Italian cakes and cookies, and picnic items like sausage rolls or a grapefruit-sized loaf of country-style white bread. It's been open fifty years and feels timeless.

874 Granville, Vancouver
Daily, 9:30-6; closed Sunday
681-3058
No Credit Cards

La Cantina di Umberto ☆ ☆ ☆

This new Italian restaurant specializing in seafood is right next door to Umberto's, both in location and quality. That means everything is just right. The restaurant is decorated to resemble a whitewashed, sun-splashed southern cafe, with colorful pottery, a profusion of plants, and a gleaming machinetta enlivening the scene. There is a smart bar for waiting patrons, while in the main room a serving counter displays some of the day's catch, fresh fruits, and cheeses.

The food lives up to the visual overture. Among the better starters are a canneloni stuffed with spinach, crab, and cheese (the other pastas are not so memorable, unfortunately); an excellent small plate of seafood antipasti; or oysters with spinach. On first visit, your main course must be the whole Dungeness crab stuffed with shrimp and spinach and cheese—outstandingly good. Otherwise, the prawns are superbly cooked, and a simple dish like fresh sturgeon emerges succulent and rich in a fine mushroom sauce and topped with a dollop of caviar. The side vegetables are fine, and the wine list rounds out the meal in style. For dessert, the house cake of the day outclasses the other offerings.

1376 Hornby Street, Vancouver
Weekday lunch, noon-2; dinner, 6-11; closed Sunday, Monday
Reservations: 687-6621
Expensive
Credit Cards: AE, BA
Full Bar

Brasserie de l'Horloge ☆ ☆

Now there's another place to go after the opera besides a dessert at the William Tell. This new brasserie stays open later and has the smart, Parisian bistro, drop-in atmosphere one looks for to stretch out an evening. There is a charming bar by the fireplace, while the main room has the small white tile floor, the bistro chairs, and the large windows overlooking Water Street in Gastown that evoke warm memories of Parisian snacks and suppers. The restaurant is operated by the people who run Chez Joel, so the food is consistent and good. Examples: quiches made from seafood or classic style, brochettes of beef, lamb, or scampi, and the de rigueur choucroute. Upstairs, incidentally, is a fine room for banquets.

Brasseries—originally the places where breweries in Alsace lured people in to drink beer with simple, snack-like dishes—are designed for quick lunches, suppers, and other times when French food is desired but without the usual three-hour duration and three-figure bill. The Brasserie de l'Horloge (the name refers to an enormous street clock installed outside) is a faithful, successful imitation of this kind of French restaurant, almost unknown in America outside of New York.

300 Water Street, Vancouver
Daily, 11-1 a.m.
Reservations: 685-4835
Moderate
Credit Cards: AE, BA, MC
Full Bar

Trader Vic's ☆ ☆

This is a good version of the famous chain; fuller details in the Seattle listing, page 88. If you get a seat by the window, your meal will be enhanced by the romantic view of the harbor. The bar features some of the best drinks in the city.

    1601 West Georgia, in the Bayshore Inn, Vancouver
    Weekday lunches, noon-2:30; dinners, 5-11:30
    Reservations: 682-3377
    Expensive
    Credit Cards: AE, BA, CB, DC, MC
    Full Bar

On On Tea Garden ☆ ☆

The impression one gets, since the restaurant is always mentioned in connection with Prime Minister Trudeau's fondness for the place, is that On On is a new spot, recently fashionable. In fact, it is eighteen years old, resolutely unfashionable (still closing early, still with no liquor license, still tiny and ugly)—and still terrifically good. So good, in fact, that it has survived Trudeaumania very nicely.

The cooking is Cantonese, with particular attention to seafood. One of the best introductions to the food here is the crab in bean sauce, a glorious, messy dinner featuring the house-special, a garlicky black-bean sauce. The cook also does nice things to fresh oysters and fish like rock cod. The menu has a conventional core to it, but the quality of the cooking soon encourages (and rewards) experimentation with exotic dishes. Prices are low. The only warning necessary is to be careful about the early closing time.

    214 Keefer Street, Vancouver
    Daily, 11-9; Sunday, 4-9; Friday, Saturday open til 10 p.m.
    No reservations: 685-7513
    Inexpensive
    No Credit Cards
    No Liquor
    —

Lili La Puce ☆ ☆

This is the prettiest of the French restaurants of Vancouver. The two dining rooms are beautifully decorated with antiques in glass cabinets, delicate, cane-backed chairs, dramatic lighting, and elegant paintings. No dining area except Umberto's makes as sudden and brilliant an impression. The first part of the meal meets one's high expectations. Lili is especially good in the fish courses: you might get a splendid bit of skate in a wine and herb sauce, or crayfish thermidor, or sole precisely cooked in beer. If these don't appeal, there is a good country pate and a quiche laced with leeks. Similarly, the meal always 'ends on a high note since the desserts — particularly the chestnut cake — are truly wonderful.

In between, however, a few problems can occur. The wine is the usual B.C. problem. The service is the usual house-restaurant slow. For a period the owner, Enrico Pietrobruno (an Italian with no illusions that his native cooking can match the French), was trying both furred and feathered game without much distinction; nor is duck very good in B.C. The red meats are well cooked and adorned with good vegetables, but we have always thought the sauces a shade thin and lacking in complexity. Still and all, it's a lovely place for a long meal and comfortable conversations, and the kitchen is unusually inventive as Vancouver French spots go.

1616 Alberni Street, Vancouver
Dinners, 6:30-10 p.m.; weekday lunches, noon-2
Reservations: 685-3924
Expensive
No Credit Cards
Wine

Napoleon ☆ ☆

This is the most ambitious of the French restaurants in Vancouver, the place to find sumptuous Parisian cooking. Accordingly, the best dishes to order are the game, such as pheasant in sour cream sauce or rabbit in cherry sauce. Both are quite good despite the necessity of using frozen game, which gets a bit dry in the cooking (good marinations and rich sauces solve most of the problems). Another good dish is the lobster tails, which are poached, finished with cognac and pernod, and then topped with a rich cream sauce. Beef dishes are less reliable, although, here too, the preparation and presentation are elaborate and done in the grand style. All this makes Napoleon a good spot for a big occasion, especially if you remember to skip lunch beforehand.

869 Hamilton Street, Vancouver
Weekday lunches, noon-2; dinners, 6-11; closed Sunday
Reservations: 688-7436
Expensive
Credit Cards: AE, BA, CB, DC, MC
Full Bar

Punjab ☆ ☆

Vancouver has a substantial East Indian Population, but so far as we know this is its one good restaurant serving that cuisine. The style is Northern Punjabi, which means the curries are not lethally hot. The menu offers tanduri chicken, numerous vegetable dishes and delicious, properly made curries of lamb, beef, and chicken; the various breads and usual pastries for dessert are of a high standard. The smallish room is prettily decorated. The Punjab has been open for five years, during which time it has attracted a steady Indian patronage: a good sign.

796 Main Street, Vancouver
Daily, 12-11; Sunday, 4-11
Reservations: 688-5236
Moderate
Credit Cards: AE, BA, MC
Full Bar

Aki ☆ ☆

The best of Vancouver's traditional Japanese restaurants, Aki is a place of long-standing, located in the heart of the Japanese district, popular among Japanese, and skilled at doing the standard repertoire well. Service is in tatami rooms. The sukiyaki is fine but you should press onward: very nice raw fish and sushi, delicious teriyakis, and a wide array of specialties you should enquire about.

374 Powell Street, Vancouver
Lunch til 2:30 p.m.; dinners, 5-11; Sunday, 5-10 p.m.
Reservations: 682-4032
Moderate
Credit Cards: AE, BA
Full Bar

Orestes ☆ ☆

At last check, it took about three weeks' advance reservation to get in here, but an expansion is underway that might improve things. The atmosphere is bright and infectious: whitewashed walls, an open spit, splashes of brilliant color. The cooking is authentic and often excellent, if not quite as good as it once was. The moussaka, the brown rolls, the roasted lamb, the spit-roasted suckling pig, the kebabs, and the Mediterranean seafood dishes (like squid or octopus in wine) are all to be recommended. You might as well make an evening of it since the mood is wonderful and the service is slow.

3116 West Broadway, Vancouver
Daily, 5-11 p.m.; Thursday-Saturday open til 12:30 a.m.; closed Monday
Reservations: 732-3515
Moderate
Credit Cards: AE, BA
Wine

Hy's Restaurants ☆ ☆

Just because you're in a major port city doesn't mean you have to eat seafood every day. Hy's three restaurants are excellent places to consume delicious beef, both for the consistently high quality and the very nice atmosphere.

Hy's at the Sands (1755 Davie, 683-2251) has the superior ambience because of its location in the West End apartment village right near English Bay; the menu is extensive, including specialties like osso bucco, pasta cooked at the table, and veal Orloff, but the reason for going is the steaks.

Hy's Encore (637 Hornby, 683-7671) is right downtown, one block from the best hotels. The menu is the same as at the Sands. There is a lovely, sumptuous bar which, along with the food, helps draw in a large portion of the expense-accounters staying at the hotels.

Hy's Prime Rib (1177 West Hastings, 684-6544) has two things going for it: the superior prime ribs, cut thin, thick, and thicker; and the gorgeous view from its perch in the Board of Trade Tower on the shore of Coal Harbour. Do a few simple and popular things this well and the results are predictable — very hard to get in.

> Lunches til 2 p.m.; dinners, 5:30-11 p.m.; Rib open Sundays, 5:30-9 p.m.
> Moderate
> Credit Cards: AE, BA, DC
> Full Bars

Kwang Chow ☆ ☆

Vancouver's Chinatown has a large Chinese population to support it, so there is no need to appease occidental tastes. If you are adventurous and not easily intimidated, Kwang Chow is where you go to get exotic food and extremely good Cantonese cooking. It is upstairs (above the Nanking, a pretty fair Peking and Szechuan restaurant), in a big, noisy room where a mostly Chinese clientele jams the place with ebullient family groups. You might spot things like lemon duck on an adjoining table, only to have the waitress unconvincingly explain that the dish is not available to you. The menu is overwhelming, with entire half-pages devoted to shark-fin dishes, fish-maw delicacies, or abalone dishes alone. It helps greatly to be, to speak, or to be with Chinese.

At any rate, the very authentic food will be very good. The duck is excellent, soups are delicious and come in endless variety, and there are some non-Cantonese specialties such as a Northern-style fried shrimp dish. The fresh vegetable dishes should not be missed. Don't dress up. This is a serious Chinese eatery; in other words, not at all elegant except for the food.

251 East Pender, Vancouver
11-10 daily; closed Tuesday
Reservations: 687-8501
Moderate
No Cards
No Liquor

Chez Victor ☆ ☆

It will take you a while to feel comfortable. Your dinner must be ordered twenty-four hours in advance — unless you just want an omelet — and that phone conversation might well end disastrously with owner-chef Victor Cote hanging up abruptly should you ask one question too many about how the oysters Italienne are prepared. Then, if you do get in, you may wonder about the shabby, tiny, three-table room. Are those *cokes* in the cooler? Be calm: the food is about to end your anxieties.

You start with soup, which is usually extraordinary. The turtle soup is full of body; the lobster bisque and the consomme are also wonderful. There are also a few appetizers, like the oysters or snails. The main course, mostly prepared for parties of four, might consist of hacked chicken in a white wine sauce, or ginger duck, or paella, or boeuf bordelaise, or shrimp diavolo, or veal. Prices run up to around $30 for four. Some nice liqueured fruits round out the meal, or, if you've given enough advance word, Victor's famous Grand Marnier souffle. The food is all meticulously prepared.

Chez Victor is a very personal place. Order is done so the chef has the convenience of going to market after the evening meals are ordered. For lunch, the choice is severe: a few sandwiches, like walnuts and cream cheese, plus excellent five-egg omelets filled with such things as artichoke hearts or sour cream and caviar. You take it or leave it — Victor won't care. Take it. Also, take your own wine to the restaurant.

614 Davie Street, Vancouver
Daily, 11:30 a.m.-3 p.m.; 5-8 p.m.; no Sunday dinner
24 hour reservations needed at dinner: 688-1822
Moderate
Credit Card: BA
No Liquor

Golden Crown ☆ ☆

Travelers to Hong Kong may be familiar with a vast restaurant complex in the main shopping district called the Golden Crown — four floors of enormous dining rooms and nightclubs. The owners of that restaurant recently opened, as their first occidental venture, a massive place just across the downtown Woodward's in Vancouver. Chefs, spirit, decor, and all, come directly imported from Hong Kong.

The Golden Crown is already a great hit for dim sum lunches, both among businessmen and shoppers. Despite its capacity for seating 1100 people on two floors, it is normally jammed by 11:30 a.m. each day. One eats in ornate splendor surrounded by dragons, phoenixes, and antiques that create a much closer imitation of tea-lunch dining in Hong Kong than, say, Asia Garden does. The thirty varieties of dim sum are better prepared than at Asia Garden, too. Lunches also feature plates of barbecued meats, including Peking duck. For dinner, the Cantonese cooking ranges from expert versions of familiar dishes all the way up to $50 servings of shark's fin soup. Five private rooms are available for special banquets and parties, and eventually this splendid establishment may offer entertainment, as in Hong Kong. Be sure to dine in the upstairs rooms.

122 West Hastings Street, Vancouver
Lunches 10:30-3; dinners 5:30-10:30; closed Wednesday
Reservations at dinner only: 688-6631
Moderate
Credit Cards: AE, BA, DC
Wine

Three Greenhorns ☆ ☆

This restaurant, in the base of the Denman Place Inn, successfully combines obvious touristic appeals—the huge curved beams, the dim lantern-light, the nautical nonsense—with quite serious continental cooking. The decor may be unnerving to some, particularly in a city like Vancouver with so many good restaurants that do not need to rely on such overkill; and the kitchen may lay on the sauces too thick and the food may lack a definite national accent. But you will certainly eat well here.

Some of the recommended dishes give an idea of the style of cooking favored by the owner, Helmut Petrak, a Viennese who once worked at Lasserre in Paris: salmon bellies stuffed with shrimp, cream and horseradish; veal kidneys prepared tableside with lemon juice, Port, mustard and pate; sole Papa Louis with cream, grand marnier, and almonds; steaks with cream sauce and walnuts; a soup of cold avocado with sherry. But there are also simple things well done, such as vegetables cooked crunchy and excellent fresh fruit for dessert. The soups and seafood are particularly good. The performance of this easy-to-ruin style of cooking is admirable.

1030 Denman Street, Vancouver
Daily, 11:30-3; 5:30-11:30 p.m.; Sunday, 5-10
Reservations: 688-8655
Expensive
Credit Cards: AE, BA, DC
Full Bar

La Cote d'Azur ☆ ☆

A few years ago, this French restaurant was generally accorded the top rank in the city, but recently it seems to have slipped a bit. The cooking is careful but not terribly original. There is a very French mood, particularly around the bar, a mood that includes some rather casual service (unordered coffee arrives, a drink with a twist comes with an olive). Like most of the small French restaurants in Vancouver, La Cote d'Azur is meant for weeknights, not the very busy weekends when the help is stretched thin and the kitchen is too rushed for finesse. Better still, this place is suited to rainy winter evenings, when you can sit by a real fire.

Our traverse of the menu would go this way: the delicious moules farcies for an appetizer; kidneys in Armagnac, the trout quenelles, sweetbreads, veal in Noilly Prat, or a filet forestiere for the main course; and a small Grand Marnier souffle to finish. The wine won't be much, but you really should spend some time in the bar, where you will feel like an American in Paris and owner Maurice Richez is normally available for an agreeable conversation and the latest restaurant advice.

> 1216 Robson Street, Vancouver
> Dinners only, 5:30-11:30 p.m.; closed Sunday
> Reservations: 685-2629
> Expensive
> Credit Cards: BA, CB, DC
> Full Bar

Venezia Gelateria ☆ ☆

Leave it to Vancouver to excel even in the humble ice cream parlor. This gelateria makes its own ice creams, using imported European flavorings and fine old recipes. It has Italian specialties—the same superb frozen cassata you will have eaten at the best Italian restaurants in town—as well as Italian drinks like chinoto and excellent cappucino and espresso made from their own machines. A city where you can take the family out for dessert, get these delicious double-scoop cones for 50 cents, top them with cappucino and then purchase one of forty-one flavors to take home—such a city can't be all bad, even if you have to drive halfway to New Westminster to get there.

> 5752 Victoria Drive, Vancouver
> Every day, 1-10:30 p.m.
> 327-8614
> No Credit Cards
> No Liquor

Chez Joel ☆ ☆

Given its location in Gastown, Chez Joel appears to be a French restaurant for tourists. But except for the summer inundations, this consistently good establishment serves a very steady local clientele, drawn by the reliability, the relaxed and less formal service, and the modest menu excellently prepared. Lacking the pretension of many of its competitors, Chez Joel often outperforms them.

The cooking is what might be called everyday French food with a provincial accent. A good dinner can be assembled from a first course of scallops in sauce Parisienne or the anise-flavored fish soup (the basis for the restaurant's esteemed bouillabaisse, which requires twenty-four hours' advance ordering); then a main course of rack of lamb or brochettes of beef and scampi topped with Bearnaise sauce; and then a dessert of fresh strawberries soaked in wine and Cointreau, or a nice vulgar bananas flambe. The food is well cooked by chef Georges Bargiel, from Lyons, and you eat it in very pretty rooms or (for lunch especially) in the sidewalk cafe in the rear courtyard; the intimacy and the courteous service complete the effect.

217 Carrall Street, Vancouver
Weekday lunches, noon-2; dinners, 6-11; closed Sunday
Reservations: 685-4910
Expensive
Credit Cards: AE, BA
Full Bar

Peppi's ☆ ☆

The name suits the place well, since dining here is genuine fun. Your spirits will be lifted by the ebullient crowds, the lovely view from the fixed up old hotel out across the Dundareve fishing pier to the harbor, and the fine, spicy Neapolitan cooking. You should time your visits with care — arriving early for a walk along the shore and then settling down so that as the dinner reaches its climax the sun is setting out one window and the harbor lights are twinkling on in Vancouver out the other.

The food ranges from adequate (like the pastas) to superb.

Stressing the latter: the stuffed mushrooms for an appetizer, the cannelloni filled with ricotta and meat and topped with luscious sauces, the delicately sauteed prawns from which the garlic has certainly not been spared, a meltingly tender veal piccata, and the stuffed chicken breasts. The evening usually ends up with lots of amateur singing, a modest bill to pay, and very pleasant memories.

150 25th Street, West Vancouver
Monday-Saturday, 5:30-11 p.m.; Sunday, 5-9 p.m.
Reservations: 922-7950
Moderate
Credit Cards: AE, BA, DC
Full Bar

Muckamuck ☆ ☆

A small restaurant with about ten tables in a basement imitation of an Indian longhouse, the Muckamuck (Chinook for "food") has the unusual specialty of serving genuine Northwest Indian food. This means the food is fresh and nutritious, and much of it is served in ceremonial baskets and bowls.

You begin, normally, with a soup: the clam chowder is a good bet. Salads come very lightly dressed and sometimes arranged in a floral pattern; or you might want to try fern shoots in butter. The bread is bannock, a crumbly whole wheat Indian specialty. The selection of fish for the main course is distinguished, all fresh except for some smoked cod and salmon. The salmon is barbecued in the proper Indian style, and it arrives on a bed of cedar boughs in a colorful wooden bowl. The wine list is miniscule, but there are delicious juices and teas. End this fascinating meal with fresh berries or a cold raspberry soup.

1060 Robson Street, Vancouver
Every day, 11-11
No reservations: 682-1210
Moderate
Credit Cards: AE, BA, MC
Full Bar

Schnitzel House ☆

German cooking is the great under-represented cuisine in the Northwest. The Schnitzel House, while a modest effort at rectifying this problem, is nonetheless an honest place to get a light supper or a good lunch of sausages and potatoes and beer, or perhaps a schnitzel and pastry with coffee. They make ten varieties of schnitzel commendably; of the sausages, only the paprika bratwurst is made on the premises, but they are all quite tasty. Pastries are fine. The one serious omission is caused by the provincial liquor authorities, who somehow have it in their heads that only one beer per foreign country should be allowed into British Columbia, so Lowenbrau is it from Germany: one country-one beer.

Take it for what it is, a nice spot to duck into while shopping on Robson Street, much as you would do in Munich for a quick plate of weisswurst. The other branch, at 816 West Pender (684-3012), is a neighborhood spot, open weekdays only from breakfast at 8 a.m. til 4:30 p.m.

1724 Davie Street, Vancouver
Dinners only, 5:30-10; Sunday, 5:30-9
Reservations: 684-1613
Moderate
No Credit Cards
Wine and Beer

Szasz ☆

The food here is merely okay, but the establishment has plenty of ambience and is an old favorite with Vancouverites in the South Granville area. The delicatessen takes up one half the place and its products are excellent. The Czech fare in the restaurant varies. The goulash and the schnitzel fail the test (the schnitzel is made from pork, unannounced), but the soups are good and so are the pastries. For a light lunch or a pastry and coffee, Szasz is a mellow busy place, well off the tourist's track.

2881 Granville Street, Vancouver
Daily, 8-8; Friday, 8-9; Sunday, 12-7
No reservations: 738-7922
Moderate
Credit Cards: BA
Beer and Wine

Tokay Hungarian Restaurant ☆

It's small and cheerful, with guests singing to the strolling violin at times. Better still, the food's good. You might start with the famous cauliflower soup and follow that with a spicy cabbage salad. Then come the very ample main courses. The Tokay plate, for example, has breaded veal, pork cutlets, home-made sausage, beef tenderloin, roast chicken, potatoes, rice, and vegetables (about $10 per person). Of course there are other combinations, plus a half-dozen styles of schnitzel. It's all quite good, loaded with paprika, and cooked more or less to order. The jolly atmosphere makes up for the lack of finesse, and the outstanding desserts round out a pleasurable evening. As for the acid test — yes, the dumplings are quite light.

> 1106 Davie Street, Vancouver
> Dinners only, 6-11 p.m. closed Sunday and Monday
> Reservations: 685-4531
> Moderate
> Credit Cards: AE, BA, MC
> Full Bar

Marine View Coffee Shop ☆

A longshoreman's cafe that serves beautifully fresh fish, Marine View has been discovered by the rest of the city. A glance out the window shows you why: a grand view of Burrard Inlet and a grander sight — the day's catch being unloaded. The chef will cook some of it to order or will open fresh oysters or make some rather good curries, at trencherman prices, very low. Nice eating, if you can find it. Directions are as follows: go east on Powell (E. Cordova); turn north onto Heatley Overpass; bear right; turn left at stop sign and go to end of the road; the coffee shop is upstairs in a corrugated building on Fisherman's Wharf.

> Campbell Avenue, Vancouver
> Weekdays, 6 a.m.-5 p.m.; fish luncheons from 11 a.m.-2 p.m.; closed
>   weekends
> No reservations: 253-9067
> Inexpensive
> No Credit Cards
> No Liquor

La Creperie ☆

Two needs are satisfied here: to find the best crepes in town for a light lunch, and to find a good place to eat in Gastown. The Breton-style crepes are done with thirty different fillings, at prices that are better than average, and you can add a nice salad and a little pastry for dessert. A dinner feature is steak pan-cooked in the French style, a good way to convince a red-blooded American steak-and-potato eater that the French know a lot more about cooking than we do. Your children might be induced to come along if informed that a railroad switching yard is clanging away right out the backdoor.

81 Alexander Street, Vancouver
Noon-2; 6-midnight; closed Sunday
Reservations: 681-7020
Moderate
Credit Cards: AE, BA,
Wine

Kobe Steak House ☆

It's the Benihana routine, except this one started sooner and has better beef and a more elegant decor, inspired by Japanese country inns. The beef, not real Kobe beef to be sure, is well-aged and then skillfully cooked on the tappan grill around which you and seven other diners sit. This is done with much flair, of course, by chefs who can twirl their knives like revolvers before putting them back in the scabbard. Nevermind: the food is excellent and cooked with a daring lightness of touch. The communal dining might bother any plans for private conversations, so it's best to go here in a large party.

1042 Alberni Street, Vancouver
Daily, 5 p.m.-midnight; open Sunday til 10 p.m.
Reservations: 684-2451
Moderate
Credit Cards: AE, BA, CB, DC, MC
Full Bar

Asia Garden ☆

Every day of the week an exotic rite is performed here at lunch. Large numbers of people walk downstairs to a huge room and take a seat. Out of the kitchen comes cart after cart, each one bearing piles of bamboo steaming baskets. The waitress exhibits the contents to the tables and you take one or pass, awaiting the next cart-parade. Such is the popular dim sum or tea lunch—so popular on weekends in fact that you had better eat very early or rather late. Asia Garden is the best place to practice this rite, but not all the dishes are equally good. The hum bow is quite mediocre, and the won ton comes in a poor sauce. But there are tasty items if you are patient: spring rolls, shrimp toast, pork meatballs flavored with coriander, rice and meat wrapped in lotus leaves, chicken feet simmered in a black bean sauce. Clamorous as a gambling casino, and you might hit the jackpot for less than $4.

173 East Pender Street, Vancouver
Lunches, 11 a.m.-3:30 p.m.; closed Monday
No lunch reservations: 682-6342
Inexpensive
Beer and Wine

The Cannery ☆

The place invites a cautious approach. The view is terrific, the interior is nicely calculated (stone fireplace in the bar, rough-hewn wood everywhere), and touted among the specialties of the chef is good old steak-and-lobster. The Irish coffee is pushed. Hmmm.

You can eat well here, however. The clam chowder is fine for a starter, as are the fresh oysters. They barbecue or poach fresh salmon carefully, and most of the fish seems to be as fresh as can be gotten. The key is to stay away from dishes like the usually atrocious bouillabaisse. To find it, drive east from downtown on Hastings; turn north on Victoria Drive and then east on Commissioner. The view back over Burrard Inlet is fine, so you might want to confine your visit here to the bar.

2205 Commissioner Street, Vancouver
Daily, 11:30-1:30 lunches, 6-10:30 dinners; no lunch on weekends
Reservations: 254-9606
Moderate
Credit Cards: AE, BA, DC
Full Bar

LODGING

Hyatt Regency ☆ ☆ ☆

From the outside, the thirty-four story building displays some of the razzle-dazzle architecture that characterizes Hyatt's famous John-Portman-designed hotels in Atlanta and San Francisco, but inside, while still good fun and full of interest, the hotel is a model of restraint and good taste. The lobby, for instance, sports a brick floor partially covered by a handsome carpet; chairs in orange suede are scattered in front of a dark-mirrored glass wall that transforms the shallow space into a grand entry without fire-code-defying bravura.

The location is another strong point. Harborside rooms have a terrific view onto busy Burrard Inlet and the surrounding mountains. Directly beneath the hotel begins a seventy-shop mall that now underlies the heart of the redeveloping core-city. The rooms are decorated in a sprightly manner — none of that tiresome autumnal-colored good Northwest taste of Western Hotels here. The amenities are complete, right down to a digital clock in the room. A rooftop restaurant offers dancing and dining; the bar is pleasant, Algonquinesque; a heated outdoor pool and a fully-equipped health club divert you in the daytime. Needless to add, all this draws conventioneers like flies.

Truffles is the restaurant of pretension in the hotel. It is decorated in a sumptuous style with oriental carpets and lustrous woods. It has waiters at every elbow. It has a strolling classical guitarist. The food, while fairly good, is somehow not wholly satisfying, in part because of the very high prices and in part because the miserable wine laws in British Columbia, misguidedly trying to protect the awful local wines, make it impossible to get good imported wines. That said, we must say the food is not bad. The turtle soup is exemplary in its smooth, rich breeding. To watch the pepper steak being prepared at your table, with Armagnac and crushed green peppers artfully deployed, is to feel $14.25 is being well spent. The menu is fairly complete, if not very unusual. Why do we quibble so? Because our recent meal for two, including a $20 bottle of wine, came to $72.

> 655 Burrard Street, Vancouver
> 687-6543
> Expensive
> Pets Accepted
> Credit Cards: AE, BA, CB, DC, MC

Park Royal Hotel ☆ ☆

This small gem of a hotel, just over Lions Gate Bridge in West Vancouver, glows pleasantly with a British ambience. Prices are fair, starting with doubles at $25, and the thirty-three-room complex has plenty of amenities: lovely gardens, a cheerful Tudor-style bar, poolside food service, and even telephones in the bathrooms. The dining room quite measures up to the rest of the place. It serves proper English cooking, from the good beef sandwiches at lunch to mutton chops or a mixed grill at dinner. Understandably, the hotel is very popular; getting a reservation at any time of the year normally requires two weeks' advance notice. The twelve riverside rooms have the finest views over the gardens, but reservations in them cannot be guaranteed.

> 440 Clyde Avenue, West Vancouver
> 926-5511
> Expensive
> Pets Accepted
> Credit Cards: AE, BA, CB, DC, MC

Sylvia Hotel ☆☆

The Sylvia is veddy English. The handsome building is old enough (built in 1912 as an apartment house) to have acquired a full growth of ivy. It is located in the proper part of town, the West End, just a few blocks from Stanley Park and even closer to the beaches of English Bay. The single guest elevator behaves in a slow, individualistic, British fashion. Telephone operators handle, when they care to, your phone calls to the outside. The best meal of the day is breakfast: blueberries in cream, scones, pancakes, eggs. And like an English small hotel, the Sylvia has a very steady clientele who have adopted the place; on some days the tiny parking lot will be almost entirely occupied by cars from Seattle.

The best bargains—among rooms that are all bargains—are the twenty-six housekeeping suites: one or two bedrooms, parlour, kitchen, bath for from $23 to $35. Prices go up a bit as you rise toward the eighth floor and if you have rooms on the north or west sides, with the best views. A double at the Sylvia, starting at $15, has to be the best hotel value in the Northwest.

If you cannot book a room and are determined to stay in the green and quiet West End, head for the less-expensive, smaller, check-the-room-before-you-take-it Buchan Hotel at 1906 Haro (685-5354).

1154 Gilford Street, Vancouver
681-9321
Moderate
Credit Cards: AE, BA, CB, DC, MC

Hotel Vancouver ☆☆

Built in the French Chateau style favored by the Canadian railways, this grand hotel comes complete with a steep green copper roof, menacing gargoyles and griffins, and rich ornamentation. Its location is the best in town, right near the big stores and overlooking the lovely little park in front of the Court House. Service is acceptable, the rooms are moderately sized and quiet, and the view from the Panorama Room, with its large windows and romantic atmosphere, is wonderful.

However, paying $45 for a double in such a place is likely to bring with it higher expectations. The lobby has been redone by the management, Hilton, and the results are tasteless in the extreme. The dowager has been made into a convention hotel, so the public spaces are swarming with conventioneers; hawkers for the sightseeing buses accost you on the sidewalk outside. The hotel, completed in 1939, is not old enough to be an antique, but it is not new enough to offer large rooms either. Dining here is good in the expensive rooms—plenty of flaming foods but also a good beef Wellington in the Panorama Room, beef dishes in the logging-decor Timber Club. The Panorama Roof is a nice place to go for a midnight supper and some dancing, and it also serves a good luncheon buffet.

> 900 West Georgia Street, Vancouver
> 684-3131
> Expensive
> Credit Cards: AE, BA, CB, DC, MC
> Pets Allowed

Hotel Georgia ☆ ☆

One block from the Hotel Vancouver is a smaller hotel with rooms as nice, a view onto Court House square as fine, and a generally more sedate feeling (except for the piles of tour-group luggage invariably cluttering the lobby). The rooms are prettily decorated, but in the summer when the air-conditioning is not up to the task, you might have to open a window onto some disturbing traffic noise. Food in the Cavalier Grill is steady and safe—Holiday Award fare—with steaks and some interesting seafood. The hotel is a nice place to be in the early evening when government workers come to drink in the popular bars. Downstairs is an English pub, authentic even to its sing-along entertainment. It's $10 a room less than at the Vancouver, and the smallness (300 rooms) means you can whiz in and out of the adjoining parking garage.

The restaurants at the similar, next-door, slightly cheaper Devonshire Hotel are a bit better: a very wide range of specialties at the sumptuous Carriage Room, and the Dev Seafood House with live trout tanks and other signs of a modest commitment to the difficult art of properly preparing fresh fish.

801 West Georgia Street, Vancouver
682-5566
Expensive
Credit Cards: AE, BA, CB, DC, MC
Pets allowed

Denman Place Inn ☆ ☆

The hotel, a felicitous mistake, which started out as a tower for apartments, is located on a pleasant, tree-lined street two blocks from English Bay and three blocks from Stanley Park. The unhotel-like, bustling residential section has interesting people on the streets and amenities like first-class delicatessens in the basement or just around the corner. Since each room contains a kitchen—stove hookup costs an extra $4 per night—you can cook up excellent meals from the nearby provisioners. The staff is very friendly. And you get complete facilities for such a small (160-room) hotel: indoor pool, saunas, putting green, and two good restaurants.

Another bargain feature at the Denman is this: in a city with fabulous views, these rooms have views as good as any and at half the price. Ask for a room on the west side and as high as is available. From your balcony on the twenty-third floor, for example, you might have a grand panorama of mountains and water for just $25 a night for a double.

1733 Comox Street, Vancouver
688-7711
Moderate
No Pets
Credit Cards: AE, BA, DC

The Bayshore Inn ☆ ☆

The eye is drawn to the view, for the Bayshore has a breathtaking setting on the shore of Coal Harbour. The eye, however, does not linger on the hotel itself, motel-like on the outside and jumbled, disparate decors within. The clientele runs heavily to the Eldorado Set.

Nonetheless, it is a splendid place from which to take in the scenic grandeur of the Northwest. The standard, lowest-priced rooms are a mistake, since their views are most likely of the sloping roof of Trader Vic's or the parking lot. Good views are in the west side rooms of the main building or, even better, the east side, such as room 920 ($49). Howard Hughes once holed up atop the Bayshore, and if you wish to emulate him, ask for the International Suite, a cavernous penthouse with a grand piano, a marble fireplace with a fake fire, and lots of plastic plants—yours for a mere $325 a night. Plans for expansion contemplate five hundred new rooms, tennis courts, saunas and an ice rink.

> 1601 West Georgia Street
> 682-3377
> Expensive
> Pets Accepted
> Credit Cards: AE, BA, CB, DC, MC

Vancouver Airport Hyatt House ☆ ☆

This three-year-old hotel offers the best accommodations near the airport, particularly if you get a room overlooking the Fraser River and a small marina. The ten-story structure is done in Hyatt's usual spiffy modern style, and there are plenty of public facilities: a seafood restaurant, a view restaurant on the top floor, and barbecues for lunch in the summer around the pool. At 412 rooms, the hotel might be a bit too busy for your taste.

> 350 Cessna Drive, Richmond
> 278-1241
> Expensive
> Free limousine to airport
> Credit Cards: AE, BA, CB, DC, MC

TOURISM

Vancouver Parks ☆ ☆ ☆ ☆

The English know better than anyone how to build parks. Vancouver, with a London climate and a more spectacular topography, is accordingly a glorious chapter in this book.

Stanley Park. This splendid park of one thousand acres, some of it still in virgin forest, was acquired by the city in the 1890s, almost at its birth. The southern portion is busiest, a children's railroad, cricket greens, tennis, a mediocre zoo, and a vast putting green. The southeast corner, Brockton Point, affords a grand view back to the downtown and also a prospect on massive ships passing eerily close. Tea rooms are on the west shore, and they are the nicest spots for a high tea. Lost Lagoon, at the park's southern entrance, provides some of the best duck-feeding (particularly in December) you or your children will ever experience. For the rest, the walks along the seawall — thirty-five years abuilding — or along the interior trails are salubrious and safe. The Vancouver Aquarium ($2) is one of the best on the continent; go on an uncrowded weekday.

Queen Elizabeth Park. Two basalt quarries have been transformed into gardens; a large triodetic dome has been erected to shelter lush tropical plants and carefully constructed small ecosystems in Bloedel Conservatory (fine for cold or rainy-day visits), and a strikingly designed indoor-outdoor restaurant, the Quarry House, serves smorgasbord for lunch and French food for dinner.

Van Dusen Botanical Gardens (West 33rd and Oak). This just-opened rolling spread of gardens is extensive and very brightly colored: gorgeous and less populated than the better-known parks.

University of British Columbia has two outstanding parks: Nitobe Gardens, an elaborate and authentic Japanese garden best seen in the spring; and Totem Park, which offers a rare chance to see totem poles as the briefly flourishing Indian artists meant them to be viewed, standing in dim light among tall trees.

Lighthouse Park (about six miles west of Lions Gate Bridge, on the north shore). You walk through virgin forest and then come to a rocky point with a lighthouse; the sublime view is back to the city, across dozens of ships standing off in the middle distance to the ranks of islands and mountains in the west.

Capilano Canyon Park. The famous suspension bridge, 230 feet above the riverbed, may be a bit unnerving for nature study, but also in this fine park is a fish hatchery and (at nearby Lynn Canyon Park, with a free suspension bridge) an ecology center with good exhibits.

Five Shopping Streets ☆ ☆

One of the truly remarkable achievements of Vancouver, for the Northwest at least, is her many blocks of excellent shopping streets, normally gay with awnings and dense with shops whose quality is kept to a high mark by a large local clientele with strong ethnic standards. Some of the streets, like Robson and Pender, may be invaded with tourists — just as Gastown is virtually ruined by them — but you can easily find others that are not and still are bustling and sociable and fascinating.

Greek Section of West Broadway. This upgraded area, stretching about five blocks west from MacDonald, has repaved its sidewalks and welcomed an infusion of shops. One of the city's best Greek restaurants, Orestes (3116 West Broadway), is the magnet; nearby are bakeries like the Broadway (across the street), and food shops like Poseidon Fish Market (2970 West Broadway) with superior oysters, or University Delicatessen (2884 West Broadway), both well-stocked in Greek specialties hard to find elsewhere.

Italian Section of Commercial Drive. This cosmopolitan stretch runs from about Napier to Fifth Avenues. The best stores are food shops such as Perri Meat Market (1501 Commercial) for veal, Renato Pasticceria (1735 Commercial), Olivieri's Ravioli Store (1900 Commercial), with its vast array of pasta, Mira Monte (1670 Commercial) with everything, and Torrefazione Coliera (2206 Commercial) for coffee. This area also has a famous spice store serving the East Indian population: Patel's (2210 Commercial).

South Granville. From West Sixth to West Sixteenth, Granville has shopping that resembles New York's upper Eastside: galleries, antiques, fine clothing, a mix of ethnic restaurants, good food stores. The best block to start with is the 3000 block. There is the best antique shop in town, the Tappit Hen (3050 Granville), the most important art gallery, the Bau-Xi (3003 Granville), with another good contemporary gallery, Galerie Allen, next door, and about the best collection of Canadian Eskimo graphics and sculpture to be found outside the Vancouver Art Gallery, at the Arctic Loon (3095 Granville). An entire fruitful morning can be passed on this one block, and the proprietors here will give you invaluable advice on other shops to the north.

Chinese Section of East Pender. The block from Gore to Main offers a marvelous concentration of Chinese stores and restaurants. You can find decorator items from Mainland China and also stock up on rare spices and sauces or just some juicy barbecued pork, freshly cut, or buy a live crab for dinner. After the stroll the custom is to relax in one of the large bustling restaurants serving dim sum lunches, Asia Garden (173 East Pender) being the most popular. Saturday morning is a mob scene worth making.

Robson Street. There's less here of value than the reputation suggests for Robsonstrasse (from Burrard to Bute). Galloway's (1084 Robson) is a first-class spice shop, with many other desirable items like glazed fruit, grains, and nuts. Two good delicatessens are Vincent's and Freybe's. Tempo Canadian Crafts is the best of the shops for Indian handcrafts. Murchie's is a famous tea and coffee store, the former being better. To revive, have a pastry and coffee at the Mozart Konditorei.

Gastown ☆ ☆

This old part of the city, rebuilt as a warehouse and business core after the fire of 1886, is named for a pioneer saloonkeeper, John (Gassy Jack) Deighton, celebrated for his lengthy monologues at his saloon at Water and Carrall Streets.

Redevelopment started in 1969, producing a hodgepodge of stores with uneven quality, several good restaurants, a large population of street people, and a modest architectural coherence. It's a nice area, but it is also one where it is fatally easy to stroll into three bad shops in sequence and thus be quickly turned off.

Architecture — The Hotel Europe at the intersection of Powell and Alexander is a lovely flatiron building dating from 1908, with original finishings still in the now-seedy lobby. The Byrnes Block, at the southwest corner of Water and Carrall, is a former hotel designed by Elmer Fisher in 1886; Fisher is the man who designed most of Seattle's Pioneer Square. Richardson-Romanesque-style buildings such as Fisher later built are represented in warehouses along Water Street, particularly in the one block west of Cambie.

Shopping — The Dublin House (Gaoler's Mews) has good Irish items; Fulano (4 Powell) imports superior Central American folk art; Karelia (97 Water) is a good specimen of the usual Scandinavian furniture store; Rambutan (Gaslight Square) has good Indonesian stuff; Yolanta Fashion Gallery (200 Carrall Street) is a very good fashion boutique; and Fox and Fluevog (2 Powell) designs interesting shoes.

Eating — DaVito's (6 Powell) is a nice spot for an Italian lunch; Honey's (on Maple Tree Square) has fine healthy food for lunch; Chez Joel, La Brochette, La Creperie, La Brasserie, and Golden Crown are reviewed in the restaurant section.

Vancouver Antique Shops ☆ ☆

For years, when the supply of antiques exceeded the demand, prices were very low for the serious collector visiting this city. Five years of boom times in Vancouver have driven up the prices, but you will still find items costing nowhere near East Coast levels, particularly older, eighteenth-century pieces.

Tappit Hen Antiques, 3050 Granville Street, 731-8021, is the best of the cluster of antique shops just across the Granville Street Bridge from downtown, a heavily-used thoroughfare hardly conducive to strolling, but the heart of the antique business nonetheless. Dr. Laurie Patrick is the proprietor, and the

specialties are pewter, silver, early English furniture, Asian antiquities, and porcelain. A fine store.

Uno Langmann Antiques and Art Gallery, 432 Richards Street,
687-1448, vies with the Tappit Hen for honors as the best shop in
town. Mr. Langmann is very reliable and knowledgeable, and his
extensive wholesale trade puts him in contact with a wide range of
items. His training is in European art, so paintings form the
centerpiece of his showroom; the other specialty is oriental rugs.

Laidler Antiques and Imports, 2415 Granville Street, 736-3731,
excells in early Canadian furniture and pine pieces; the shop also
makes reproductions.

T.J. Watkins, 2306 Granville Street, 733-8809, is a fine small
place whose proprietor is the city's authority on porcelain.

Swift's Antiques Ltd., 8211 Granville Street, 261-1616, also a
small shop, specializes in eighteenth-century furniture, probably
the best single category Vancouver has to offer the collector.

Old Books. Vancouver has several excellent shops, most of them
specializing in old books about the Northwest Coast. Bond's (523
Dunsmuir Street) has the largest stock and is popular with
collectors; it commands very high prices. McLeod's (350 Pender
Street) is strong in old prints; Ahren's (746 Davie Street) has fine
art books; and McIntyre's (833 Davie) is solid in books about the
western provinces.

The Antique Map and Print Gallery (3030 Granville Street) is
the place to go for a wide selection of old maps.

Vancouver Architecture ☆ ☆

Major Buildings. The Provincial Court Building, 22 Main
Street, is a contemporary monument in concrete (by
Harrison/Plavsic/Kiss). Victor Gruen's Pacific Center, Georgia
and Granville, is an unpopular Miesian essay in dark glass, adjoining the stark white Eatons. The CBC Broadcasting Centre,
Georgia and Hamilton, by Thompson/Berwick/Pratt, has a
dramatically angled facade in a brutalist design. Broadway
Centre, 805 West Broadway, is a strong concrete highrise with a
distinctive pointed roof (by Vladimir Plavsic). Robert Rapske

designed tiered apartments of strong lines: The Thirty-Nine Steps, 770 Great Northern Way. Somewhat similar are new apartments by Downs/Archambault in the west end of Van Duesen Gardens, Oak and W. 33rd. And there is the ungainly hanging Westcoast Building, 1333 West Georgia Street (by Rhone and Iredale).

Arthur Erickson. Vancouver has a master builder, an architect of great power and verve. His MacMillan Bloedel Building, 1075 West Georgia Street, is a masterpiece with load-bearing walls of honeycombed concrete. Nicholson Tower, 1115 Nelson Street, and Harley House and Sutton Place, 1230 Nelson Street, are residential towers in the West End. The Sikh Temple, 8000 Ross Street, is a marvelous expression of geometric formalism. Simon Fraser University, atop Burnaby Mountain, was master-planned by Erickson (in conjunction with his former partner, Geoffrey Massey), whose central mall and powerful overall design unifies the dissonant works by other architects. Erickson's new provincial government complex, stretching for two blocks behind the old downtown courthouse, 800 West Georgia, may do for Vancouver when it is complete what Boston's City Hall did for that city.

Older Buildings. One area for viewing grand homes in tudor, shingle, and classical revival styles is The Crescent, starting at 16th and Granville. The 1100 block of Comox Street preserves the early twentieth-century style of wooden housing in Vancouver. The Marine Building, 355 Burrard Street, deploys handsome Art Deco motifs in its ornament.

Culture in Vancouver ☆ ☆

Visual Arts. The Vancouver Art Gallery (1145 West Georgia Street) is the center of things. Its own collection is nothing special, but it mounts imaginative contemporary shows at frequent intervals, and the noonhour recitals, films, poetry readings, etc. are very much worth attending.

The painting scene in Vancouver is currently quite impressive. The two leading galleries are Bau-Xi (3003 Granville), managed by Paul Wong and stressing excellent works by the best local artists; and the Ace Gallery (1724 Davie), managed by Doug Christmas and exhibiting with a strong New York bias. Also important are Equinox (West Sixth and Granville), and the Mido Gallery (936 Main Street) noted for wall hangings and tapestry.

Theater. Some excellent British-trained actors settle in this town, so it is worth inquiring what's doing. The fare at the Playhouse in the Queen Elizabeth Theater complex has been reliably dull in recent years but is now improving. Much better are the plays mounted by various groups at the Vancouver East Cultural Center, a large project designed to bring the blue-collars culture, but taken over instead by the experimental crowd; you can find classical plays, musicals, or premieres here, all at low prices and normally at high levels of excellence. Then there are two intriguing outlets for light entertainment, skits, Noel Coward fluff, and suchlike. One is City Stage (591 Howe Street), with shows at 12:15 and 1:15 p.m. — bring your own brown bag; the other, with evening shows, is the Arts Club (1181 Seymour Street); both are well done. The latter, incidentally, is where the theater crowd hangs out for a drink after 10 p.m.; "for members only," but lightly enforced.

Opera. Richard Bonynge (Mr. Joan Sutherland) is the distinguished new director of the hitherto mediocre Vancouver Opera Association. That should be very interesting, especially to aficionados who wish to see infrequently performed fine operas as well as Sutherland debuts.

Ballet. The top show in town is the Anna Wyman Dancers, a totally modern, Martha-Grahamesque troupe now getting invited for European and New York tours: always worth going to.

Sports in British Columbia

Golf. In the Vancouver area, the finest courses are all private, but if you are a member of a private club in the states your card will probably get you on the course. Capilano Golf and Country Club is the most beautiful course, a very tight one too; Point Grey Golf and County Club is the most testing — narrow, with good length, and large greens; Marine Drive Golf Links is short and tough; Shaughnessy Golf and Country Club is long and more open; Seymour Golf and Country Club, a short, demanding course, is open to public play Mondays and Fridays. Vancouver Island has excellent golf open to the public: Nanaimo is long and hard; Royal Colwood in Victoria provides the best golfing challenge in the province; Uplands, also in Victoria, is a nicely balanced test; and Victoria Golf Club, edging the sea, is easy unless there's a wind, when it's very tough. Best inland courses are Penticton Golf Club, a testing layout; Kelowna Golf Club, very pretty and short; and the well-rounded Kamloops Golf and Country Club—all open for public play.

Fishing. The major draws are: the Kamloops area for trout, May to October; Vancouver Island for salmon, year round; the Skeena River for steelhead, September to November; and the Cariboo country, particularly the Dean and Horsefly Rivers for fly-fishing for trout. The Fish and Wildlife Branch, 4529 Canada Way, Vancouver, can supply you with a list of guides.

Hunting. Best in the Cariboo and Tweedsmuir Provincial Park: moose, deer, ducks, grizzly bears. An outfit like Northwest Safaris Lt. (985-3638) will take parties of two into the grizzly country for $2500, but all openings are booked for the next few years.

Spectator Sports. Horseracing at Exhibition Park in Vancouver is at a pretty track, only a half-mile, which someday soon may revive harness racing (April-October, Monday, Wednesday, Friday, Saturday only). For more unusual sports: cricket at Brockton Point in Stanley Park, curling at Vancouver Curling Club (call in advance: 874-0122), lacrosse at various indoor arenas, rugby at Brockton Point. The obvious ones: NHL contender Vancouver Canucks are sold out, but standing-room tickets can be had; the B.C. Lions, for Canadian-style football, early August to November; and the middling-rank Whitecaps of the North American Soccer League.

Indian Art ☆ ☆

There is keen interest in Indian art in this city, particularly Eskimo carvings and prints. The interest is so keen that you can very easily be taken. The following three shops offer fair value and have superb art on display.

Best is the gift shop in the Vancouver Art Gallery (1145 West Georgia; 10-5 Monday-Saturday, open til 10 p.m. Wednesday and Friday; 2-5 Sunday), which sets the standards for price, range, and quality throughout the Province.

Tempo Canadian Crafts (1029 Robson Street; 687-5411) has a strong selection of jewelry and good connections with Indian artists far and wide.

Arctic Loon (3095 Granville Street; 738-9918) is a shop with small, high-quality pieces, particularly Eskimo prints; and the owners are most helpful.

Nightlife in Vancouver ☆

For a period, Vancouver was one of the few cities of its size actually to book the big name acts into town, usually at The Cave, but those days are past and the Age of Discotheque has set in.

Oil Can Harry's, 752 Thurlow, is the magnet for the best groups, with a new jazz room upstairs. The most popular spot for the young crowd in Gastown is Pharaoh's, 364 Water Street, with pizza and good rock. Of the disco palaces near the downtown hotels, a good bet is the plush Sugar Daddy's, 645 Hornby. For folk music and Irish entertainment there is Blarney Stone in Gastown, 218 Carrall Street; while a more mature crowd heads for the Town Pump nearby, 66 Water Street. If you just need a nice bar for talking, the bar at Truffles (Hyatt Regency Hotel) is subdued and luxurious, while the one on the top floor of this hotel makes an excellent Irish coffee, spaces the chairs nicely, and offers a pretty view.

SECHELT

Casa Martinez ☆

Spanish restaurants of any worth are difficult to find in the
Northwest, and eateries of merit are rare on the Sunshine Coast —
so Casa Martinez is a most welcome oasis. The food is authentic,
especially the paella, which comes in large and richly varied
portions but must be ordered a few hours in advance, and the
sangria ($10 for two). The Martinez family is much in evidence
and very friendly once they let you past the locked front door, but
the distinction of this place comes from the care taken in finding
fresh ingredients. The vegetables come from a neighbor's garden,
the bread from the oven, and even the dairy products are made
and churned according to specific instructions. Just drinking a
glass of milk here can be a pleasure again.

> Route 1, Sechelt
> Daily, noon-2 p.m.; 6-9:30 p.m.
> Reservations essential: 885-2911
> Moderate
> Credit Cards: BA
> Full Bar

Lord Jim's Lodge ☆

The rooms in the lodge are particularly attractive, offering a
lovely marine view from private patio or balcony. The cottages
also have views, but the furnishings are not so fine. As the name of
this place might suggest, it is a lodge for the more adventurous.
Families with fisherpersons, golfers, horseback riders, and
swimmers will particularly enjoy it. Even the pinball games are
athletic versions. There's a full bar; the food in the dining room is
middling.

> Route 1 at Halfmoon Bay, 8 miles north of Sechelt
> Closed Christmas Week
> Reservations essential: 885-2232
> Expensive
> Credit Cards: AE, BA, MC

ALTA LAKE

Whistler Mountain ☆ ☆

The skiing here can be fantastic — if you are not a novice, and if it doesn't rain that day. The mountain has an extremely long vertical drop (4,280 feet), and the skiing is challenging enough to have attracted a World Cup event recently. If you want still more excitement, you can be helicoptered to glaciers for breathtaking runs.

The resort area, seventy-five miles north of Vancouver, has been going through rapid changes, with three of the leading lodges currently in financial turmoil (the best is Cheakumus Inn — 932-5521 — worth checking). A good bet among the stable ones is Highland Lodge (932-5525), which is a small motel with nice housekeeping units and open year-round. The new Whistler Inn opens in late 1975 and promises to be a fine resort, with forty-four comfortable condominium units for rent (932-5756). A large family can rent a condominium with three bedrooms from Slope Haus Condominiums (932-5829). Summer offers fishing, horseback riding, and hiking into the fabulous wilderness nearby. Food at Whistler is mediocre.

HANEY

Century House Antiques ☆

Wayne Clark has collected more than five thousand handsome antiques, mostly Victorian originals, and displayed them in this enormous antique store thirty minutes upriver from Vancouver. It is not only the largest such establishment in Western Canada; Century House contains many quality items, most of them dated, and all at very reasonable prices. The fourteen thousand square feet of showroom area allows the furniture to be displayed in an uncluttered fashion. Since the stock changes regularly, you would be well advised to sign up for the monthly newsletter sent to regular customers to inform them of newly arrived items.

22653 Dewdney Trunk Road, three blocks east of Haney Center, Haney
Daily, 10 a.m.-5 p.m.; closed Monday
463-3323
Credit Cards: BA, MC

Vancouver Island

VICTORIA

RESTAURANTS

Chez Pierre ☆ ☆

Victoria restaurants have long been poor, as you would expect in a town aimed point-blank at the daytime tourists and a little too close to sophisticated Vancouver to be able to compete without inviting devastating comparisons. Well a good French restaurant, small and Vancouveresque, has now managed to make it.

Chez Pierre, with only about 15 tables, can get somewhat crowded, but it is pleasantly furnished and lit. The staff has been well drilled by owner Jean-Pierre Mercier. You may start with a commendable house pate, an avocado with curried mayonnaise or perhaps a crab crepe with a flavorful Hollandaise. With this, you can enjoy very good, very authentic French bread. The soups are also fine, whether the lobster bisque, a wonderfully thick vegetable soup, or a dense, piping-hot gratinee. The best item of the whole place comes next — a perfect salade vinaigrette that is so meticulously made as to be one of the best we've ever eaten.

For main courses there are many interesting dishes. The duckling is served in a cherry sauce (a shade too sweet?). Luncheon lamb chops have been inferior, but for dinner there is a New Zealand saddle of lamb that comes pink and juicy, adorned

43

with peppercorns, garlic and rosemary. As good is the rabbit chasseur, seasoned with sage, mustard and dill. Desserts, coffee and wine list are all acceptable.

512 Yates Street, Victoria
Weekday lunches, 12-2; dinners, 6-10; closed Sunday, Monday
Reservations: 388-7711
Expensive
Credit Cards: AE, BA
Full Bar

Chauney's ☆

The room is smashingly decorated with high burgundy ceilings, panels of an English Art Nouveau wallpaper, potted palms, and elegant brass and glass in the bar. You will find it inside the restored Belmont Building, now an office building but originally built as a hotel just before the Empress arose across the street and struggling in unfair competition ever since.

The kitchen concentrates on the seafood in which the region abounds and the food easily surpasses that at the Empress. The results have been uneven, according to our first-year reports, but it is still worth a try. The seafood chowder is particularly delicious, as long as you can digest lots of garlic. The more ambitious dishes fare less well than a simpler plate like poached black Alaska cod. Cracked crab comes in a characteristically full-flavored veloute with marsala, cayenne and garlic. Desserts, particularly the coupe Turc, are fine. Due to the unevenness in the kitchen, a few words with manager Dominique Chapheau might be wise before ordering.

614 Humboldt Street, Victoria
Dinners only, 6-10 p.m.; closed Monday
Reservations: 385-4512
Credit Cards: AE, MC, BA
Moderate
Full Bar

Princess Mary ☆

It does look like a tourist trap, this landlocked liner in an ugly section of Victoria. And the tourists are all there, ranged about a pleasant two-level dining room. The surprise is this: the seafood is quite often good and nicely served up by sprightly waitresses. There is halibut, salmon, sole, shrimp (some fresh) from various locales, scallops, oysters, crab, lobster, and a few grills. It also has an outstanding bakeshop, where you can purchase items for a later picnic or breakfast in your hotel room.

Nearly everything is to be recommended, starting with terrific cocktails. The clam chowder is fragrant and fresh. Howe Sound shrimp are dressed in a tangy curry sauce and accompanied by a grand chutney, garden-fresh peas, and a basket of marvelous hot biscuits. You can even restore your faith in an old standard like oysters wrapped in bacon and skewered with mushrooms. On no account should you eat so much that there is not plenty of room left for the desserts: perfect fresh strawberry pie for instance, or a raspberry cheesecake, or—best of all—the pineapple pie.

344 Harbour Road, Victoria
Daily, 7:30 a.m.-10:30 p.m.; closed Sunday
Reservations: 386-3456
Moderate
Credit Cards: AE, BA, MC
Full Bar

Coq au Vin ☆

Our candidate for a back-up French restaurant in this city, after Chez Pierre, is this similarly-decorated one in Bastion Square. Some corners are now being cut: an ordinary salad has replaced the salade nicoise of before, and the good French bread is missing. The once-good omelets are not so reliable now, sometimes emerging far too dry. But there is still plenty to praise. The pate is very good, mildly seasoned and smooth. A lobster bisque is exemplary (far better than the gratinee). A lot of heavily-sauced fish dishes have recently been added, but we prefer the meat dishes, in particular the boeuf bourguignoune.

Our other recommendation for back-up French cuisine is *La*

Petite Colombe (604 Broughton Street, 383-3234, closed Sundays). It is another cozy place with a limited menu. Snails and salmon are good; sweetbreads and lamb are commended; the standouts in this menu are the wondrously fresh vegetables.

516 Bastion Square
Daily, 11:30 a.m.-2 p.m.; 6-10:30 p.m.; closed some Sundays
Reservations needed: 388-9414
Moderate
Credit Cards: BA
Wine and Beer

LODGING

Oak Bay Beach Hotel ☆ ☆

Oak Bay is the loveliest — and most British — part of Anglophile Victoria, a nice place to stay if you want to avoid the swarming tourists downtown. This Tudor-style hotel overlooking the Strait of Georgia evokes another world: ladies dress for dinner, and guests are treated as if the twentieth century had not yet arrived. The claim that Rudyard Kipling stayed here is quite believable. Handsome antiques dot the comfortable public rooms. The private rooms are spotlessly clean, and those that have balconies overlooking the sea are lavishly furnished. The location is secluded and quiet, but some noise can pass through the thin walls or drift up from a loud lounge.

The dining room is prettily done, overlooking the gardens, and the food therein is delicious and nicely served. The menu is not ambitious, but they do a roast beef with Yorkshire pudding, or salmon, that could hardly be improved upon. Also in the hotel is The Snug, one of the coziest bars in the whole city, where you can sit before the fire and feel for all the world as if you have successfully penetrated the inner circle of this most class-conscious city. If you require additional status assurances, you can walk across the street and play Victoria Golf Club, one of the few courses on the Coast that actually is a Scottish-style links, complete with windswept holes dramatically bordering the sea.

1175 Beach Drive, Oak Bay, Victoria
598-4556
Pets can be arranged for in advance
Moderate
Credit Cards: AE, BA, DC

Olde England Inn ☆ ☆

It looks awfully hokey, this faithful recreation of Elizabethan cottages, an English village lane, and a manor house. But inside, there is a collection of splendid antiques, ranging from authentic room furnishings to jousting armor. You can stay overnight in rooms that are really great fun and very comfortable — and outfitted with thoroughly modern baths. The rooms are decorated to the teeth in various styles, including Louis XIV and Tudor rooms complete with a massive sixteenth-century four-poster. The Elizabethan Room is one of the most desirable. Some suites have kitchens.

Just as good is the food, served in another authentically decorated room and offering some of the best English food you can find this far from the mother country. There are proper English breakfasts as well as superior high teas. The scones and crumpets will amaze you. Dinner boasts — what else? — Yorkshire pudding with the beef and a splendid trifle at the end. These meals are also served to non-residents. Service can be impolite.

The Inn is supervised by Squadron Leader Sam Lane (ex-RAF) and Mrs. Lane, "late of Yorkshire, England." They see to it that the gorgeous gardens are well maintained and the armor frequently polished. A short walk away are a beach and authentic replicas of Shakespeare's birthplace and Anne Hathaway's thatched cottage. Things are laid on a bit thick, and the Inn is popular with honeymooners, but don't let this deter you.

429 Lampson Street, Esquimalt, west of Victoria
Open year round
382-8311
Expensive
No Pets
Credit Cards: AE, DC

The Empress Hotel ☆ ☆

We don't recommend actually *staying* at this venerable old hotel, since the prices are too high for what you get, but you should certainly make use of it. The Library Bar, for instance, is a most civilized corner for an afternoon drink, particularly as you smugly watch the swarms of Americans departing on the "Princess Marguerite." The high tea with violins in the main lobby is not worth the wait. The food at the famous Sunday brunch is badly outclassed by the decorative splendors of the main dining room in which it is served. The Bengal Room is beautifully paneled but cluttered and badly decorated, nor is the food any compensation. The Garden Cafe, pleasant and airy,offers very formal service and food that is not half-good. The Dining Room is gloriously ornate. Service is formal and glacially paced, but we can recommend only a few items, like the seafood crepes, the roast beef, and the grills.

Our main recommendation would be to sit and read the paper in the flower-filled conservatory, have a drink in the Library, and then find somewhere else in town to eat. As for the rooms, if you take a cheaper room, at about $35 a double, you will be disappointed. By spending a few dollars more you will have real antiques, a view, a claw-footed bathtub, and a semblance of the Imperial style that once created this ivy-clad fortress.

721 Government Street, overlooking the harbor, Victoria
384-8111, (toll-free reservations: Zenith 6375)
Expensive
Credit Cards: AE, BA, CB, DC

Chateau Victoria ☆

Downtown is the place to be in Victoria, near the shops on Fort Street and near the splendid Beacon Hill Park. But you'll want a little breathing room from the tourists who fill up the Empress or the Executive House. Our choice is the Chateau Victoria, a small hotel cleverly disguised as an apartment tower. The lower five floors are rented as hotel rooms, and these accommodations are spanking new, tasteful, and quiet, if a bit dear at $32 a double. Besides a modest view, you get free covered parking and an indoor swimming pool. Service is fine, since a large staff is on hand to keep the rest of the building humming. There's a coffee shop as well as a rooftop restaurant (specializing in beef) and a cocktail lounge. There are a few drawbacks as well: the noise from the buses lining up for tourists below your window can be annoying, and the walls are too thin.

740 Burdett Avenue, two blocks inland from the Empress, Victoria
382-4221
Restaurant hours: 11:30 a.m.-11 p.m.
Expensive
Credit Cards: AE, BA, MC

Helms Inn ☆

One of the nicest sections of Victoria for lodging is along the edge of beautiful Beacon Hill Park, where you can stroll into the park on a summer afternoon, or walk just a few blocks to the downtown, the harbor, and the Empress. The Helms Inn, with a modest twenty-two rooms, satisfies these needs and also saves you money. The new side of the hotel has balconies, kitchenettes, and a view of the park, while the older portion has large rooms and some antiques among the furnishings. Best rooms to request are 101, 201, and 301, and you will have to book well in advance if you hope to get in during the season. If you are turned away, best choices nearby are the Shamrock Court (675 Superior Street: 385-6768) or the modern Queen Victoria Inn (655 Douglas: 386-1312; expensive).

668 Superior Street, Victoria
385-5767
Moderate
No Cards
No Pets
No dining facilities (eat at the Glenshiel)

TOURISM

The Connoisseurs Shop ☆ ☆ ☆

British colonials used to stop off at Victoria, en route home from the Far East for a year of holiday or recuperation. Many of them took note of the verdant Victoria, and later retired there. This pattern has given the town its more-British-than-the-British air and also made it a fine town for finding antiques.

The best shop is The Connoisseurs Shop, supervised in dignified accents and grand knowledgeability by Faith Grant and her daughter, Felicity Graham. It is a beautiful shop for browsing. Each of the rooms in the rambling old house is arranged with great care, so you will not feel exhausted after a few cluttered rooms. The collection is splendid, at fair prices. The specialties are Georgian silver, Sheffield plate, pewter, paintings, old books, old glass, and of course fine furniture, the best of which is from the eighteenth century. You will pick up a lot of information by osmosis in a place like this, the perfect start for a day of antiquing and the best place to learn about other good purchases around town.

The two best other antique shops in the city, in the event you have any money or time left after your visit with Faith Grant, are:

Vanhall Antiques Ltd., 1023 Fort Street. Silver, rare maps, oriental porcelain.

Michael Cotton Antiques, 946 Fort Street. English items.

Old Books. There are two good stores in town where you can find Canadiana and some collectors' items: The Haunted Bookshop (822¼ Fort) has a fine stock of anthropological books about Northwest Indians; Poor Richard's (923 Fort) has an extensive collection of hard-to-find fiction interspersed among the occult books.

1156 Fort Street, Victoria
10-5; closed Sunday
383-0121

Provincial Museum ☆ ☆ ☆

This legacy of the Canadian Centennial (funding for which puts the American Bicentennial to shame) is the best museum in the Northwest. Allow time enough to soak it up, and try to go in the morning before the American boatloads pile into town.

The Indian carvings are uncommonly fine. Many of the pieces are on a grand scale, such as the totem poles of sinuous, interlocking design. These works, among the most under-appreciated triumphs of the world's art, are unfortunately executed in a highly perishable medium (cedar set in heavy rain forests). The well-funded artistic and archeological staff of the museum continuously enriches this treasure, and a new display area of Indian culture will soon be open.

The natural-history displays, mostly stuffed animals, are so-so. But on the top floor is a most impressive recreation of British Columbia history, with an elaborate street scene from seventy years ago, as well as haunting, imaginative dioramas that depict early logging operations, mines, and desolate, snowbound farms in the interior valleys. The displays are particularly good for children, but they are no insult to the intelligence of adults.

Downstairs is an excellent giftshop, a place for lunch or tea, and the best bookstore for Northwest art you'll find anywhere.

> Belleville and Government Streets, Victoria
> Daily, 10 a.m.-8 p.m.
> Free

Victoria Shopping

Somehow the whole downtown seems designed to make you buy a gift. You need not buy a bad one.

George Straith Ltd. (921 Government Street) is the best clothing store in the city, an institution since 1917. It offers both men's and women's imported clothes and accessories, mostly from England and Italy. Cary Grant gets an occasional suit here, which is good enough for us. The major lines in men's fashion are Chester Barrie of London and Brioni of Italy, and it is possible to have a suit tailored in London and shipped to your home (costing more duty this way). The specialties for women are Jaegar and Burberry of London. It is not as easy as you might think to get British clothes in Victoria; many of the stores offering such lines are actually selling clothes of Canadian manufacture. Not Straith. Nor W & J Wilson Clothiers, 1221 Government.

Windmill Toys and Hobbies, 1175 Douglas Street (Bank of Commerce Building), has great European toys: Holland dollhouses, German clockwork toys, Dutch puppet theaters, English miniature zoos and farms.

Edinburgh Tartan Gift Shop, 1003 Government Street, sells outstanding fabrics, mohairs, Scottish tartans, and distinguished sweaters; expensive but not overpriced.

English Sweet Shop, 739 Yates Street, has it all: black currant pastilles, marzipan bars, Pomfret cakes, sesame-dipped peanut brittle—about 100 varieties.

Hand Loom, 625 Trounce Alley (and in Empress Hotel lobby), specializes in Canadian handcrafts. The woven goods are fine, as are the carvings in jade and argillite, the New Brunswick fabrics, and the Eskimo art. Prices are high.

Butchart Gardens ☆ ☆

Robert Pim Butchart was a pioneer cement manufacturer who built his estate around a limestone quarry thirteen miles north of Victoria. Apparently the gaping pit eventually got to Jennie, his wife. She undertook a massive reclamation project, filling in the pit, hiring a small Chinese army of workers, hauling in topsoil, scouring the world for rare flowers, and finally—over a 65-year period—making a 25-acre stretch of beautiful gardens. The quarry itself is an alpine garden; there are also formal Italian gardens, an English rose garden, and a Japanese garden. It's enough to keep 150 gardeners busy and well worth perusing.

The problem comes from the busloads of tourists who are disgorged at the place each summer day, set to noisy wandering, and then whistled back to the buses. Hence you should go before June 15 or after Labor Day. If you are there in summer, wait until about 5 p.m. You can have a two-hour look-around, then get a light supper at the Floral Restaurant in the old mansion, and possibly catch a garden sunset concert by the Victoria Symphony. To top it off, you should walk the gardens at dark, when hidden lights transform them to a wonderland.

800 Benevenuto Road, north of Victoria
Open year round

VANCOUVER ISLAND

SOOKE

Sooke Harbour House ☆ ☆

Sooke—nice name—is 21 miles west of Victoria. A big white house is waiting there, with comfortable rooms looking out over Whiffen Spit—nicer name—the Strait and Washington's Olympics. Best rooms are numbers 3 and 4, with balconies and good views; prices are great. It's a fine place for walking, botanizing, beachcombing, salmon-fishing, or a little golf.

What makes this spot unusually attractive is the superb cooking Mara and Prit Dhillon concoct in the dining room. Mr. Dhillon, the manager, was born in the Punjab; he is determined to preserve the traditions of Indo-Pakistani cooking he grew up with. So, each night, there will be a chicken dish like a tanduri, lamb, or a delicious beef dish prepared with yoghurt, coconut milk and almonds. All their condiments are fastidiously prepared at home. As if this were not enough, classic French cooking is also offered, such as fresh trout, fresh sole in a cream sauce, stuffed salmon, salmon crepes, or lobster thermidor. Everything on the small menu is meticulously prepared. Lunches are modest soups and omelets.

One detail indicates just how determined the owners are to do careful cooking: dinners must be reserved in advance, at which time you must decide between French and Kashmiri cuisine. That way Mr. Dhillon can start his preparations in advance, assured of serious diners.

1528 Whiffen Spit Road, Sooke
Restaurant hours, 5-8:30 p.m.; closed Monday and Tuesday
Resort closed January and first half of February
642-3421
Moderate

SIDNEY

Deep Cove Chalet ☆

About five minutes from the Vancouver ferry (take the first right when you get off) is a venerable chalet perched picturesquely above the water west of Sidney. There you can sit out on the deck in good weather and partake of a luncheon smorgasbord of cold salads and seafoods and the day's roast. In the evening the menu turns seriously French, despite the rustic Swiss atmosphere within.

Chef Pierre Koffel is particularly skilled at preparing seafood. The ingredients are always scrupulously fresh, including the local shrimp, the Dungeness crab, and the clams. One fine dish consists of clams steamed in wine and topped with cream and cognac. The meat dishes are enhanced by nice fresh vegetables, and the pheasant, while frozen (thanks to provincial laws), comes in a nice vigneronne sauce. The wine list is extensive, and with provincial prohibitions against private importations about to be relaxed it may well become a very good list. All in all, it is a distinguished if expensive place, not content to let its 2,000 feet of prime waterfront substitute for dedication in the kitchen.

11190 Chalet Road, Sidney
Daily, 11:30-11 p.m.; closed Monday
Reservations: 656-3541
Expensive
Credit Cards: AE, BA
Full Bar

SALTSPRING ISLAND

Booth Bay Resort ☆

The Gulf Islands, lying north of the American San Juans, comprise a lovely archipelago of secluded beauty, more treed and less developed than the American counterparts. They were formerly used for growing fruit and vegetables for the transcontinental railroads to serve, and several of the smaller islands still display the remnants of fastidiously cultivated small farms developed before the war, when the Japanese were thrown off their land. Now the islands are dedicated to fishing and yachting and summering—plus occasional inundations of their few provincial parks on holiday weekends.

Another factor that keeps the Gulf Islands modestly developed is the lack of any first-class resorts. The best place we've found is Booth Bay Resort, an old house with four modest sleeping rooms and eleven units on a bluff facing west on Saltspring Island (the westernmost and most populous—3,200—of the islands). The duplexes, which have the best view, are cedar cottages furnished with overstuffed chairs and complete with a kitchen (dining out on the island is poor). The two units with double bedrooms have heat in the bedrooms and are a best bet at $25 for four persons. Clamming and oystering are available on the beach below, and golf or fishing are nearby. A complimentary continental breakfast is served by the courteous Scottish owners each morning in the main house.

3 miles north of Ganges, Saltspring Island
Closed November 1-Easter
537-5651
Moderate
No pets in July or August
No Credit Cards

DUNCAN

The Village Green Inn ☆

This pleasant, medium-size motel just south of Duncan offers rooms furnished with quality Mexican pieces and balconies that overlook the swimming pool or the putting green. There's also a single tennis court. But the major draw here is a branch of Hy's steakhouses, where the usual excellent prime rib and steaks are served amid the usual red plush decor. It's a bit hotel-like and it's not on the water, but the amenities and the good taste make this a recommended stop if you're en route up the island.

Highway 1, just south of Duncan
Open year round
746-5126
Expensive
Credit Cards: AE, BA, DC, MC

COWICHAN BAY

Wilcuma Resort ☆

Cowichan Bay is about 35 miles north of Victoria, and here is a nice place from which to enjoy it. The handsome lodge, built in

1902 in Tudor-style, is situated at the end of a quiet road, facing the Bay, and set among lovely trees and gardens. The rooms are moderately attractive, some with fireplaces and a few antiques; there are also a few beach cottages. A heated, outdoor pool, an elaborate marina with rental boats for the excellent fishing, steelheading nearby, even some of the rare grass tennis courts in the Northwest offer plenty to do. The dining room is licensed, with dancing on weekends.

Lanes Road, on Cowichan Bay
Closed November 1-March 1
748-8737
Moderate
Credit Cards: BA, MC

PARKSVILLE

Island Hall Hotel ☆

Parksville is 20 miles north of Nanaimo at the turnoff to the west coast; if you wish to stay here, this is your best bet. The large motel is plasticky on the outside, but on the other side it faces a lovely, sandy, sheltered beach. There are plenty of facilities, should you tire of the beach: tennis (two courts), an exercise room, a children's playgroom, outdoor barbecue, sauna, and indoor pool. The food is not recommended, except for the pastries baked on the premises. The motel has 103 units, so you may find it more crowded than you wish. The beach is fine for children.

Route 19, Parksville
Reservations advised: 248-3225
Moderate
No Pets

Cathedral Grove ☆

The historical drama of the Northwest, such as it is, revolves around the loss of its old trees. When the old forests were here— 200 feet high, 500 years old, rendering all light into filtered mists—they were the last great virgin forests in western civilization. Appropriately the Northwest Coast Indians, cleared along with the trees, were the ones who discovered the artistic equivalent of this natural beauty by setting cedar totem poles among these dim cathedrals.

If you were to fly over Vancouver Island you would see how heavy has been the cutting even here. But one magnificent stretch has been preserved for easy viewing: Cathedral Grove of the MacMillan Nature Park. There are haunting walks through the towering Douglas firs and cedars, and you can then sit down for a picnic along nearby Cameron Lake, or at the park near Little Qualicum Falls. The Grove is 10 miles west of Parksville, on Route 4 heading for Port Alberni.

CAMPBELL RIVER

The Austrian Chalet ☆

Campbell River, just up the highway, is a popular town for salmon fishermen, but it has sorely lacked for good lodging and food. Dieter von Schellwitz, a widely experienced chef, has now taken over this nice motel at Willow Point, and in the spring of 1976 he will open a proper German restaurant that should do a good deal to remedy the situation. The motel is quite nice, with all rooms having views across the road to the private beach. For about $30 you can stay in a townhouse, with sleeping in the upstairs room and a kitchen, bath, and living room downstairs.

More rooms are going in, along with an indoor pool, in order to complete the project, but the big undertaking is to found a good restaurant. The chef plans to demonstrate good cooking of the local seafood in the summer and then concentrate on Bavarian cooking the rest of the year. The facility will have a nice room for breakfast, a cocktail lounge, and the Austrian-style dining room. Von Schellwitz is also a good person to ask about another new restaurant due to open soon, a French dinner-house south toward Courtenay.

462 South Island Highway, south of Campbell River
Open year round
923-4231
Moderate
Credit Cards: AE, BA, MC

QUADRA ISLAND

April Point Lodge ☆ ☆

This famous resort draws serious fishermen from far corners of the world; even John Wayne occasionally steams in. The fishing for salmon is extremely good, with bluebacks in April and May, tyees in July to September, and cohos in October. The island is a short ferry ride from Campbell River, halfway up the east shore of Vancouver Island, and it is a lovely spot for hiking and beach walks, particularly in Rebecca Spit Provincial Park.

The cabins facing to the west are spacious, beautifully furnished, and graced with large fireplaces; they can also run up to $95 a day for the two-bedroom suites in cabins A and B. On the other end of the scale are thin-walled tenements overlooking the marina, where late-drinking and early-rising fishermen in adjoining rooms can keep you sleepless. The food served in the sunny dining room is, on occasion, outstanding. In short, this is one of British Columbia's best resorts—if you love fishing and if you have booked far enough in advance to get a good cabin.

April Point, Quadra Island
Closed November 1-April 15
285-3329
Expensive
Credit Card: AE
Full Bar

BAMFIELD

Aguilar House ☆ ☆

Bamfield is a tiny fishing village and the northern terminus of the old Life Saving Trail (originally for shipwrecked sailors and now for iron-legged hikers) along the southern part of Western Vancouver Island. The view out over Barkley Sound and the Pacific and the off-shore islands is magnificent, and this little lodge (three units in the house plus one cottage) will give you the seclusion and the panoramic views appropriate to such a wild and inspiring beach. The large rooms are modestly furnished; the public rooms are not much, but an improvement scheme is underway; bring your own booze. Meals are served family style in the dining room, by Florence and Bob Peel, the owners. A couple of boats can be rented for fishing, but the recommended activity is walking the beach or hiking. Reserve a month in advance.

Another attraction of the place is the fun in getting there: you catch a boat from Port Alberni (leaving Monday at 6 a.m., Tuesday and Thursday at 8 a.m., and Sunday at 9 a.m.), cruising with the loggers, four hours down the Sound to the edge of the world.

Bamfield, Vancouver Island
Closed November-February
728-3323
Moderate
No Credit Cards
Pets in cottage only

UCLUELET

Wickininnish Inn ☆ ☆ ☆

This splendid inn, with just 22 units and requiring at least six weeks' advance reservation to get in during the summer, is situated on a rocky promontory jutting out over the sandy, driftwood-tangled Long Beach, half-way up the wild west coast of Vancouver Island. The beach, which is part of a national park known as Pacific Rim, rivals Waikiki or Acapulco in size and the Australian beaches in grandeur. Mountain-girt and sea-tossed, this is one of the most beautiful areas on the continent. And here is a resort to match.

The rooms are comfortably furnished in a rustic way. All have sea views, with the preferable rooms being those on the second floor with balconies. One two-room suite can handle a large family. Rates for doubles are surprisingly low: $28-up. Owners Robin Fell and John Allen have tried to make the place a retreat. Newspapers, radio, television, and room telephones are banned; tennis, games, and other organized activities are avoided. Thus rid of temptation, you will find much better ways to occupy your time. The wet-suit surfing is the best in Canada (with surfboards available for rent). There are miles of lonely beach to hike, with a resident naturalist to explain the sea life you collect and a skilled chef to cook it for you. Nearby is a lake-fishing, beachcombing, bird-watching. Or you may just wish to sit in the bar or at the afternoon semi-high tea and listen to the sea lions barking on the rocks.

You are a virtual captive audience in the dining room, but fortunately the food here at the end of the earth is a delight. A new chef, Ken McCloud, was just arriving as we prepared this review, but we would expect the same high standards to obtain as before. The kitchen concentrates on the marvelous fresh seafood: scrupulously fresh oysters or crab for a starter, and poached fish with French wine sauces, or served naked, for entrees. The meat courses are also fine. You might get loin pork chops topped with sugar-cured ham and robed in a tart cherry sauce, or lamb chops done with French provincial vegetables. Vegetables are fresh, and desserts, baked daily, are outstanding. The wine list is the usual B.C. disaster. Lunch offers daily specials, a seafood chowder, and a sandwich of the day.

The road over the Island is much better than it used to be, but you may still wish to fly into the Tofino airport or take the MV "Lady Rose" on its enjoyable cruise from Port Alberni to Ucluelet. The Inn will meet you at airport or dock. Should there be no room at the Inn, the best backup motel is Pacific Sands Resort at Tofino—moderate, clean, and overlooking Cox Bay (725-3322).

> Box 250, Ucluelet
> Closed, Octoboer 31-Easter
> Dining room open, 8-10 a.m.; 12:30-2 p.m.; 6:30-9:30 p.m.
> 726-4244
> Expensive
> No Credit Cards
> Pets tolerated

TOFINO

Clayoquot Lodge ☆ ☆

The lodge was once the handsome, rambling estate of a Canadian mining tycoon, the only buildings on heavily treed Stubbs Island. You reach this remote spot by a "water taxi," a euphemistic description for an old speedboat, which departs from the government dock at Tofino. The lodge has recently been remodeled, so each of the six handsome rooms now has a private bath. A few cabins, more rustic in accommodations, are also scattered around for larger parties. All is spotless, and the cheerful public rooms are filled up with plants, comfortable old furnishings, and a grand fireplace. A double room, including three meals a day, costs $60 for two, $40 for single occupancy.

During the days there are books to read and the island to explore. But the real pleasures come at table. The lodge is managed by an attractive young couple, Yves Margraff, a Belgian ex-journalist who doubles as chef, and his wife, Ghislaine Gauthier, the hostess. Breakfast is served at 9 a.m.—English style and modest. Lunch comes at 1 p.m.—normally soup and an omelet. Dinner, which is open for non-residents as well, comes at 7 p.m.—and it is often a quite good, full-dress, seven-course French repast. A typical meal might be eggs stuffed with whitefish, a freshly made cream soup, a coquille of local fish, coq au vin, a fresh spinach salad, a cheese board, and a parfait: $12 per person. Check about the wine license: if it hasn't arrived yet, you will want to bring your own from the mainland. The food is quite good, but the feeling of immense self-satisfaction to be eating such fare on a remote island, while conversing with these intelligent cosmopolitans, is almost as keen as the ocean air. You should be warned, however, that the proprietors insist on promptness at all meals and don't seem eager to please visitors they do not take a liking to.

Stubbs Island, 400 yards by boat from Tofino
Open year round; dinner at 7 p.m.
725-3284
Expensive
Pets in cabins only
No Credit Cards

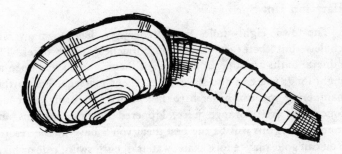

Interior British Columbia

Harrison Hot Springs ☆

The town, eighty miles from Vancouver, has too many fake chalets, but there are certain nice touches at the hotel. The mineral baths are superb, all three of them, and they're open all night long; you can also have an excellent massage. For further pampering you can order breakfast in bed, featuring such nice touches as fresh orange juice, kippered herring, muffins and marmalade (this will be the best meal you'll have at the resort). You can golf, play tennis, skate, waterski, curl, swim, ride or hike.

Of course, most people seem drawn to the overpriced 288-unit resort to eat the dull hotel food or to listen to the whistling accordionist in one of the two dining rooms. We don't recommend much of this, although the bar is a very congenial place for passing the evening. Best rooms to reserve are in the Tower West Wing. You might well inquire which breed of conventioneer is going to predominate when you wish to come.

On Harrison Lake, Harrison Hot Springs
796-2244
Expensive
All Credit Cards

NARAMATA

The Country Squire ☆ ☆ ☆

You need to do some advance planning in order to get a seat here, calling beforehand to discuss the chef's-choice menu with Walter Strehlin, the owner and chef, and learning how to find this handsomely restored house on the southeast shore of Okanagan Lake. When you arrive you will be warmly received by your host and treated to what must be the best cooking in all of interior British Columbia.

Everything is meticulously prepared by Strehlin, who offers prix fixe dinners that change frequently according to the availability of ingredients. A winter meal might consist of an avocado filled with shrimp, a golden chestnut soup with ginger in the whipped cream, beef Wellington accompanied by tomato-halves stuffed with fresh asparagus, and pastries for dessert. Or, in summer: scallops in red wine sauce, a soup of watercress and chervil, duckling in sauce cardinal, and an iced souffle. The wine list is good and the wine, like everything else, is served with great care. During February and March, the Squire offers outstanding clam and lobster bakes, with lobsters flown in fresh from Nova Scotia.

10 miles north of Penticton at Naramata
Dinner only: winter, Friday-Sunday; summer (May 30-September 1),
    Monday-Saturday
Advance reservations required: 496-5416
Expensive
Credit Cards: AE, BA, DC
Full Bar

KELOWNA

La Mission Motor Inn ☆

Okanagan Lake bears an unfortunate resemblance to the New Jersey Shore in many places, so you might have trouble finding decent lodgings. This motel is pleasantly decorated, spacious, and located in a relatively secluded spot alongside Mission Creek, near the Lake. In case you catch a fish, the kitchens in the suites are particularly nice. Plainer rooms are—plain.

> 579 Truswell Road, at Lakeshore Road south of Kelowna
> Open year round
> 764-4127
> Moderate
> Credit Cards: AE, BA, DC, MC

Capri Lodge and Motor Hotel ☆

The town of Kelowna is pleasant enough with its several nice shops and, in the summer, sidewalk stands to display the valley's luscious fresh produce. In addition the town boasts fine water and snow skiing. The best place to stay in town is the glossy Capri Lodge—185 comfortable, moderately priced rooms hard by a shopping center.

The chief reason for staying here is the food in the dining room, which is many notches above the local standards. The steaks are superior, and you can augment the meal with fresh vegetables and an excellent salad. There are also more ambitious dishes if you're steak weary.

> Highway 97, Kelowna
> Noon-10:30 p.m.; no lunch on Sundays
> 762-5242
> Moderate
> Credit Cards: AE, BA, CB, DC, MC
> Full Bar

ROCK CREEK

Edelweiss Restaurant

This little chalet, whose boxlike rooms and proximity to the highway make it undesirable for lodging, offers solid fare in the dining room. For breakfast you can get home-cured ham or bacon to go with (usually) farm eggs. There are no lunches, but the dinners are worth stopping for. The steaks are commendable, but the star attraction is fondue, either beef or cheese. You must order one two days in advance, however, and arrive early enough to enjoy it in leisurely style: the dining room closes early.

Route 3, Rock Creek
Daily, 7-9 a.m.; 5-8 p.m.
446-2400
Moderate
No Credit Cards
Beer and Wine

GRAND FORKS

Yale Hotel Dining Room ☆

The Faminov family purchased this innocuous hostelry a few years ago and set about to do peasant-style Russian cooking with the excellent local produce of the Okanagan Valley. The results are pretty good. Borscht comes in a traditional Russian (non-beet) style, made from cauliflower, cabbage, onions, tomatoes, and carrots, seasoned with dill. Then come dumplings stuffed with cheese, vegetable tarts, and cabbage rolls. Desserts feature pies with the local fruits. Not everything is flawless: the tarts can be made with poor pastry, the salads are uninspired, and the wine list is hopeless. But this makes a very nice respite from the greaseburgers along most of this route, and some of the dishes, like the cabbage rolls, are very good.

> 416 First Avenue N.E., Grand Forks
> Daily, 11 a.m.-9 p.m.;
> 442-2144
> Moderate
> Credit Cards: BA, MC
> Beer and Wine

FAIRMONT

Fairmont Hot Springs ☆

This resort certainly does not lack for attractions. The rooms are good to begin with, especially the poolside rooms or those with a view of the mountains. Then there are the hot springs, cooling off a bit, it is suspected, but still quite soothing at 106 degrees. There is an 18-hole golf course surrounding the resort. There's a modest ski hill, with two others not far away. Then there is Columbia Lake alongside, the headwaters of the Columbia River which in this remote part of the world flows north. Down the road a piece is Fort Steele, an interestingly renovated townsite where once the North West Mounted Police established their western-most post. And Kimberley, a Bavarianised town. The main at-traction, however, is the well-laid-out resort, modern in design but with a nice big fireplace in the old lodge and decent cooking in the restaurant.

Route 95, Fairmont Hot Springs
345-6311
Expensive
Credit Cards: AE, BA, MC

VERNON

Hy's ☆

Good old reliable Hy's, here in the gastronomic wilderness, is a very welcome sight. The dining room is located in a nice new motel, and you eat amid the usual seemly ostentation of Hy's establishments. The menu is familiar, too: excellent (if a bit expensive) steaks, some carefully prepared seafood, and for dessert the home-made ice cream is topped with the luscious local fruit. The roast-beef buffet lunch is another reason for pulling off the road at this juncture.

Highway 97 at Silver Star Road, Vernon
Daily, 11:30-11:30; Sunday, 5-11:30
Reservations: 545-1777
Moderate
Credit Cards: AE, BA, DC, MC
Full Bar

Vernon Lodge Hotel ☆

Vernon is a prosperous and pretty town at the north end of Okanagan Lake. Polson Park is one of the nicer attractions, with its famous floral clock changing colors with the seasons, its Japanese gardens, its eating pavillions and summer-evening band concerts. The architecture of the civic complex is notable, and you can catch symphonic and theatrical performances there now and then. If you wish to skate or to observe that peculiar Canadian passion, curling, head for the community center.

The town also boasts an unusual motel, one which looks as if it were designed by some backwoods John Portman. It features a large, four-story-high, inner courtyard, all decked out in Polynesian splendor and traversed by a natural stream. The stream overflowed its banks just after the motel opened, so now it trickles through tamely, behind ungainly heavy buttresses. Each of the 135 rooms in this piney version of a Hyatt Regency overlooks the central courtyard, which has—in addition to the stream—whirlpools, a swimming pool, and a lounge. The rooms are nicely decorated with cedar, the service is attentive, and the rates are surprisingly modest.

The dining room, called The Pepper Tree, is another plus. The cooks have a nice way with fresh local trout. They can also do a decent steak Diane at tableside, or refrain from overcooking the fresh vegetables. Even the wine list is fairly good, quite ambitious by Canadian standards.

   3914 32nd Street, Vernon
   Open year round
   545-3385
   Moderate
   Credit Cards: AE, BA

KAMLOOPS

LeJeune Lodge ☆ ☆

For years, and for a very good reason, the splendid interior country of British Columbia has lacked lodgings to equal scenery—the reason being the short season for tourism. And so, in the Kamloops area for one, the fishermen may net lovely trout by day but by night they sit around their woodstove cottages and wonder why.

Roy Turner, the owner of LeJeune Lodge, twenty-two miles by paved road southwest of Kamloops, decided two years ago to try a big gamble; he tore down the 1910 lodge and spent $750,000 in constructing a new facility of deluxe motor-inn style. He added a hot pool, a ski slope (a paltry 800-foot drop), boats, horses—and soon will put in a tennis court and a swimming pool. It's quite grand for a fishing lodge—about the grandest in the province—and he even capped it off by offering cherries jubilee in the dining room (since dropped). The cedar-board cabins came out the best bet for lodging, followed by the fireplace suites with kitchenettes in the older fourplex.

The fishing is good, although the lake gets heavily fished during the peak months of July and August. Even better is the cross-country skiing, which takes place over thirty-six miles of groomed trails in lovely, rolling ranch country on snow made very dry by the nights when the temperature regularly drops below zero. The food is quite good, too, especially if it's your own Kamloops trout the chef is preparing that night.

Lac LeJeune Road, 22 miles southwest of Kamloops
Open year round
374-2165
Expensive
Credit Cards: AE, BA, MC

---

100 MILE HOUSE

---

108 Recreational Ranch ☆ ☆ ☆

The Cariboo country, a popular vacationland for the professional classes of Vancouver, has not been noted for its resort facilities or its dining—the superb fishing, the hunting, the dry air of the high plateau have amply sufficed. This new ranch, built at the center of a large development and golf course, does certainly provide the best lodging in the vast and extraordinary country. It's a 200-mile drive from Vancouver, or there is PWA scheduled service to the ranch airfield.

It is preferable to stay in the original lodge, whose rooms are large enough easily to take families of four; the two best rooms are numbers 21 and 22, with high ceilings. The new motor-lodge will have smaller rooms. The rooms are very tastefully furnished, some with kitchens, and they all look out over the excellent golf course and into the sunsets.

In addition, the Ranch offers fine facilities: a heated pool, a sauna, a stable with fifty horses, thirty miles of trails for riding or the superb cross-country skiing in the winter, a clubhouse with good food, and of course access to the marvelous nearby fishing and hunting. A popular time to visit this year-round resort is in the fall, when frustrated Easterners can watch bright foliage, and frustrated cowboys can ride along on the annual cattle drive down the old trail. Spring flowers are best in April and May; cross-country skiing is best in January and February.

Highway 97, 8 miles north of 100 Mile House
Open year round
395-2411
Moderate
Credit Cards: AE, BA, MC

BARKERVILLE

Barkerville ☆ ☆

This historic town was, in the 1860s gold rush, the largest town north of San Francisco. Now, after years of desolation, it is turning into one of the finest restoration projects. The town makes a fine way to cap a trip up the Cariboo trail past all the old ranches and cabins that characterize this long-settled, remote region.

Sixteen miles away is another notable attraction. Bowron, Spectacle, Sandy, Lanezi, and Isaac Lakes form an almost perfect rectangle that in turn makes an almost perfect 100-mile canoe trip with modest portages. You can begin and end the circuit at Becker's Lodge (write Box 129, Bowron Lake), a nice facility with housekeeping units and plenty of canoes.

PRINCE GEORGE

Inn of the North ☆

Prince George, in the midst of splendid hunting and hiking country, is not the finest of cities in itself. This ten-story Delta hotel is rather grand, however, and if you secure one of the spacious corner rooms with a balcony ($32 a double), you will be well-fixed. The hotel also offers a free health spa, three cocktail lounges, and some of the fanciest cooking in the north in the Club Car Grill, where a Dutch chef produces some respectable tableside cuisine.

There are a couple of other places in the area also worth dining at. The nearby Schnitzel House (611 Brunswick Street) offers good German cooking, and if you go six miles east you can have a dinner of carefully prepared steaks and roasts in a country inn overlooking a lake: The Log House (Six Mile Lake).

> 770 Brunswick Street, Prince George
> 563-0121
> Expensive
> Credit Cards: AE, BA, DC, MC

FRANCOIS LAKE

Glenannan Lodge ☆

The fishing is marvelous in François Lake, particularly just after the ice breaks in early May. This lodge, consisting of six cabins with fairly modern facilities (propane cooking stoves, Franklin heating stoves), is right on the lake in a pretty setting. You can sit around the barbecue at night, or throw a few horse-shoes, or talk over fine points with Slim Walsh, the owner, but the real stars of the place are named Rainbow, Char, Dolly Varden, and cutthroat.

> East end of Francois Lake
> Closed October 15-May 1
> 699-7715
> Moderate
> No Cards

TELKWA

Round Lake Resort ☆

Here you can stay in prefabricated log cabins with two bedrooms, a bath, and a kitchen. The setting is on a lake, where you can fish for rainbow and cutthroat trout; or you can hire a guide and go hunting or hiking into the snowcapped mountains. The five units are very neat, prettily set amid poplars. The Danish owners of this small resort, the Karelis , no longer guide into the countryside, but they are still most courteous and informative about this remarkable, remote district. All this makes the resort an ideal spot for breaking from the highway and staying a day or three.

> Highway 16, five miles east of Telkwa
> Closed October 1-June 1
> 846-5383
> Inexpensive
> No Credit Cards

PRINCE RUPERT

Crest Motor Hotel ☆

Prince Rupert is a fascinating city with the rawness of the frontier everywhere. It rains a lot here, of course, but in the clear patches you have splendid views of the harbor. The Museum of

Northern British Columbia (First Avenue and McBride) has an excellent Indian collection, but even more stirring is the sight of the bustling fishing port where Indians, Portuguese fishermen, and Anglos fill the streets.

The best place to stay is the Crest Motor Hotel, offering standard rooms at $27 a double, but some have a nice overlook of the harbor. Tourists are a captive market in the summer here, so prices may surprise you, and the seafood served in the "halibut capitol of the world" may not be the fresh delight you've imagined during the miles of driving down the Skeena. If you go to Smiley's Cafe on Cow Bay (624-5636, and check to see if it's open beforehand), you will be able to get the freshest of seafood, simply prepared in a small joint.

222 First Avenue West, Prince Rupert
Open year round
624-6771
Expensive
Credit Cards: AE, BA, CB, DC, MC

The Prince Rupert Loop Trip ☆ ☆ ☆

One of the great motor tours in North America is the loop from Vancouver, through the Hell's Canyon of the Fraser River, up through the high Cariboo to Prince George, then west through unimaginable wilderness to Prince Rupert, thence by steamer back to Vancouver Island. (The car ferry is run by B.C. Ferries, 816 Wharf Street, Victoria, 656-1194; reservations in the summer must be made months in advance.)

The attractions of the Fraser gorge, the Cariboo, Barkerville, and fishing on Francois Lake are detailed elsewhere. Possibly the least publicized and most satisfying part of the trip occurs in the Valley of the Skeena, coming into Prince Rupert. The gorge has scenery that puts even the mighty Columbia gorge to shame, and inland one can observe Indian civilization in a way that does justice to its haunting and subtle art. At Hazelton, for instance, there is 'Ksan, an Indian craft village with authentic Indian longhouses and good artifacts produced at the village for sale. Just north is Kispiox, an Indian town with awesome totem poles.

Eastward is Moricetown, where a canyon forces salmon to jump high over the rapids as they ascend, and Indians gather to catch the mythical fish in the ancestral way. It is a wondrous area to hole up in for a few days, soaking up the remoteness and the grandeur of the frontier and reading the obligatory book evoking this region, Edward Hoagland's *Notes From The Century Before* (Random House).

Customs Regulations

For Americans visiting Canada, the following regulations should be kept in mind:

1. If you stay more than 48 hours, you can bring back merchandise for personal use worth $100 fair retail value in Canada without paying duty; families can combine exemptions for those in the car—thus a family of four could bring back a single item worth $400. In addition, under the 48-hour rule, you are entitled to 100 cigars, unlimited cigarettes, and 32 ounces of liquor duty-free.

2. If you stay less than 48 hours, duty-free merchandise is limited to $10 per person, 10 cigars, 50 cigarettes, and four ounces of alcohol; family exemptions cannot be combined.

3. Gifts or other items shipped from Canada are subject to duty if worth more than $10.

4. To take a dog into Canada, you must produce its rabies vaccination certificate, showing a vaccination within the past year.

5. Common items that cannot be brought back to America without a permit: unprocessed plants, seeds, and cuttings; meats or fowl and their byproducts, even if processed; certain endangered wildlife and their byproducts (such as whalebone sculpture); goods originating in Communist China, North Korea, North Vietnam, or Cuba.

6. Owners of American trademarks may restrict importation of foreign-made merchandise with that trademark, although many allow a small number to be brought in (three Nikons, for example). Be careful in these areas: cameras, musical instruments, jewelry, perfumery, timepieces, tape recorders. Customs has a handy pamphlet, "Trademark Information."

Washington

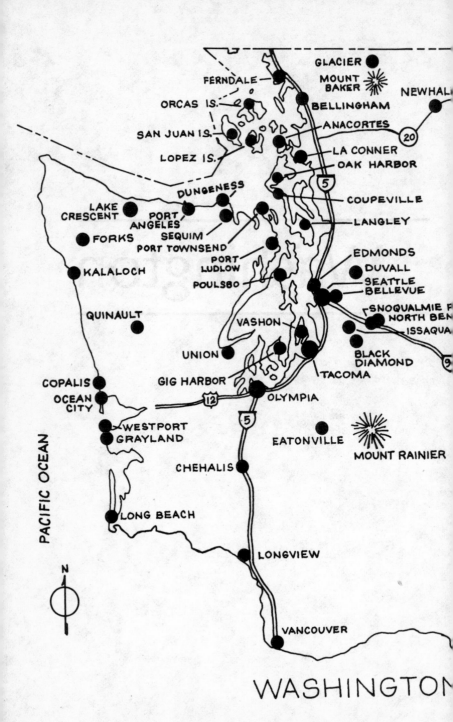

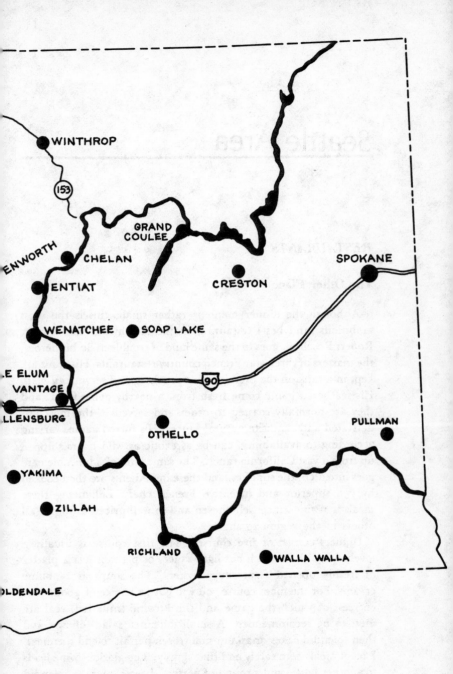

WINTHROP

153

GRAND
COULEE

ENWORTH   CHELAN

ENTIAT

WENATCHEE   SOAP LAKE

E ELUM
VANTAGE

LLENSBURG

YAKIMA

ZILLAH

RICHLAND

OLDENDALE

SPOKANE

CRESTON

90

OTHELLO   PULLMAN

WALLA WALLA

TATE

Seattle Area

RESTAURANTS

The Other Place ☆ ☆ ☆ ☆

   Although the dinner menu is rather small, this is the most ambitious (and best) restaurant in the Northwest. The owner, Robert Rosellini, goes to the same kind of trouble as do his heroes, the masters of three-star French country restaurants. His trout are kept in a tank on the premises, for poaching and serving *au bleu*. His feathered game come fresh from a nearby game farm, and they are normally roasted to order and served in the most understated and exquisite natural sauces. His furred game, varying according to availability, can be as exotic as wild boars shipped up from a vast California ranch. The same kind of admirable care goes into all of the supplies, and these ingredients are then cooked by two superior and inventive French chefs. Enhancing these meals is a wine list so well-chosen and so well-priced as to put all others in the region to shame.

   Dinners consist of five courses. The first course is usually a lovely fish dish in a rich but light sauce, or perhaps just a platter of freshly opened Canterbury oysters. The soups are sublime creams. For the main course you will have a choice of about four entrees, of which the game and the Provimi (milk-fed) veal are most to be recommended. A small julienned salad follows, and then splendid cakes or an unusual frozen parfait to end the meal. Except meals here rarely end that simply. The glorious wine leads to another bottle and a round of perfect cheeses, and the splendid Crofts ports are hard to deny on such an occasion. Accordingly, while the prices are extremely fair, meals so good tend to run up a handsome tab.

The restaurant is much less good for lunch, when the closely packed tables and the uninspired menu can annoy. (Of course, a serious eater, by consulting with the helpful Rosellini, can always get something special from the kitchen.) For dinner it helps to have one of the best waiters (Mike or Jean-Paul or Manuel) since the service can be complicated, and to select a quieter table (like numbers 5, 26, 34, or 24) in order to avoid mood-spoiling neighbors. Beyond that, you simply need to trust Rosellini's very candid description of the evening's offerings and his solid recommendations about the wine.

319 Union Street, Seattle
Daily, 11 a.m.-midnight; closed Sunday
Reservations: 623-7340
Expensive
Credit Cards: AE, BA, MC
Full Bar

The Mikado ☆ ☆ ☆

This wonderful restaurant fully honors the Japanese devotion to good seafood, a tribute made a bit easier by the fact that the owner's father works for a major fish supplier. You can dine at the high-backed chairs along the front counter, where Japanese businessmen often drop by for a few off-the-menu appetizers, or in a regular sit-down dining room, or in the handsome, modern tatami rooms. And you can choose your level of sophistication. This ranges from a simply broiled crab (batayaki) or steak in a garlic sauce, on through salt-broiled (shioyaki) specialties like chicken or salmon, a pork cutlet with a rich dipping sauce (tonkatsu), or a steamed dish of vegetables and meat cooked at your table in a clay saucer (toban-yaki), and then on up to the authentic feasts. These feasts must be ordered a day in advance, and if you are not Japanese you would do well to insist on a few authentic items. The dinners reveal the power of the kitchen: delicate liver pates, custard dishes with full-flavored ingredients, salt-broiled little trout presented in a beautiful composition, and marvelous raw fish.

The prices for this are very reasonable; indeed you can eat a good meal of rice and an omelet with chicken (domburi) for about $2. The special feasts cost $8-10 per person. The service is cheerful, and the Yoshimura brothers are attentive managers whose advice on what to order should always be solicited.

514 South Jackson Street, Seattle
Dinner only, 5:30-10 p.m.; closed Sunday
Reservations: 622-5206
Moderate
Credit Cards: AE, BA, CB, DC, MC
Full Bar

Brasserie Pittsbourg ☆ ☆ ☆

Put an old gentleman out front shucking oysters for sale, and you would be at a brasserie in Paris. The restaurant is a faithful adaptation of an old Seattle soup kitchen into a Parisian brasserie, complete with white-tile floors, a pressed-tin ceiling, art-galerie posters, butcher-paper on the tables, bursts of flowers, and magnificent copperware scattered about. The din may be too much for a quiet dinner or a serious talk at lunch (though the tables in the front alcove are less loud), but the decibels give the place its smart, clubby feel.

The food can be wonderful, but it requires some precaution. At lunch you stand in a slow line passing in front of the steam tables; there is a choice of two not-terribly-exciting items each day, or a slice of the day's omelet, made twenty-five eggs at a time. In the summer they do some cold plates which are more successful than the hot dishes with their mushy vegetables. If you wish table service, that can be arranged, and you might then create an elegant luncheon with the house pate, the excellent salad (whose dressing chef Francois Kissel makes in a secret, double-locked room), and then a paella, or some sausages, or a little chicken with a very good wine. At any rate, lunches at the Brasserie are an institution in Seattle, where all the aspiring young lawyers, government-workers, journalists, and architects put in weekly appearances and busily scribble on the butcher-paper, plotting the next bold maneuver to save the city.

Dinners shift to classic French cooking—full dinners, not brasserie suppers—nicely served at your table by a marvelous corps of waiters and waitresses. When Francois is in the kitchen—he has two other restaurants, plus a catering business—the food is wonderful and it may include a seasonal delight he has found up at the Pike Place Market, like skate or crayfish. For the rest, it is perfectly good, although one might hope for a more complex sauce here, more careful preparation there, more variety, and better wines. The food hovers between being classic cooking with delicate sauces and being French suppers slightly elevated. Among the best bets: duckliver mousse, the assorted appetizer plate, the stuffed trout, the pork with calvados, the lamb provencale, the red snapper, the chocolate mousse for dessert. It is a fine place for before the opera, but if you come back afterward or are making an evening of it, be sure to finish with one of the eaux de vie, extraordinary clear fruit brandies.

602 First Avenue, Pioneer Square, Seattle
Lunch, 11:30-2:30; dinner, 5:30-12; closed Sunday
Reservations: 623-4167
Expensive
Credit Cards: BA, MC
Full Bar

Prague ☆ ☆ ☆

The setting is very up to date: contemporary paintings on scraped brick walls, flower-print hanging lamps over the polished-wood tables, and a location in chic Pioneer Square. But the standards are Old School, Old World. The meat is all cut by the chef, Peter Cipra. The waitresses are extremely well drilled. And the standards for the food are about the highest in town. Thus, while not the most congenial place in town, and while Czech and Hungarian cooking is not everyone's favorite cuisine, the Prague is one of the Seattle restaurants most deserving of acclaim.

Lunches are very nice, whether the definitive wiener schnitzel, or a salad, or a piece of sole, or an open-faced sandwich with one of Cipra's unsurpassable soups. The atmosphere at lunch is both bustling and conducive to long conversations. At dinner the food is better, but the place is often a bit underpopulated. Nearly all of the dishes can be recommended. The pork dishes, whether in cream, a paprika sauce, or with green peppers, are particularly good as are the veal plates, notably the veal Orloff with slivered pickles and capers in a piquant cream sauce. Lately, new dishes have been making their way onto the small menu: a spicy duck, sole with ham, and a peppercorn veal steak. All of the dishes come with excellent vegetables and potatoes, with the entire composition artistically presented on the plate. The usual objection to this style of cooking, that it is too heavy, is considerably tempered by Cipra's devotion to the lighter forms of middle European cuisine, as anyone who has tasted his feathery dumplings will agree.

Cipra may, incidentally, be moving his restaurant uptown about the middle of 1976, so diners reading this report after that date should check to see if there is a new location. It's doubtful that the standards will have dropped the slightest.

309 First Avenue South, Seattle
Lunches 11-3; dinners 6-10; closed Sunday
Reservations: 682-1624
Expensive
Credit Cards: BA, MC
Full Bar

Jake O'Shaughnessey's ☆ ☆ ☆

No restaurant in Seattle has been more carefully thought out. The Irish decor is carefully understated. The bar is just noisy enough and irresistably appetizing as you gaze on the high wall display of every brand of booze the state carries. The help, all virginal in terms of restaurant experience, is fresh and enthusiastic and well-coached. The specially made sourdough bread is kept warm by a concealed hot marble chip in the basket, while the chilled salad comes with an icy fork, no less. Yet, despite all the painstaking care, Jake's does not come off as overwrought or mechanical. The place is wonderful fun and invariably good. And prices are great.

The food is just splendid, thanks to the care in preparation and the limited menu. Best is the saloon beef, reviving a pioneer method of roasting beef in a thick crust of roasting salts at a very low temperature for seven hours. It emerges moist and flavorful, warm even to the pinkest, rarest center; and it comes with the expected extra touch—freshly grated horseradish. A close contender is the alder-roasted fresh salmon, a filet cool-smoked to a delicate fragrance over alder for hours, then microwaved for a few seconds before being served moist and hot. The beef and fish stews are also very good.

The evening draws to a close with ice cream (very rich, especially the vanilla) and coffee served in heated cups. But evenings here don't really end that easily, unless you're heading over to see the Sonics or the theater across the street. There's a round of perfectly made Irish coffees to be enjoyed. Then perhaps another bottle of what must be the best $5 cabernet in America, Pedroncelli. Then a fine cigar from the distinguished collection. And then—what the hell—a few more hours in the best bar in the city.

100 Mercer Street, in the Hansen Baking Company complex, Seattle
Monday-Saturday, 5-11 p.m.; Sunday, 5-10 p.m. (may open for lunch
   soon)
No reservations (may change soon): 285-1898
Moderate
Credit cards: AE, BA, MC
Full (really full) bar

City Loan Pavilion ☆ ☆ ☆

The most beautiful restaurant in the Northwest, City Loan is entered through Occidental Park in Pioneer Square. You can sit in a greenhouse jutting into the park—very nice on a sunny day, with the louver rising automatically as the temperature does—or in a sumptuous room adorned by Persian murals and a massive chandelier rescued from an ornate movie palace torn down for the Washington Plaza Hotel. To the rear is an elegant small bar where you sit amid antique pewter and romantic eighteenth-century murals. It is all done with such taste and assurance that it does not even come as a surprise to learn that the green velvet dining chairs once graced the Waldorf Astoria.

Oddly, the food served here is quite modest. It is in its way as much an expression of the owners' personal preferences as the decor is. Chef Francois Kissel once cooked in Algeria in the French Army, so there is an Algerian soup (vegetables, avocado, eggs) and an Algerian version of salade Nicoise (topped with peanuts and peppers). Julia Kissel has Kentucky roots, so there is chicken dipped in cornmeal and then deep-fried and topped with a lively sauce of tomatoes, onion, bacon, and garlic. And so it goes — remarkable new combinations everywhere: clams put into potatoes Dauphine; apple fritters with a honey-and-lemon sauce; steak tartar deep-fat fried and transformed by splendid sauces into a sublime hamburger; lentils wrapped up in a slice of ham. Plus simple good things like a pan-fried steak, French style, fresh Kumamoto oysters, and grilled sausage in herbed dressing. The Pavilion is designed for a short visit and a light supper, say before the theater; but the bar is so inviting, the food so intriguing and the room so bold and so right, that it is hard not to make an afternoon or an evening of it.

206 First Avenue South, Pioneer Square, Seattle
Daily, 11:30-midnight; closed Sunday
Dinner reservations only: 624-9970
Moderate
Credit Cards: BA, MC
Full Bar

John Nielsen Pastry ☆ ☆

John Nielsen was a respected baker in Copenhagen before he moved to Seattle, and he brought with him the high standards of Danish baking. His little shop in downtown is a wonderful substitute for a late breakfast at the nearby hotels, a splendid spot for coffee and a pastry while you rest from shopping, and a good source for traveling food or treats for a hostess.

You can buy breads like rugbrod — the base for Danish sandwiches — or delicious cookies or many-layered cakes. But the best products are the Danish pastries such as mazarines (a soft little cake with almonds and pistachio puree), Napoleon's hats (with a nugget of almond paste in the center of the cookie dough), petits fours, and "potatoes" made with custard and cream inside a puff of pastry topped with a micrometer-thin pane of almond paste rolled in cocoa powder. Such baking is a high art, and it's yours in this cheerful place for about 30 cents.

1329 Third Avenue, near Union Street, Seattle
Daily, 10-6; closed Sunday
622-1570

Rosellini's 410 ☆ ☆

This restaurant, a new, Italian version of a famous closed namesake downtown, opens after this guidebook comes out, but our knowledge of the people involved and a peek at advance plans make us confident that it will be a good place, and that it will earn at least the two stars we give it provisionally at this time.

Several aspects are bound to be very, very good. The bar should quickly re-establish Victor Rosellini's reputation as the premier manager of convivial bars serving peerless drinks. There will be a trattoria where you can get a freshly carved sandwich or a plate of hot Italian food like lasagne; adjoining this room will be counters to buy take-out food, pastry, Italian specialties, and some of the pasta the kitchen will make for the restaurant. The service is sure to be superb. Whether the main dining room will do authentic Italian cooking remains to be seen, but we would expect it to do so. Each day about a dozen pastas will be offered, many of them made fresh and all cooked to order (al dente), as in Italy, and then topped with classic sauces. There is a determination to serve very good veal, another touchstone. And the kitchen, which will also be set up for small banquets, boasts that it can do "anything" with enough advance word. The menu will also have continental dishes, and the wine list at first will be small but quite well-chosen. The decor will be elegant, comfortable, and slightly countrified.

2515 Fourth Avenue, Seattle
Daily, 11:30-11
Reservations: 624-5464
Moderate
Credit Cards: AE, BA, MC
Full Bar

Trader Vic's ☆ ☆

Trader Vic's starts off as a restaurant for tourists and expense-accounters: thick Polynesian decor, cute drinks, an exotic menu. It can be a lot better than that, but for many diners the meals stay firmly at the level where you can experience curt service and such absurdities as the ceremonious dumping of A-1 sauce into a chafing dish that has beautifully cooked a lovely piece of steak. Yet there are numerous excellent dishes on the menu, and if you go on an uncrowded night and somehow get into the good graces of the management, it is possible to dine regally: noble unlisted wines appear from the cellar, the waiter will tell you about an unexpectedly fine liver that the kitchen can prepare especially for you, and the maitre d' might consent to toss the limestone lettuce salad with exquisite care. Trader's is a place that rewards very well those members who have joined the club by dining there regularly—but it's an expensive initiation fee.

For probationary members, we have a few tips. One good first course is the crab crepe, followed closely by the crepe with morels; salads are also by and large good. For main courses the best bet is the lamb, whether the Indonesian lamb lightly smoked in the Chinese ovens, or the Mongolian lamb of juicy chunks in a subtle brown plum sauce. Lunches are also good bets; the room is agreeably busy and the oyster dishes are commendable. The famous novelty drinks are over-rated, and the desserts are disappointing. Our general advice is to order conservatively (not risking, for instance, a dish like veal Cordon Bleu) and to stick with the roasted meats and a good wine.

Washington Plaza Hotel, Virginia and Westlake, Seattle
Daily, 11:30-10:45; Sunday, 5-10
Reservations: 624-8520
Expensive
Credit Cards: AE, BA, MC
Full Bar

Mirabeau ☆ ☆

Mirabeau is much better than you would expect a restaurant to be that sits atop the tallest bank tower in town. The baked alaskas are here, of course, along with the prom couples, and the $100 bottles of Chateau Latour that certain Arab parties order every visit. Service is somewhat uneven, and the decor is no better than unobjectionable. But it is also a French restaurant of high standards.

One of the best aspects is the lunch menu — four new specialties each day, with the list changing through the month. These are well-priced and very well-prepared, with occasional rarities like squid in a lobster sauce, or superior sweetbreads. Such a meal, accompanied by the salad with its excellent house dressing and a glass of the house wine, will cost no more than about $5. And of course on sunny days the view out over the Bay is worth the $5 alone. A true bargain.

For dinner one is confronted with a huge menu, too large really. The scampi provencale are a first course that cannot be bettered. After that, one would do well to order some of the game, such as the squab in a natural sauce or the quail in a sauce of gin and cream. A menu so big means that many of the items will be coming out of a freezer or from various states of partial preparation, so it makes sense to discuss the order with the manager, the very affable and helpful Gilbert Barth (formerly of Ondine in the Bay Area). You can also get good guidance through the moderately sound wine list. For dessert the souffles are very good. An extremely pleasant bar, with plush seats and the dazzling view, makes a fine ending to the evening.

Fourth Avenue and Madison Street, Seattle
Weekday lunch, 11:30-2; dinners, 5:30-11; closed Sunday
Reservations: 624-4550
Expensive
Credit Cards: AE, BA, MC
Full Bar

Chez Paul ☆ ☆

This is Seattle's one good restaurant on the model of Vancouver's small house restaurants. As far as the decor goes, it is completely successful. The foyer has the proper note of serene formality, there is a tiny, comfortable bar in the front room, and then there are three dining areas with elegant prints accenting the pale walls and well-spaced tables precluding large parties. Maitre d' Paul Kyer is a suave and charming host, a particularly good companion if you happen to be an opera buff.

The food has not been consistently good. It was delicious at first when the other Paul, the chef, was in command, then suffered from overcooking and underseasoning when a new chef was installed (since departed), and lately it has recovered its balance once more. It's a fairly small menu. For starters there are pate, ratatouille, quiche, snails, and a good salmon mousse. The entries get a bit more imaginative: an excellent pork roast stuffed with prunes, a passable duck with olives, and medallions of lamb in herbs. The wine list is outstanding, and the vegetables with the meal are also very good. When the food matches the quiet dignity of the setting, the evening is hard to beat.

1107 Dexter Avenue North, Seattle
Monday-Saturday, 5:30-midnight; closed Sunday
Reservations: 285-5000
Expensive
Credit Cards: AE, BA, MC
Full Bar

Canlis ☆ ☆

Peter Canlis, founder of this the second but best of four restaurants with similar menus on the coast, learned his trade in Hawaii. Canlis has a correspondingly international feeling: kimona-clad waitresses (extremely good at their trade, by the way); a Roland Terry interior design of glass, fieldstone, and natural wood; a French wine list; and a menu which, when you come right down to it, suggests a glorified steak house. It all fits together surprisingly well, although the steep bill for such a meal may mean the only happy diners here are those on generous expense accounts.

Dinner normally begins with a short stop in the elegant bar, since the thirty-two tables are usually heavily booked for dinner. The seafood appetizers at dinner can be superb, such as the mahimahi in a butter sauce or the terrific steamed clams in a wine and nectar sauce; the salads, especially the Canlis special (a bargain-priced Caesar), are also commendable. The entrees are simply cooked and served with one of the few sauces the house meticulously prepares. The salmon, when it is fresh (be sure to ask), can be expertly poached. The lamb we have had suffers from a house weakness—overcooking. Best are the steaks, carefully selected from choice cuts, grilled precisely to order, or served as a steak au poivre that could scarcely be improved. The beef also goes well with the best part of the wine list, numerous Medocs of good vintage (not actually on the list but kept in a special listing at the maitre d's desk). Desserts, except for the cheese cake, are another high point.

2576 Aurora Avenue North, Seattle
Dinners only, 5-11:30 p.m.; closed Sunday
Reservations: 283-3313
Expensive
Credit Cards: AE, BA, CB, MC
Full Bar

Crepe de Paris ☆ ☆

They do these things very well at this pleasant place—actually two places now, one downtown not far from the Washington Plaza and the other (Crepe de Paris au Bord du Lac) at the Lake Washington end of Madison Street in the pretty urban village of Madison Park. The crepes are made crisp in the Normandy style, and they are folded over some very good ingredients. In addition, the side dishes are superior: a thickly crusted onion soup, a small coquille packed with seafood, or a delicious large luncheon salade Annie. Since the crepes are a shade sweet, it makes sense to order some of the more assertive fillings such as the veal, the ratatouille, or the shrimp in bechamel sauce. Dessert crepes come bulging with a luscious vanilla ice cream and strawberries, chestnuts, raspberries, or a marvelous chocolate sauce. The wine list is a disappointment, but you can order a nice mildly alcoholic cider. Take a big swallow before you look at your bill, which will be high for mere (however delicious) crepes.

1802 Seventh Avenue, 1927 43rd Avenue East, Seattle
Downtown branch: daily, 11:30-11; Friday, Saturday til 12:30 a.m.;
   Sunday, 5-11; Au bord du lac: daily, 11-11; Friday, Saturday til 12:30;
   Sunday, 10-11.
Reservations: 623-4111 (downtown), 329-6620 (lake)
Moderate
Credit Cards: MC (both), BA (lake)
Beer and Wine

El Gaucho ☆ ☆

There are three gauchos here. The first is evident at lunch, which is expensive and very good. This is a steak house, so you are best advised to have a steak sandwich or the chopped sirloin in a proper mushroom sauce; the barbecued ribs in a tangy sauce are even better. You eat in semi-darkness, but everything—the good Roquefort on the salad, fine daily specials like a Creole omelet—is very well managed.

Then comes dinner, when the service gets more stately, you can see the handsome, well-arranged room, and the prices rise toward the ceiling. You are best advised to stick with the steaks, since the place shows little skill in the seafood appetizers or with some of the non-beef offerings like the lamb chops with kidneys. The steaks are superb, and you can enhance them with an excellent Caesar salad and a wine from the extensive, well-chosen wine list.

Finally, there is the hunt breakfast, starting around midnight and going to 4 a.m. For once, here is a place that understands that this meal should consist of very good, if small, portions. The fruit is splendid, the rolls and muffins are perfect; then you might have a half an omelet, a bit of sausage, a morsel of steak, and a few chicken livers with a tiny pile of excellent home-fries.

624 Olive Way, Seattle
Weekday, 11-4 a.m.; Saturday, 5-4 a.m.; closed Sunday
Reservations: 682-3202
Expensive
Credit Cards: AE, BA, MC
Full Bar

Maximilien's ☆

The Pike Place Market has always had everything except a proper cafe where one could get a bowl of onion soup and watch the passing crowd. Now it has it—or so we hope, since this tiny cafe is wedged into such a small space that the economics may close it down during the life of this book; and standards now vary.

Maximilien's is named for the family cat of Francois and Julia Kissel, and true to that spirit, the place is a highly personal version of the French cafe. Fish and chips, for instance, don't really belong at a French cafe, but since you can get such lovely fresh cod at the Market they make the dish—transform it would be a better word. Second-best item is the good old American hamburger—similarly put through an alchemical process. If you still insist on being French, you can have the onion soup, an outstanding salade Nicoise, or croissants (imported from Spokane!) with your morning breakfast. It's hard to get in at lunch, but the mid-afternoon is a nice time to catch a little sun through the windows as you gaze out over Elliott Bay.

Lower Level, Pike Place Market, Seattle
Daily, 10-5; closed Sunday
No Reservations: nearest phone, 464-9960
Inexpensive
No Credit Cards
No Liquor

Koraku ☆

Everybody knows Seattle has a good Chinatown; less well known are the good Japanese restaurants. For lunch there is a particularly fine choice of cheap, healthy, non-fattening ones that have plenty of atmosphere and are patronized by so many Japanese customers that standards remain very high.

Our favorite for lunch is the most authentic one, Koraku. (For dinner, See Mikado entry.) Few Caucasians go to the tiny place, which is poorly marked. The cooking is wonderfully palatable. Each day there are one or two specialities—a broiled fish, teriyaki, tempura, things like that. They come on a black tray with five other fixed items: an excellent soup, raw spinach (best when doused with a table hot sauce), bean cake in various artistic versions, rice, and pickled radishes. The cost is about $2.50; there is no charge for the excellent background music or the Japanese pornographic magazines.

419 Sixth Avenue South, Seattle
Monday-Friday, 11:30 a.m.-5:30 p.m.
No Reservations: 624-1389
Inexpensive
No Credit Cards
No Liquor

The Cedars ☆

What we have in this unlikely location, a recycled burger pit, is an authentic Lebanese cafe complete with Lebanese clientele (mostly students) and a proprietor dedicated to cooking proper Lebanese dishes with few concessions to American tastes. Portions are rather small and quality can be variable, but on a good day you can find delicately-spiced Shish Kebab, stuffed grape leaves, and oddities like a sandwich of garbanzo beans, fava beans, and sesame-seed butter on Syrian bread. Prices are very low, and the atmosphere could not be more atmospheric.

2312 North 45th Street, Seattle
Daily, 11 a.m.-1 a.m.
No reservations: 632-7708
Inexpensive
No Credit Cards
No Liquor

Vietnam Dynasty ☆

Vietnamese cooking, with its distinctive use of fresh herbs, is a distinguished cuisine almost unknown in the Northwest. This restaurant, small and struggling, makes a modest stab at providing some examples. The meals start well with thick soups, crisp imperial rolls (never to be missed), and nice salads. For the main course, you might have chicken breasts in mushrooms and wine or, if you have ordered a banquet in advance, the Vietnamese version of Peking duck, flattened and marinated. The plates are lacking the sprinklings of fresh herbs you may expect, and they are not hot enough. But the two proprietresses, Mrs. Padgett and Miss Canh, will gladly help you bring the dishes to fiery life by dosing them with nuoc mam, a sauce compounded of salt and rotting fish and aged for up to fifty years.

914 East Pike Street, Seattle
Daily, 11 a.m.-2 p.m.; 5-10 p.m.; closed Mondays
Reservations: 322-4080
Inexpensive
No Credit Cards
Beer and Wine

The Russian Samovar ☆

The restaurant, glimpsed behind the leaded glass in the handsome Loveless building on Capitol Hill, looks very inviting. The lunches, however, are modest buffets—fried chicken, meatballs, cheese slices—that have only the low price to recommend them. But dinner affords a chance to eat some good Russian items. The chicken Kiev is very nice, as are the cabbage rolls, the stroganoff, and for that matter the veal cordon bleu. (Skip the piroshki and the pelmeny.) As for the acid test, the borscht comes off very well as a nice bouillon with a delicate flavoring of beet puree. Desserts are acceptable; the wine list is not. The place is a bit uneven because it gets jammed, keeps costs quite low, and is actually a revival of a Russian restaurant started in 1931, changed to a tea room, and then reinstated fourteen years ago by Martin Farrar, who learned the cooking out of books.

806 East Roy Street, Seattle
Daily, 11:30-2, 5:30-9:30 p.m.; closed Sunday
No Reservations: 323-1465
Moderate
Credit Cards: AE, BA, DC, MC
Beer and Wine

Tien Tsin ☆

Consistency is not a strong point at this Mandarin restaurant near the University District, which seems to vary in quality depending on whether or not owner Bob Swei is in the kitchen. But the virtues are considerable: a menu with 168 items, including some items rarely seen in these parts (sea-cucumber, for instance), very good dishes made from chicken or prawns, a bold way with spicy Northern Chinese and Szechuan cuisine, modest prices, and a cheerful cafe-atmosphere in the front part of the place. It's enough to make it Seattle's second-best Chinese restaurant. We particularly like the Tien Tsin for lunch, when you can have such items as nice dumplings, a delicate serving of prawns in garlic and ginger, and perhaps one fiery dish. Banquets of ten courses or so are popular in the evening; they require advance notice of a day and are not of uniform quality.

1401 North 45th Street, Seattle
Lunch, Tuesday-Friday, noon-2; dinner, 5-10 p.m.; Saturday, 4-11;
    Sunday, 4-10; closed Monday
Reservations: 634-0223
Credit Cards: BA
Beer and Wine
Moderate

Java ☆

Indonesian cooking can be so good and so reasonably priced that one wonders why it is so rare in the Northwest. This struggling little place is the best we've found.

The mainstays are sates: skewered, bite-size pieces of chicken, pork, beef or lamb, grilled with vegetables and pineapple and served with a mint sauce or a wonderful peanut sauce. Since portions are small (and cheap), you can also order for your dinner such delicacies as sweet-and-sour chicken Indonesian style, nasi-goreng, or huzarensla — a savory blend of ground beef, tangerine slices, lettuce, grapes and a mustard sauce. The proper ending to this novel and compelling combination of flavors is an avocado pudding. There's also a ten-course Rijsttafel at $3.52 — merely acceptable.

Most of these dishes, in smaller portions, are also available at lunch, when you will be eating with a crowd of young lawyers. The enjoyable atmosphere is enhanced by the congenial and hard-working Tjoa family, who run the place.

212 Fourth Avenue South, Seattle
Weekdays, 11:30 a.m.-8 p.m.; Saturday, Noon-9 p.m.
Reservations: 622-9135
Inexpensive
No Credit Cards
Beer and Wine

Norseman Cafeteria ☆

Seattle has a large Scandinavian population, but it must be an eat-at-home group, since there are no outstanding restaurants serving this cuisine. Our favorite small spot is this cafeteria in the heart of Ballard. You can get tasty open-faced sandwiches with salmon, herring, shrimp, cheese, or beef, and there is a rich, sweep soup called rommegrot that is not to be missed. On Fridays and Saturdays, the menu blossoms into a smorgasbord particularly strong in fish dishes. The desserts are extensive and excellent, particularly the lefse, a soft, potato-flour pancake.

If the pastry whets the appetite for more of the same, then head over to Oscar Mathisen's Scandinavian Bakery (8537 15th Avenue Northwest, 784-6616, open 9-6), where there is a magnificent selection of breads, cookies, and cakes. It is a great place to visit in the holiday season.

2301 Northwest Market Street, Seattle
Daily, 8:30-5; closed Sunday
No Reservations: 783-5080
No Credit Cards
No Liquor (but great coffee)

Benihana of Tokyo ☆

This Benihana is just like the others in the chain. You sit around three sides of a table, among strangers usually, and after a round of drinks the chef appears, makes some jokes, and proceeds to carve and clatter and spin and meanwhile lightly grill your dinner on the large, stainless-steel griddle that is your table. The food is really very good—excellent beef cut into chunks, fresh vegetables cooked crunchy, exemplary bean sprouts, a fragrant soup, prawns and chicken chunks made delicious by the light cooking and the two good dipping sauces. This is not the best way to have a private dinner conversation, and the meal is a bit overpriced, but it's well cooked, and the setting of this restaurant, looking out into the courtyard of the IBM building downtown, enhances the tasteful decor. The bar is dark and pleasant, too. The lunches offer light cooking, when the speed-up style of dining seems less objectionable.

Fifth Avenue and University Street, Seattle
Weekday lunches, 11:30-2; dinners every night, 5:30-last seating at 9:45
Reservations: 682-4686
Moderate
Credit Cards: AE, BA, CB, DC, MC
Full Bar

Atlas Cafe ☆

As a rule, the best Chinese cooking to be found in Chinatown comes out of this tiny cafe. Over the years it has been a family kind of a place, with mostly Chinese families crowding the few tables and the counter. Now expansion is underway which will double the size of the cafe when it reopens in late 1975, so some of the agreeable funkiness may be departing.

The best dishes tend to be the daily specials, which are usually fresh fish like a sweet and sour rock cod or fish balls made from perch. On occasion there will be exotic dishes like pigtails and peanuts, gelatinous but good. The regular menu is fairly extensive and Cantonese. Caucasians will often be in a small minority in the Atlas, but they are not made to feel unwelcome.

424 Maynard Avenue South, Seattle
Dinners only, 4-10 p.m.; closed Monday
No Reservations: 623-0913
Inexpensive
No Credit Cards
No Liquor

Italo's Casa Romana ☆

Everything looks promising. The chef, a man of appropriate girth, lives upstairs. He is a gregarious fellow who enjoys talking about food, and table-hopping. The clientele is somewhat Italian. The tablecloths are red-checkered.

And on certain nights the place lives up to its promises. The fettucine comes out lightly cooked and with a distinctive bite of garlic. The saltimbocca is alive with fresh sage. The zabaglione is in perfect balance. But it is not always so, and therefore it pays to establish a good working relationship with Italo before placing the order. If Italo is given enough time and knows that he has an appreciator of his native cuisine on his hands, he will usually see to it that the food is not cooked American style.

One item requires no such pains: the pizza. It is delicious, with a high, bubbly crust. Even better is a calzone, a pizza made soft and folded over a filling of cheese and eggs.

38th South and Empire Way South, Seattle
Daily, 11-11; closed Monday
Reservations: 722-0449
Moderate
Credit Cards: BA, MC
Full Bar

The Earl of Sandwich ☆

As the name suggests, this place is dedicated to the humble sandwich, but its standards are lofty. The ingredients, from the fresh-baked bread to the Snohomish-made jack cheese, are uncommonly good and combined in fresh ways with fresh touches, such as the lemon juice whipped into the cream cheese for the smoked salmon sandwich.

But what makes this cheerful restaurant in a refurbished house the best sandwich shop in town are the accompaniments. There are excellent home-made soups, particularly the fresh mushroom. The breads and baked goods are superior. A simple thing like cider is the best local brand, Wax Orchards of Vashon. Dinner is another plus, served from a single nightly special at a modest $2.95; these meals make a genial start to a night at the Center across the street. Another good time to drop by is for Sunday brunch, with quiches, breads, fruit, and newspapers. Then at least, you'll get right in; during lunches the popular Earl almost always requires a short wait.

Hansen Baking Company, First North and Mercer Street, Seattle
Daily, 11-8; Friday, Saturday, 11-9; Sunday, 11-7
Evening Reservations: 284-8382
Inexpensive
No Credit Cards
Beer and Wine

Le Pigalle ☆

Only a single star now; the restaurant opened just after presstime for this year, so we could not judge the food. However, we know the chef, Jacques Jarriault, and know his work to be very fine, particularly the sauces, so we can assume it will be quite a good place.

Lunches will focus on crepes, which you might augment with a slice of Jarriault's outstanding pate, formerly served at Crepe de Paris and to our taste the best in the city. For dinner the menu looks like a classic array of established favorites: sole chambertin, salmon in champagne, pork with sauce pruneaux, and sweetbreads with sauce porto. The boneless stuffed duck should be very good. The wine list looks most interesting. The restaurant is medium-sized, located in the University district on a nondescript street. Both the Jarriaults are very charming, so the dining will be an unformidable excursion into first-class French cooking.

1104 Northeast 47th Street, Seattle
Lunches, 11:30-3; dinners, 5:30-11; closed Sunday
Reservations: 525-1525
Moderate
Credit Cards: BA, MC
Wine, aperitifs and beer

The Turbulent Turtle ☆

For several years, Don and Lea Andersen ran a tiny hamburger stand out by Shilshole Marina, favored by yachting folks and also by a band of hamburger scholars who considered the meticulously made, outrageously mammoth, daringly combined burgers of this stand to rank among the world's leaders. Now the family has gone big time, opening up a large establishment in University Village, the very heart of the gourmet community in Seattle.

The famous burgers are still here, like the wurstburger (liverwurst, pickles, and cream cheese sauce), the hushburger (with hushpuppies and chili), and the tostadaburger (salsa, guacamole, and chili). In addition, there is a fountain with homemade ice cream, a delicatessen, and a bakery. It is much bigger, but the same zany, nautical decor pertains as at the old stand, along with the same congenial fanaticism about doing things the right way. It should be a perfect place for a lunch, or for morning coffee with some pastry just out of the oven, as well as for an inexpensive supper for the family.

University Village Shopping Center, Seattle
Daily, 9 a.m.-8:30 p.m. (other details not yet available).

Mr. D's ☆

A few years ago Seattle actually had a fine Greek restaurant, Mr. D's — named for the multi-talented, easily distracted Demetrios Moraitis. Then it closed and went into hibernation for a couple of years. It has recently reopened, thus ending a long fast by Greek food lovers.

Mr. D's is a very funky place, with fish in numerous aquaria, zany paintings on the walls (by the chef himself), and so much assorted memorabilia that it looks more like a junk shop than a restaurant when you first walk in. There is plenty of time to contemplate the decor, since the service is slow and D takes his time with careful preparation of the orders. The results amply justify the wait: juicy skewers of souvlaki, a delicious first-course dip of minced cucumber and yogurt called tsiziki, a brightly flavored avgolemono soup, fragrant meatballs in tomato sauce, souzoukakia, and some new items, mostly seafood dishes. The two best items are standards you would probably order anyway: the moussaka and the baklava. With this comes some nice Greek wine and, often, a few songs performed by D.

> 1001 First Avenue, Seattle
> Daily, 11-10; closed Sunday (hours vary)
> Reservations: 622-4881
> Moderate
> No Credit Cards
> Beer and Wine

Mr. Pickwick's ☆

This Pioneer Square restaurant fills the need both for good English cooking and for a warm and cheerful place on those rainy, Londonlike days that characterize Seattle winters, falls, and springs (and sometimes a good part of her summers as well). The fire is real, the pewter pieces scattered around would pass for real, and the accents of the owners aren't bad either. More important, the cooking is proper British fare. At lunch you can have cheese, salads, fruit, a brisket of beef with a nice mustard, or a bit of steak and kidney pie along with your pint of Watney's. Dinners are fairly simple affairs, with meat pies, soups, and some outstanding desserts, notably the perfect bread pudding. At times, too, you can get scones and crumpets to go with delicious tea.

Negotiations are under way with prospective new owners, but we are informed that if the sale does go through, few changes are contemplated, except to expand the idea of doing solid English cooking in a publike atmosphere not laid on too thick.

> 222 South Main Street, Seattle
> Daily, 11-9; Friday and Saturday, 9:30-1 a.m.; closed Monday night and
>   Sunday
> Reservations: 623-1841
> Moderate
> Credit Cards: BA, MC
> Beer and Wine

Der Adler ☆

This restaurant, located in the basement of the new Peoples Bank office tower downtown, does not quite know whether to be a real German place or not. At lunchtime you can get an excellent bratwurst and a splendid German meat salad, but most of the menu is American sandwiches. At dinnertime, when the shining woods and bright colors contradict the mood for a good dinner, the menu offers serious German cooking but with such jarring notes as an insistent accordionist, a list of beers shy on German offerings, and only moderately knowledgeable waiters. But chef Wolfgang Grutzmacher is one of the few serious German chefs in the Northwest.

The dinners are particularly notable for the care that goes into all the side dishes — perfect potatoes, a red cabbage that is steeped in rich flavors, fine relishes, etc. There are several standout plates: the rouladen, the veal paprika, the sauerbratten, and the rabbit hunter's style. The wine list is well-chosen, and Der Adler offers you a chance to have a glass from each of three bottles for a modest price, so that you can progress to a sweeter wine with dessert (inferior pastries, by the way). When making a dinner reservation, ask for one of the small rooms.

> 1415 Fifth Avenue, Seattle
> Daily, 11-11; closed Sunday
> Reservations: 622-1432
> Moderate
> Credit Cards: AE, BA, CB, DC, MC
> Full Bar

Ray's Boathouse ☆

Pleasantly decorated with raw wood, hanging plants, and fabrics on the wall. Ray's offers two things tourists ardently desire when in Seattle: pretty good seafood and a view of the water. The restaurant is next to Shilshole marina, looking west, so if you go for dinner you are likely to see the sun setting over the mountains and the sailboats.

Ray's does moderately careful cooking and gets good ingredients, but the kitchen is not up to the subtlest preparations.

You are better off getting a simply broiled piece of salmon (or for that matter the excellent prime rib) than attempting the complicated thing they do with the prawns. Salads, appetizers, wines, desserts, and service are all quite good in this very well-managed place. The bar is blessed with one of the finest views in town.

6049 Seaview Avenue Northwest, Seattle
Weekday lunches, 11-2:30; dinners, 6-11; closed Sunday
Reservations: 789-3770
Moderate
Credit Cards: BA, MC
Full Bar

King Cafe ☆

By and large, we are not very impressed by the Chinese food served in Seattle's Chinatown, at least during the present period of economic uncertainty in the District due to the impact of the nearby new stadium. The Atlas Cafe, with a separate entry in this guidebook, is the best place; Sun Ya, while discouraging to occidentals and soon to relocate, is another good-enough one; Four Seas is Americanized but can do some excellent rock cod; Lin Yen is cheap and respectable; and there is the very popular Tai Tung with a huge menu of items, most of which taste alike. You do better eating Japanese food in Chinatown, or going out of the area for distinguished Chinese cooking.

In exception to this mediocrity is King Cafe, a crowded little place specializing in dim-sum pastries. The range of pastries is not terribly great, but the hum bow and the shrimp balls, along with a half-dozen other carefully made dishes, make the spot well worth visiting for a light lunch. The Sunday brunches are particularly good, but getting in is lots of trouble.

723 South King Street, Seattle
Daily, 11-5; closed Wednesday
No reservations: 622-6373
Inexpensive
No Credit Cards; no checks
No Alcohol

Ivar's Salmon House

There are places that don't overcook the salmon, as often happens here, and places like Jake O'Shaughnessey's that know how to do the alderwood smoking with far greater delicacy, but Ivar's is still not a bad spot to know about. The view over Lake Union is exceptional, and the prices in this family-style establishment are quite good: $4.95 for the complete dinner. In addition, Ivar Haglund has insisted that the decor in this imitation Indian longhouse adhere faithfully to the traditions of Indian carving and design.

> 401 Northeast Northlake Way, Seattle
> Weekday lunches, 11:30-2; dinners, 5-10
> Reservations: 632-0767
> Moderate
> Credit Cards: AE, BA, DC, MC
> Full Bar

The Merchants Cafe

The food here has never amounted to much, but the restoration of this former German restaurant, originally opened in 1889, is the handsomest in Pioneer Square. The downstairs, under-the-sidewalk bar is intimate and as much of the Underground Tour as you should allow yourself. The food, under the current new management, is at least underpriced, and the soups are well-made. Have the cioppino for lunch or dinner and enjoy the ornate surroundings. The best sandwich is one called two meats and two cheeses.

> 109 Yesler Way, Seattle
> 11:30 a.m.-2 a.m.; closed Sundays
> Reservations: 624-1515
> Inexpensive
> Credit Cards: AE, BA, MC
> Full Bar

LODGING

Washington Plaza Hotel ☆ ☆

If you get a room above the twentieth floor in the tower of this hotel and on the west side with the view of the Sound outside the tall windows, you will have found the best room in the city. As usual with new Western International Hotels, the rooms are well appointed with features, generously apportioned and tastefully, conservatively decorated. Expensive, too: $40 a night for that double, and on up to $135 a night for the penthouse two-level suites.

Otherwise, the hotel is as ungainly as its corn-cob architecture. The lobby has the requisite plush chairs and chandeliers, but since it is wrapped around the base of the round tower, leading nowhere, no one uses it. The Library Bar is acceptable, and Trader Vic's gives the ground floor whatever class it has, but the other rooms are decorated with little verve and serve mediocre food. The adjoining Ben Franklin offers overpriced rooms in a nice older hotel that seems rather forgotten. Service is variable, and the hotel sometimes seems dominated by conventioneers. The hotel's location, near the Monorail and close to the best shopping, is a definite plus.

> Fifth Avenue at Westlake, Seattle
> 624-7400
> Expensive
> Credit Cards: AE, BA, CB, DC, MC
> Small pets permitted

Olympic Hotel ☆ ☆

This famous Seattle institution was built in the 1920s, when fashion called for ornateness within and without. Public rooms like the Spanish Ballroom still show evidence of this grandeur, and the main lobby with its golden arched vault has a kind of composure amid the bustle that even the plastic globe, the clanking baggage carrier, and the fake flowers cannot efface. But after this positive first impression, one must exercise care.

The rooms in the east wing (odd-numbered rooms) were built in a later addition designed for commercial travelers and they are depressingly small; if you draw one of these you would be well advised to seek another hotel. Other travelers paying $30 a night for a double might find the absence of a view, now that tall office towers have grown up around the hotel, a bit of a shock. But the rooms in the west wing are generally quite nice, decorated with taste, and with modernized bathrooms. If you select a suite in the 54 series (Fourth and University corner), you will have a view of the Sound above the eighth floor—and a bill from $75 a night up to $200 for the presidential suite.

Downstairs there is a fine sense of being at the center of town, which is exactly where you are. There are ample facilities, although none of them is outstanding. The nicest bar (of three) is in the Golden Lion, a dinner place serving uneven international-hotel-style food. The English pub is a congenial place for a glass of stout, but here too you should not expect too much from the kitchen. The attractions of the hotel, in short, are that you get a nice quiet room, you are close to good restaurants and shopping a few blocks away, and you've done your bit for historic preservation.

Fourth Avenue and Seneca Street, across from the airline terminal, Seattle
682-7700
Expensive
Credit Cards: AE, BA, CB, DC, MC

University Tower Hotel ☆ ☆

This older hotel was intelligently designed to give every room a bay window, so if you get up on the higher floors with a southern exposure, you will have a sun-filled room with a pretty view of Lake Union, the University of Washington campus, and Lake Washington. The rooms are decorated in standard fashion and are good-sized; suites are only marginally larger than the standard doubles. You are better advised to take a standard room and save some money. The lobby downstairs is not very attractive, but the hotel does an excellent job preparing food for conferences—a good sign. The nearby University Avenue is a good place for shopping and strolling, and downtown is ten minutes away. The

University Tower, in short, is the best place to stay near the University and one of the best bargains in the city.

> Brooklyn Avenue NE and NE 45th Street, Seattle
> 634-2000
> Moderate
> Credit Cards: AE, BA, CB, DC, MC
> Pets Limited

Airport Hilton ☆ ☆

Hiding behind an ugly, mammoth sign is a motel with some unusual features. This fifteen-year-old, small motel was designed by the prestigious firm of Skidmore-Owings-Merrill, and its interiors were supervised by the noted Seattle designer Roland Terry. The results are very pleasing: strong functionalism in the architecture, a deft use of Northwest materials such as fieldstone within, and a sense of scale around the courtyard that is comforting and rare. The landscaping is mature and attractive.

Parts of the motel are getting a bit tacky now as the management prepares to construct a large hotel tower in the area, but if you stay in the south wing (the 400 series), you will have a view of the inner courtyard from a very large room attractively redecorated. The 100-series wing, on the other hand, is rather poor and too close to the noisy crowd that comes to dance in the lounge. Food at Henri's has been terrible, but it is improving.

> 17620 Pacific Highway South, across from the airport, Seattle
> 244-4800
> Expensive
> Credit Cards: AE, BA, CB, DC, MC
> Pets Limited

Mayflower Park Hotel ☆

This fifty-year-old hotel, located right between the two big department stores downtown, is showing distinct signs of rejuvenation: a new lobby, a smart new restaurant and lounge called Oliver's about to open, and up in the average-sized rooms, some very tasteful modern decor. There's no air-conditioning, and the lower level rooms might get a bit of street noise; but the walls are thick, and if you get up above the ninth floor on the north side you will have a bit of a view of the Sound. The proportion of tour-groups and convention-goers is acceptably small. It adds up to a major bargain: fine location, a small, older building with character, and $20 a night for a double.

405 Olive Way, Seattle
623-8600
Moderate
Credit Cards: AE, BA, CB, DC, MC

Edgewater Inn ☆

This lure here is the waterfront location on Elliott Bay a few blocks below Seattle Center. The waterside rooms overhang the Bay, so if you get one of the rooms with a balcony and on the lower floors, you can actually do some fishing for dogfish. The decor is glossy, but the rooms are spacious and quiet. Fourth floor rooms are undersized, and the inshore rooms overlook a dreary parking lot. The rooftop nightclub has dancing for the middle-aged, and the restaurant has a passable luncheon buffet.

2411 Alaskan Way, Pier 67, Seattle
624-7000
Expensive (waterside)
Credit Cards: AE, BA, CB, DC, MC
Pets Permitted

TOURISM

Pike Place Market ☆ ☆ ☆ ☆

Not only is this the best attraction in Seattle; the sixty-year-old Public Market is the finest remaining farmer's market in the country. It is a moving tribute to an old streak of social-welfare idealism that set it up (as a way around middlemen), to an aggressive preservationist movement in the city that narrowly saved it, and to the indomitable individualists who keep the shops and produce stalls going. It is worth an extended visit for many reasons. Crowds of interesting people come, particularly on Saturdays, to shop and mingle. You'll have the best shopping for food and gourmet items, splendid views of the harbor below the bluff on which the Market perches, the nice spots for lunch, and a bazaar-like profusion of sensory detail.

Like any bazaar, the Market has its pitfalls where an unsuspecting buyer can get inferior goods slipped in by a fast-talking hawker. The absence of signs and the rabbit-warren architecture also make it a difficult place to shop intelligently; hence the following guide to the best places. The numbers start at the main entrance to the Market, at Pike Place and First Avenue. Numbers in boxes refer to attractions on the lower level of the main building; all others are on street level.

1. DeLaurenti's: a Mediterranean delicatessen, dominantly Italian.

2. Little Bread Company: exotic breads and fine bagels.

3. Mondo's: specializing in oddities like fennel, coriander, ginger root.

4. Alice Signey: delicious locally grown fruit.

5. Randall's Bar-B-Q: wonderful, crusty chicken and ribs.

6. Don and Joe's: the best meat market—veal, innards, fresh turkeys.

7. Pike Place Fish: great quality and some rare finds.

8. Roy's: the best local fruit and fine non-local vegetables.

9. Rotary Bakery: fresh goods from upstairs and superb macaroons.

10. Rufino Ordonio: a family vegetable stand of high standards.

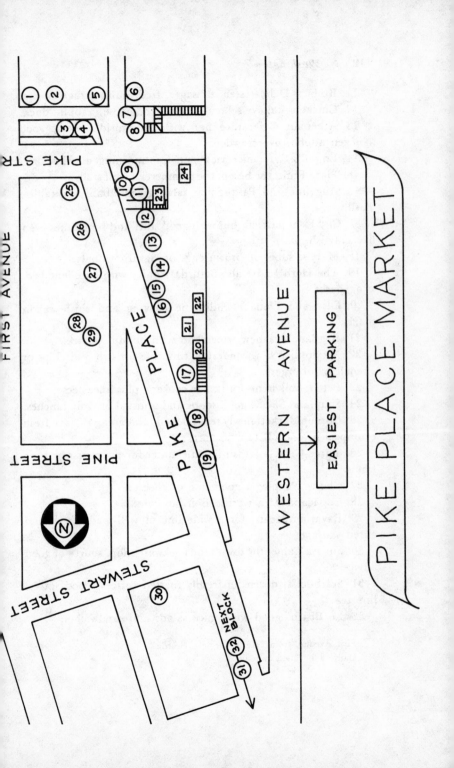

PIKE PLACE MARKET

11. Brehm's Delicatessen: sausages, fresh bulk cottage cheese.

12. Chicken Valley: schmaltz, chicken, goose, rabbit, duck.

13. Athenian Cafe: nice bar with the world's beers, good chicken adobo, overcrowded.

14. Lowell's Cafe: nice view and fine morning muffins.

15. Plaza Fruit: the best of the commercial fruit stalls.

16. Angelina and Pasqualina: salad greens, baby vegetables, basil.

17. City Fish: harried, but with good stuff and sometimes even live crayfish.

18. Mary's: superior brown eggs on Saturdays only.

19. The Herb Lady: also Saturdays only, with excellent bedding herbs.

20. Elisa and Elena's: Philippine cooking and shish kabob snacks.

21. Bagdade's: a new wine shop with helpful service.

22. Maximilien's: a wonderful, tiny cafe for fish and chips or French hamburgers.

23. Pete's: bulk items for Italian cookery, plus fine cheese.

24. Soup and Salad: good soups and unusual organic lunches.

25. Corner Market: newly redeveloped, and going to have fresh crumpets in one of its new stores.

26. Three Girls: a Jewish lunch counter for liverwurst or tuna sands.

27. Cheese People: a good line of cheeses.

28. Copacabana: a terrific Bolivian cafe.

29. Bavarian Meats: for a wide line of well-made fresh and cured sausage.

30. Sur La Table: the town's top cookware shop, source of good advice.

31. Starbuck's: dozens of freshly roasted coffees, good spices, fine tea.

32. Le Bistro: good wine, nice salads and sandwiches.

First Avenue, from Pike to Virginia, Seattle
Daily, 9-6; closed Sunday

Port Chatham Packing Company ☆ ☆ ☆ ☆

Our variant of the custom of "sending a salmon back home" is to go to this authentic salmon-smoking company in Ballard and buy for yourself and to send to your friends a version of smoked salmon that impresses us (Julia Child was recently converted, too) as just about the finest we've eaten.

Erling and Norman Nilson carry on a family tradition started in the 1930s: they smoke the salmon ever so carefully with alder sawdust, at lower temperatures, with less salt, and for fewer days (about two) than is the custom. The result is a buttery, very subtle, luscious salmon that normally makes instant converts. It sells for around $4.90 a pound, or you can bring in your own freshly caught salmon from Westport and the Nilsons will work their magic for a mere $1 a pound. It can be semi-frozen, well-packed, and then shipped airmail-special-delivery anywhere in the country with good results for about $7.50 a pound, including fish, smoking, and delivery. You can also buy it canned, or smoked Portlock style (a little stronger), or you can get salmon jerky to chew on. The shop and smokehouse, knee-deep in fish, are great fun to visit in their own right.

632 Northwest 46th Street, Seattle
Weekdays, 8-5; Saturday, 8-noon; closed Sunday
783-8200

Seattle Waterfronts ☆ ☆ ☆

More than any other American city, Seattle is surrounded by busy and beautiful bodies of water. The deep and cold Puget Sound forms the western boundary, an arm of the Pacific Ocean whose navigability and beauty have been marveled at by nearly everyone since Captain George Vancouver sailed into it in 1792. The eastern border is eighteen-mile Lake Washington, a fresh-water "mountain lake at sea level" prettily flecked with sailboats in search of its non-existent winds. Much of this waterfront is readily accessible to visitors.

Central Waterfront. You will feel squeezed by tourists and railcars, but the views of the Sound are as bracing as the salt air.

Ye Old Curiosity Shop, at the foot of Yesler, is a campy apotheosis of the souvenir shop; the fish and chips are good at the Sourdough Restaurant (Pier 57); just north are an evolving Waterfront Park of strong design that is fine for promenades, and the new Public Aquarium, which should open in late 1976 as one of the finest in the nation.

Boat Tours. Hour-long harbor tours leave frequently from Pier 56 (adults, $2.25, 623-1445) and since the harbor is a busy one and the captains are very knowledgeable about the traffic, this is an excellent tour. You can cruise across the Sound to Blake Island for Indian dancing and Indian-style roasted salmon (Pier 56, summers only, $11 adults, 322-6444). A more dignified version of this tour goes to the beautifully landscaped Kiana Lodge on Bainbridge Island, with a twilight cruise back to downtown (summers only, $14.50 adults, 682-1234). Easiest of all is simply to take a round-trip walk-on cruise aboard a Washington state ferry to Winslow—a lovely, 75-minute lunch break for $1.50 (Pier 52).

The nicely refurbished "Princess Marguerite" sails at 8:30 a.m. each summer day to Victoria, four hours away. The cruise is very nice, with decent food in the dining room, an enjoyable bar, and a sunset on the way back. Unfortunately the boat returns after only five hours in Victoria, so unless you plan to spend the night (which we recommend), you may be herded through Victoria like so many tourists being fleeced. (Canadian Pacific Ferries, Pier 64, $14 adults round trip, 623-5560).

Ship Canal. The city is bisected by a canal and Lake Union, connecting Puget Sound to Lake Washington, where a thriving waterside industry was once envisioned. Here you can watch the boat traffic close-up. Government Locks (Northwest 54th Street and 32nd Avenue Northwest) provide a manicured landscape for enviously watching yachts. Fisherman's Bay Salmon Terminal at the south end of Ballard Bridge (175 West Thurman) is a marvelous maze of salmon, halibut, and crab boats you can walk among, photograph, or admire from the bar in the Wharf Restaurant. Franco's Hidden Harbor Restaurant is set amid enormous yachts moored in Lake Union. At the eastern end of this waterway you can walk along the embankment beneath rustling poplars (start at the park just north of the Seattle Yacht Club,

1807 East Hamlin); or rent a canoe from the University of Washington Canoe House, just south of Husky Stadium (543-2217).

Lake Washington. The Olmsted brothers, sons of the famous designer of Central Park, laid out some of Seattle's fine parks and boulevards, a notable example of which stretches south from Madrona Drive along the lake; it makes splendid biking (rent at Velocipede, 3101 East Madison). Swimming is nice in the lake at this point, after July; the Sound is always too cold. The bar at the Hindquarter (102 Lakeside) has a romantic view of the lake and the marina at Leschi.

Longacres Racecourse ☆ ☆ ☆

One of the best small race tracks in the country, Longacres offers several unusual feature. The track, built on springy tidal loam, is extremely fast. The setting is lovely, and the track is famous for the care it lavishes on maintenance. The clubhouse is a fascinating mixture of buildings where one can find variety and calm away from the crush. The horses are of good quality, sportingly matched. Best of all, the races are held at twilight on weekdays, so you can combine a nice meal and a sunset with the entertainment.

There are several unusual places from which to watch the races. The Gazebo offers outside terraces for sunny days. There are smaller lounges back in the clubhouse, like the Garden Room and another bar with outstanding Currier and Ives prints. Best bar is the old one in the original clubhouse, with a fireplace and timber beams.

Route 405, one mile east of I-5, Renton
Mid-May to Mid-September, Wed.-Sun.; weekday post time, 4:15 p.m.;
weekends, 1:15 p.m.
624-2455
Grandstand admission: $1.75

Sports in Washington ☆ ☆ ☆

Golf. In the Seattle area, the best private courses are Sahalee (north of Issaquah), a very narrow, sporting course of great beauty; Meridian Valley (Kent), a course with exceptional greens requiring very intelligent play; Seattle Golf Club (north end), with a hilly layout and a fairly easy play; and Broadmoor (Madison Park), quite pretty and too easy. For a beautiful public course that will boost your ego, play Mount Si at North Bend.

Outstanding courses elsewhere in the state are: Sudden Valley (east of Bellingham), with a marvelous setting, fine greens, and two contrasting nines; Port Ludlow, tight, beautiful, and simply superb; Meadow Springs at Richland, a desert course in magnificent shape and very difficult; Tumwater (Olympia) looks wide open, but the fairways are cut narrow; Indian Canyon at Spokane, a dazzling public course; Fircrest (Tacoma) is hilly and well-groomed; and Tacoma Golf and Country Club, a short, mature course with old-style, umbrella greens.

Fishing. Besides salmon from Westport and Ilwaco, there are bass near Castle Rock, Moses Lake, and on the Snake River, and fine trout in the Okanogan region. The masochistic local obsession is for steelhead, a sea-going rainbow trout normally pursued in bone-chilling rains, sleet, or snow. The north fork of the Stillaguamish is restricted to fly fishing for steelhead; another good area is in the south, along the Kalama and Toutle Rivers. Steelhead guides hang out in Forks on the Peninsula and Sedro Woolley on the Skagit.

Hunting. Eastern Washington has a long fall season for fowl: Othello for ducks, Moses Lake for pheasants, Tri-Cities for geese, Okanogan and the Snake River for chukar, and Yakima for quail. Blacktail, whitetail, and mule deer are hunted all over the state; there are substantial elk herds in the Olympic Peninsula and near Cle Elum; and black bear in the two mountain ranges.

Skiing. Crystal Mountain, near Mount Rainier, has the greatest variety and some runs of international caliber for experts; Alpental is the best of the facilities at Snoqualmie Pass, with a large vertical drop; Mission Ridge at Wenatchee is blessed with dry snow, and offers some runs for advanced skiers, but sometimes windy. Also notable are Mount Baker, for spectacular scenery; Stevens Pass, for lots of variety; 99 Degrees North at Chewelah, for dry snow and a new resort; and Schweitzer Basin in Idaho.

Alpinism. Hiking in Washington's two mountain ranges is among the finest in the world, and there are enough areas open so that crowding is not a major drawback. Start by buying the paperback guides *101 Hikes, 102 Hikes,* etc., published by The Mountaineers; then ask the Forest Service and the National Park Service for more detailed advice. Equipment can be found at Recreational Equipment Inc. (1525 11th Avenue), which has absolutely everything, or at Eddie Bauer (1926 Third Avenue), a fine shop specializing in top-quality down products and expensive gear and clothes. Best months are August and September. If you hike into the mountains off season taking snowshoes and cross-country skis, do it in Eastern Washington where the snow is dry.

Spectator Sports. The SuperSonics basketball team is a genuine contender in the NBA, playing Bill Russell-style team ball. The Sounders are one of the better soccer teams in the NASL. An NFL football team, the Seahawks, debuts in 1976 in the Domed Stadium, a bare-bones facility with excellent viewing lines. Some years the U.W. football team is not too outclassed by the California members of the PAC-8.

Pioneer Square ☆ ☆

Architecture—Two factors created and preserved this unusually large and coherent old town at the south end of Seattle's downtown. After the fire of 1889 destroyed the area, one architect, Elmer Fisher, took virtually complete charge of designing the masonry structures that replaced the wooden city. When the downtown leapfrogged uptown, the area was drained of economic value, so the buildings survived rather than being torn down for modern offices. Now they're back in style.

That style is Victorian Romanesque Revival, laid on so thick by Fisher that the buildings have a comic, parvenu spirit about them. In a major building like the Pioneer Building, 606 First Avenue, each story has a different way of treating windows. Zany as these buildings are, Fisher's strong sense of urban design imposed a

pleasing unity: a pedestrian-enhancing scale of broad streets
setting off relatively low buildings, and unifying design elements
like rusticated arched major entrances to most buildings. Walking
south on First Avenue South, one can observe the evolution of
American architecture from Fisher's 1890s decadence to the
Sullivanesque style in warehouse buildings south of Jackson Street.
Best restorations: Pioneer Building, Maynard Building (117 First
Avenue South), Grand Central Hotel Arcade (First South and
South Main), and Occidental Avenue South, from Main to
Jackson.

Shopping—As usual in such sections, the quality is variable.
The Grand Central Arcade (First South and South Main) is a good
place to start: Courtney Branch for pottery, David Ishii for old
books, R. David Adams for plants, Tribal Arts for jewelry, and
Grand Central Mercantile for cookware. Additional unusual
shops in the area are: Glasswater Leathers (11 First South) for
handbags and jackets; Design Products (217 First South) for
European plastics; Compleat Cookery and other shops in the St.
Charles Hotel project (81 South Washington); The Seattle Air
Force (166 South Jackson) for kites; and The Wood Shop (402
Occidental South) for toys.

Eating—The Brasserie Pittsbourg, City Loan Pavillion,
Prague, Mr. Pickwick's, and Mr. D's are listed separately. In
addition: the best spot for outdoor dining is The Salad Gallery
(312 Second South); the nicest spot for coffee and a pastry is
Amstelredamme Cafe (81 South Washington); the best gimmick is
The Breadline (325 Second Avenue South), where old folks serve
excellent soups.

Nightlife—Best bars are City Loan Pavilion (on Occidental
Park), chic and quiet; The Salad Gallery for marvelous fruit
daiquiries; and The Central Tavern for beer with the
bureaucrats. You find good bluegrass at Inside Passage (200 First
South), disco at Shelly's Leg (300 Alaskan Way South), and
dancing at Bombay Bicycle Shop (116 South Washington Street).

Seattle Parks ☆ ☆

None is quite grand enough or well-kempt enough to be remarkable, but the park system offers a great variety of rewarding experiences.

U.W. Arboretum (Lake Washington Boulevard and Madison) is most beautiful in the late spring. The Japanese Garden is quite authentic; Azalea Way is a fragrant stroll in the spring; and the northern section features a wonderful walk along marshland and waterways.

Volunteer Park (15th East and East Prospect) is a Victorian throwback, with the Seattle Art Museum, a botanical conservatory, mature trees set on sweeping lawns, and an inspiring view from atop the old water tower.

Woodland Park (North 50th and Aurora Avenue North) is the busiest park: lawn bowling, a so-so zoo, a rose garden, playing fields, and a perfect jogging path around lovely Green Lake.

Gas Plant Park (North Lake Union) is a daring concept: the promontory has a peerless view back to the city over busy Lake Union, and set into the park is a magnificent complex of old cracking towers for the gas plant, creating a haunting industrial sculpture.

Discovery Park (Magnolia Boulevard and West Emerson Street) is a converted Army fort with grand views from the southern bluffs, beach walks, and fine wilderness for picnics.

Schmitz Park (Admiral Way Southwest and Southwest Stevens) preserves fifty acres of virgin forest.

Seattle Center (Denny and Broad), the architecturally jumbled legacy from the 1962 World's Fair, has the best people-watching and several good attractions: the Pacific Science Center has moderately instructive displays and a fine book and gift shop; the amusement rides are good; the Northwest Craft Center (just west of the big fountain) has an outstanding collection of works by Northwest craftspersons; the Seattle Art Museum Pavilion offers top-notch traveling shows of modern painters. Two tips: confine your visit at the Space Needle to the bar or the observation deck; and steer around the fast-food emporium known as the Center House.

Seattle Antique Shops ☆ ☆

The serious student of antiques will be interested in this city not so much for the depth and range of the items as for the possibility of finding extraordinary bargains in quality pieces. The reason is simple: the area does not have serious collectors constantly going over collections as in the East. Best choices:

Globe Antiques, 1524 E. Olive Way. This is consistently the most interesting shop, strong in English and Continental furniture, oriental rugs, Georgian silver, and some simple country pieces. Owner Betty Balcomb is the queen bee of the Seattle antique business.

William L. Davis, 1300 Fifth Avenue. Pieces here are very expensive but invariably in superb condition; the English furniture is the top line.

Unique Antiques, 700 Olive Way. The name is valid: this shop has the unusual specialty of eastern European antiques, plus paintings.

Rosen-Colgren Gallery, 1814 Seventh Avenue. The best porcelain in town is here, along with good rugs (some Navaho) and silver.

Bushell's Auction House, 2006 Second Avenue. Mixed in with plain old stuff are some excellent antiques that you might get at the weekly Tuesday auction for a steal.

The Legacy ☆ ☆

Northwest Coast Indians had high aesthetic standards and their creations in carving and design rank among the finest in American Indian art. These designs combine animism, an elaborate formal patterning into cellular units, and a vivid metamorphic imagination. Some of this can be studied at the Burke Museum at the University of Washington, but there is also at least one very good gallery where you might learn more and find a nice gift.

In some areas, The Legacy is tops in the Northwest — Indian baskets, old Eskimo materials, and contemporary Indian and Eskimo prints. But it also has a good representation of jewelry, old Indian materials, and carvings. A helpful owner, John McKillop, and a good rack of books on the subject complete your needs. Another good collector and dealer in town, who operates more on an appointment basis, is Michael Johnson (108 South Jackson, 622-0084).

71 Marion Viaduct, near the waterfront, Seattle
Monday-Saturday, 10-5
624-6350

Asian Art ☆ ☆

Seattle has a long history as a port serving Asia, since it is the closest American mainland port to Japan. The Asian influence pervades the city's domestic architecture and interior design, thus further encouraging good shops with Asian artifacts. Three notable examples may be found.

Benavi Asian Arts (606 First Avenue, Pioneer Square: 622-8899) is a small shop managed by Frank Bennett, who has assembled over the past dozen years a remarkable collection of Asian antiquities. By concentrating on finds from the Philippines, where masterpieces traded from Asia were often buried with the dead, he has discovered pieces of great age and value, many of museum quality. His large, resonant Martaban jars, used by Chinese traders, are outstanding. Bennett is normally in the shop from 10 to 2 each day, is quite learned, and his prices are extremely good.

Mariko Tada Inc. (519 Olive Way, by Frederick and Nelson: 624-7667) is another shop with pieces (particularly ceramics) of quality rarely encountered outside of New York City. The shop displays its pieces as if it really were a museum and specializes in Chinese, Korean, and Japanese works from before the nineteenth century. Takao Sugiyama is the curator.

Japanese Antiquities Gallery (200 East Boston: 324-3322) specializes in fine examples of Japanese folk art, many of museum quality; Gene Zema is the owner of this most unusual shop.

Culture in Seattle ☆ ☆

Visual Arts. Some of Seattle's serious art sales galleries are within easy strolling distance of each other in the Pioneer Square area, Foster-White Gallery (311½ South Main) represents big Northwest names like Tobey, Graves, and Callahan as well as a strong stable of younger talents. Just across the hall from Foster-White is Dootson-Calderhead's tiny space, the main showplace for nationally-known, established contemporary artists. D/C shows and stocks prints and multiples as well as original works. Other showplaces are less consistent but often worth a visit: check the gallery listings of the papers to see what's on view at Polly Friedlander (97 Yesler Way) and Linda Farris (322 2nd South). At less central locations are Francine Seders (6701 Greenwood N.) and Gordon Woodside (803 East Union).

The Seattle Art Museum has two homes: the small Art-Deco jewel-box in Volunteer Park is the home of the renowned collection of Oriental art, well-worth a number of visits; the Modern Art Pavilion at Seattle Center is mainly an exhibition space for ambitious touring shows reflecting the contemporary art scene. The Frye Art Museum collection is a spotty but fascinating assembly of the kind of 19th century "bad art" (Bougereaux, shepherdesses, genre paintings of sheep, Pre-Raphaelite allegory) which is currently undergoing a revival. The true American avant-garde, from video art to body pieces, finds its home at obscurely-located and/or gallery (1525 10th Avenue).

Theater. The two established theater stock companies share the year between them. A Contemporary Theater (locally called "ACT") runs from June to October with a subscription series ranging from revived "American classics" to original scripts. Their heavy production schedule of a new show every three weeks or so makes their batting average spotty, but they score several times a season. The Seattle Repertory Theater's subscription season runs from October to April with a mainly staid line-up of classics, comic crowd-pleasers, and a leavening of new though usually New-York tested material. Both companies are highly subscribed, so getting single seats can be a problem, but it's worth a try.

Off the beaten path are three theaters worth a visit. The Rep now has a small second theater, 2nd Stage, (Eighth and Union), which is intended to perform more "experimental" pieces than can be mounted at the main theater. On Capitol Hill near downtown, The Empty Space Association (919 East Pike) has a strong track record and a devoted audience for their unusual and energetically theatrical presentations of both classic plays and new American and European drama. The Intiman Theater presents highly polished revivals of early modern plays at various theaters.

Music. The Seattle Symphony Orchestra seems to be on the rise again after a long fallow period: their work is still erratic, but if you catch them under the right guest conductor the experience can be richly rewarding. (Ticket information, 447-4736.) Seattle Opera presents five productions a year during the season, five performances in the opera's original language, two in English. Some of these productions are highly enjoyable.

Music lovers should also check the papers for events at the University of Washington: they're badly publicized off campus, but some are very worthwhile, mainly chamber music performances by The Contemporary Group, the Soni Ventorum Wind Quintet, and the school's quartet-in-residence, the Philadelphia String Quartet.

Fish Stores ☆ ☆

Visitors from afar often want to buy good seafood, particularly fresh salmon, for a gift or for cooking at a vacation home, boat, or campfire. Here's our list of the best local fishmongers. (See also the entry for Port Chatham Salmon.)

Pike Place Fish Company, is the southernmost of the fish stores in the Pike Place Market and the one with the most consistent quality. Manager John Yokayama is always worth asking if he has any unusual specialties, like skate. (682-7181).

Sandy's Seafoods, 10528 Greenwood Avenue North, is a cost's-no-obstacle shop, operated by Sandy Hanson, who knows many captains well enough to get the choice of their catch. (362-6868).

University Seafood and Poultry Co., NE 47th St. and University Way, is operated by Dale Erickson, and it is invariably reliable; it is one of the few places with unfrozen Dungeness crab. (632-3900.)

Mutual Fish Company, 2335 Rainier Avenue South, is a very large supplier with a great range of fine fish, but you will not have quite the same personal service and reliability; you can get fresh salmon for a longer season here.

Four Shopping Districts ☆ ☆

Downtown. Frederick and Nelson (Fifth and Pine) is an unusually large, unusually good department store for any city's downtown: sedate, deep in merchandise, traditional. Supporting it with younger, less expensive lines is the equally huge Bon Marche (Third and Pine). Nordstrom (Fourth and Pine) is a fashion department store with striking decor, superior buyers, and merchandising moxie that impresses even *W.* Two fine, small shops for clothes are nearby: Butch Blum (Fifth and Union) for men's clothes, and Traina Michael (just south at 1328 Fifth Avenue), a women's boutique.

Capitol Hill. This smart section specializes in home furnishings, with Broadway East the main street. Del Teet's (127 Broadway East), Keeg's (310 Broadway East), and Mobilia (301 East Pine) are the best shops for furnishings. The nearby Recreational Equipment Co-Op (1525 11th) run by Jim Whittaker, is probably the world's largest store for outdoor equipment: camping, mountaineering, skiing gear, everything. A good spot for lunch in this district is The Deluxe Tavern (625 Broadway East); for a drink, Boondock's bar (611 Broadway East).

University District. The main shopping street, University Way Northeast, is the magnet for hip shops like Bluebeard's (4241 University Way) and Bench Leather (4223 University Way). There are some other fine shops: Miller-Pollard (4538 University Way) for home furnishings, La Tienda (4138 University Way) for superb folk artifacts, and University Book Store (4326 University Way), which ranks just after the Harvard Coop in size. Have breakfast at New Orleans Sandwich Shop (4718 University Way), lunch at The Frankfurter (4527 University Way), and do your drinking with the students at the College Inn Pub (4000 University Way).

A few blocks east is a notable shopping center, University Village, with several bests-in-town: For wines, La Cantina and Free Run; for cheese, The Cheese Shoppe, one of the best such stores in the country; for records, Orpheus, a model of completeness, knowledgeability, and effective display; and for baked goods and hamburgers, The Turbulent Turtle.

Seattle Center Area. Under "Seattle Parks" we discuss the Center itself; just to the north is a very agreeable specialty-shop complex called The Hansen Baking Company. The Men's Room has good clothing; La Belle Liberte is a women's boutique. Pier 70 to the west (foot of Broad at Alaskan Way) is a pleasant browse among mostly touristified shops: Gold Balloon for toys, Gretchen Hill for leather, The Principal for a bar.

Seattle Architecture ☆

What modest distinction Seattle architects have achieved is in domestic architecture, hidden from view. Works that can be seen and are worth the trip are: Condon Hall (the University of Washington Law School, 12th Avenue Northeast and Campus Parkway), a striking example of the Philadelphia School style, by Romaldo Giurgola; Red Square on the U.W. Campus, a difficult marriage of Siena and Brutalism by Kirk-Wallace-McKinley; the Weyerhaeuser Headquarters Building at Federal Way (twenty miles south of Seattle off Interstate 5), one of Skidmore-Owings-Merrill's finest office buildings; and the new Freeway Park (I-5 at Seneca Street), which puts a Lawrence Halprin waterfall in a one-block complex bridging the downtown freeway.

Nightlife in Seattle ☆

Best Bars. Jake O'Shaughnessey's is busy and has such admirable touches as single-malt Scotch whiskey; Canlis has a nice view and lots of comfort; Mirabeau is posh and forty-six stories up; Rosellini's 410 will offer the best-made drinks; the Downtown Hilton is the zoo; Deluxe 2 (5401 26th Northeast) is the place with the University crowd; City Loan Pavilion and The Salad Gallery are the best in Pioneer Square; and the Boondock's bar (611

Broadway East) is the handsomest on Capitol Hill.

Music. Pioneer Banque, on Pioneer Square, offers the name jazz groups for a stiff cover charge. The two spots on Pier 70 have fine jazz and rock groups, and often Overton Berry, the city's top jazz pianist. Sunday's, at Hansen Baking Company, will be a lively spot in a recycled church. Doubletree Inn, at Southcenter, sometimes books good groups. The Golden Lion bar in the Olympic Hotel atones for weak drinks with a good pianist, Tubby Clark. Bellevue's Greenwood Inn books big names.

BELLEVUE

Le Provencal ☆ ☆ ☆

You can get better French food in the Northwest, but in certain moods this is probably the most pleasant of French restaurants. You are greeted with a professional touch at the door by Phillipe Gayte, owner-manager and once a waiter at Henri Soule's famous Pavillon in New York; he helps you immediately to leave all the week's cares behind you. There are two small rooms, nicely decorated in modest rusticity; the meal proceeds with calm order, quiet and assured. It's a fine place for a romantic meal for two.

The menu is limited — another reason why the cooking is unformly reliable — with occasional seasonal augmentations of trout or duck well worth ordering. Nearly everyone has the house specialty for the first course, oysters Corsaire, small Canterbury oysters cooked in a cream sauce with spinach and topped with a fine Bearnaise. The next sure-fire dish is the *tournedos en feuillete,* a rosy filet enveloped in a marvelous pastry and accompanied by the usual excellent vegetables. Just as good is the veal in a cream sauce — normally the best veal at any local restaurant. The wine list is good, nothing more. Desserts are not quite up to the rest of the meal, so you might choose instead a slice of the excellent Brie.

A final positive note comes with the bill: prices are very

reasonable for such a cuisine. A skilled marketer, M. Gayte knows, for instance, how to turn lesser cuts of beef into a slowly simmered *daube Avignonnaise* (a tribute to his native region of France), or how to find superb vegetables and serve them in delicious small portions, thus keeping the bill in line. The one problem is that you must usually dig deep to afford a wine to match the meal.

212 Central Way, Kirkland
Monday-Saturday, 5:30-11 p.m. (no lunches)
Reservations needed: 827-3300
Moderate
Credit Cards: BA, MC
Full Bar

Yangtze Szechuan Restaurant ☆ ☆

Incongruously located alongside of Herfy's in Crossroads Shopping Center, the Yangtze has served some of the finest meals we've ever eaten. The cuisine is Szechuan, from a western province of China noted for its very hot spicing with garlic, ginger, and peppers, as well as the great decorative beauty of the cooking and slicing. In its opening year, the Yangtze had the services of an extraordinary chef, Chiukao Peng, since departed to Los Angeles. A simple call a day or so in advance to manager Paul Yang, a Boeing scientist by day, would enable the chef to create a ten-course banquet (for only about $7.50 per person) that was normally sensational. It might start with hacked chicken, a splendid, palate-awakening dish. Shellfish would come in a baked noodle basket. Abalone would be fluted for tenderness. There might be chicken with softened walnuts and murderous bits of red peppers. Duck smoked with tea leaves. Ginger beef. A soothing platter of creamy vegetables and a few tiny eggs. Then a decorative fish, sculpted, deep-fried, and festooned with colorful shards of vegetables. A winter-melon soup and glazed bananas would end the complexly orchestrated meal.

The food is still very good, but there has been a definite decline since the chef moved south. No longer is the spicing as daring, and on occasion a poorly prepared item will intrude. But what remains is still excellent. The lunches and simple family-style dinners are tasty and novel. The bar serves excellent drinks. The service is extremely good, and the decor of the restaurant, converted from a former House of Pies, is tasteful and cheery. And the devoted Mr. Yang will be glad to steer serious diners to some of the best items on the menu, in particular the duck dishes (Peking duck requires a day's advance notice), the mushroom plates, the servings with meat and walnuts, the fish, the dry pork, and the soups. The banquets are still offered for parties of six or more, and they remain the best bet.

1320 156th Avenue Northeast, Bellevue (Crossroads Shopping Center)
Tuesday-Saturday, 11-11; Sunday, 5-11.
Reservations or take-out: SH 7-2404.
Moderate
Credit Cards: BA, MC
Full Bar

Domani ☆

This restaurant possesses a good Swiss chef, capable of excellent Italian cooking. The devotion to that exacting cuisine, however, is less than total. Recently Domani moved from a small location to its present large spread in downtown Bellevue, and the menu was augmented with numerous French and continental items that seem to be straining the kitchen. Still, we have been able, on occasion, to get a creamy fettucine, a splendid fritto misto, and a flavorful chicken breast stuffed with cheese and ham. It is worth taking extra pains to insist that the food be cooked properly, even if it takes longer, since the evidence indicates that the chef clearly knows how to do it right.

The new location lacks the intimate charm of the old Kirkland spot, but the rooms are nice, particularly the bar. The main room is dark, so dark that flashlights are sometimes provided to enable one to read the menu. Service is shaky. The wine list is a definite plus, as is lunch with its wide selection of interesting Italian dishes.

604 Bellevue Way NE, Bellevue
Weekdays, 11:30 a.m.-11 p.m.; weekends, 5 p.m.-2 a.m.
Reservations: 454-4405
Moderate
Credit Cards: BA, MC
Full Bar

Ole

It's not for Mexican food freaks, but Ole does have some positive points. The room is most attractive, a tall cedar-lined chamber overlooking a greenhouse. Prices are good. And there's the capacity for good cooking in the kitchen, along with an ability to do quite bad cooking. You might start a meal with freshly made guacamole, then order up a plate of great quesadillas to go with your excellent Marguerita, made from fresh limes. After this it gets tricky. The enchiladas and the tamales are unreliable, while the chili relleno is an unsuccessful variant. Tacos are fine, and the refried beans and rice are good. At least there's a wide selection of Mexican beer to get you through this portion, and a nice cheese cake to end the meal.

If you want to be more careful, you can have some good oyster dishes, a well-made Caesar salad, or, for lunch, sandwiches with only a slight Mexican accent. The Sunday brunch serves an acceptable huevos rancheros.

Trident Square, 11838 N.W. Bellevue-Redmond Road, Bellevue
Monday-Saturday, 11-11; Sunday, 10-9.
Reservations: 455-4441
Moderate
Credit Cards: BA, MC
Full Bar

Holiday Inn ☆

The architectural design of this Holiday Inn is very good for a change, but inside, the rooms are the usual thing for this chain. The Inn has a heated pool and plenty of meeting rooms. We advise staying out of the "gourmet" restaurant, Jonah and the Whale, since the excellent service cannot compensate for the astronomical prices and uneven cooking; but the coffee shop is good, with fine daily specials, a good chowder, and a nice fruit salad.

> 11211 Main Street, Bellevue
> 455-5240
> Expensive
> Credit Cards: AE, BA, CB, DC, MC

Thunderbird Motor Inn ☆

The exterior is garish and it seems too close to the freeway, but it is a pretty good place. The rooms are varied and uniformly attractive; those which overlook the well-planted interior court-yard are the most desirable. In all, a good value.

> 818 112th Avenue NE (at I-405 and 8th St) Bellevue
> 455-1515
> Credit Cards: AE, BA, CB, DC, MC
> Moderate

Bellevue Food Stores ☆

There's not much to do in Bellevue, so people garden and cook a lot. The list of good food stores is not difficult to master:

Johnston's Seafoods, 210 106th Place NE, is one of the best fish shops in the region, with a selection both wide-ranging and very well handled. Dry-ice packing is available.

Bud's Meats and Mike's Produce, 202 106th Place NE, is right next door. The meats are first-rate, and the store makes its own lunch meats, sausage, and pizza, as well as pre-prepared chicken-almond rolls, canelloni, and veal cordon bleu. The produce is slightly erratic, but there are good local items.

Medina Grocery, 800 Evergreen Point Road, Medina, is a costly little store catering to the gold coasters nearby. They sometimes get the best fresh fruit you can find anywhere, and the shop, with its well-worn floors and bursting shelves, makes for a nostalgic visit.

Brenner's Bakery and Delicatessen ☆

This is as close as you can come in the state to a typical Beverly Hills deli. Sandwiches start with the excellent fresh rye baked on the premises; then you might add pastrami, corned beef or chopped liver. Cabbage rolls, gefulte fish, matzo ball soup, cold borscht, and salads are also at hand. Food is served cafeteria style.

An equally good reason for going to Brenner's is to buy food to take home. There are frozen knishes, blintzes, potato pancakes, or kishkas, plus a big line of baked goods. You can even stock up on rendered chicken fat, celery tonic, and Israeli wine.

120th NE and NE Bellevue-Redmond Road, Bellevue
Every day, 8-8.
744-0600

EDMONDS

Chez Claude ☆

This Edmonds restaurant, just changing hands as we go to press, will be continuing some of the traditions of its previous incarnation as Henri de Navarre: the famous rack of lamb in a mustardy persillade, the impeccable steak au poivre, and the meltingly good sweetbreads a la Lyonnaise. In addition, the undistinguished decor has been greatly improved by the addition of copper and plants and countryside touches that recall the owner-chef's birthplace of Lyons. The service will probably be more gracious than at Henri I.

Among Faure's new items are several very inviting dishes. He will prepare his escargots with a cream sauce; the coquille of seafood is prepared without cream and baked in a pastry shell—

Faure's concession to the new French cooking and the less-fattening cuisine it espouses; the trout will be served in a champagne sauce; and his pheasant comes with sauerkraut. The meals are quite inconsistent, however. Sauces tend to be over-salted, some of the combinations (such as veal and artichokes) are oddly out of balance, and the wine list has too many expensive nullities.

417 Main Street, Edmonds
Every day, 5:30-11 p.m.
Reservations: 778-9888
Expensive
Credit Cards: AE, BA, MC
Full Bar

Henri de Navarre Riviera ☆

This long-established Parisian restaurant in Edmonds has moved down the street to a location at the ferry dock, complete with a summertime sidewalk cafe. Additions to the old menu include more seafood, as well as a luncheon menu of salads, sandwiches, and quiches. Based on our long experience with the original Henri and its owner, Jean Branaa, we recommend your trying the new place.

Henri de Navarre does some things very well, and presumably these items will be easily transplanted to the new location. The house pate is good. The sole Nantua is fine, and the excellent new chef, Pierre Schaar, will be adding a sole Florentine. The duckling is crisp and delicious, and the steak au poivre has always been outstanding. The rack of lamb, the house specialty, remains in an honored position. The new dishes will be seafood delicacies, such as a preparation of fruits de mer in a pastry shell. Wine and vegetables are quite up to the high standards, but desserts have not been strong points in the past.

On the negative side of the ledger have been occasional inconsistencies, high prices, and the sometimes overbearing manner of the manager. The new rooms are cheerful, but they seem somewhat awkwardly carved out of the recycled building and they can be too loud.

101 Main Street, Edmonds
Seven days, 11 a.m.-2 p.m.; 5:30-11 p.m.
Reservations: 778-1171
Expensive
Credit Cards: AE, BA, MC
Full Bar

Olympic Peninsula

LONG BEACH

The Ark ☆

This restaurant aspires to become one of the few good seafood places on the Washington coast, and it has made some promising first steps. The oysters come from an oyster plant just across the Nahcotta dock, so they are good if the chef has not turned them into oysters Rockefeller or fried them. The fresh fish comes from nearby boats, and it is often lusciously cooked and superbly fresh. In season, you can get fresh Dungeness crab right out of a tank in the lobby. The wine list is hopeless, but some of the other accompaniments are not bad, particularly the cranberry cream pie, the ranch fries, and some of the salads.

The one severe drawback of the place is its refusal to take reservations in the summer season, which can often necessitate a mood-ruining wait in the lobby with dozens of steamed-up tourists; you can get reservations before 6 and after 10 p.m., however. The service turns over customers very fast—another drawback. Lunch is less crowded, but the menu is much less interesting.

> Peninsula Road, Nahcotta
> 11 a.m.-11 p.m.; closed Mondays
> Reservations only Oct.-June 15 (665-4700)
> Full Bar
> Moderate
> Credit Cards: BA, MC

Chatauqua Lodge ☆

Between the 1966 Washington state court decision saying that accreted sand dunes in front of private homes belonged to the owners (not the public) and recent federal tidelands legislation making development virtually impossible, there was a fear that the state's coast would be lined with condominiums. Fortunately it didn't happen, but here is one of the few erected out in the dunes. Ecologically reprehensible it may be, but the lodge is still the nicest place to stay on the Long Beach peninsula.

The rooms are a shade narrow and the decor is straight out of the motel-management catalogs, but the view of the ocean five hundred feet away is incomparable—especially during off season when there may be a storm brewing. You also get a lot of deluxe features at this condominium doubling as a motel: a heated swimming pool, an acceptable dining room and bar, sauna, billiards, kitchen units and fireplaces (fed by gas). Prices are a bit high, but in off season you can often get the second day of a weekend stay free. A double unit for $40 can handle a large family, with no extra charge.

If the ecological intrusion bothers you, you can atone. Instead of joining the parade of cars driving along the beach (and normally getting stuck every few miles), you can rent a saddle horse at the Seaview Riding Academy.

205 W. 14th, Long Beach
624-2244 (reservations needed one week in advance)
Expensive
Pets $1
Credit Cards: AE, BA, MC, CB, DC
Restaurant hours 7 a.m.-10 p.m. (4 a.m.-11 p.m. in summer)

The Anchorage ☆

Long Beach developed around the turn of the century as a posh Cape Cod for Portland society, which arrived by steamer and railroad. When this genteel life passed, the peninsula put up a series of family-style tourist courts shortly after World War II. Now many of these have declined, replaced by in-town motels—jarring retreats where kids yell at poolside all day long and the fishermen drink all night. One nice remaining court is The

Anchorage. It is spotless—ovens are cleaned after each stay—very spacious inside, and small enough (ten units) so kids can come and play in safety away from the road yet not dominate. Lovely dunes and the beach are just outside some of the windows. The kitchens are well-equipped, so if you don't get any razor clams, you can stock up on excellent seafood at Cornell's Market (three miles south). Owner Max Marasko is a friendly guide to the attractions of the peninsula.

> 1 mile north of Long Beach on Route 103
> 642-2351 (reservations difficult in summer)
> Moderate
> Pets accepted
> Credit Cards: BA

Nature Study ☆

Long Beach is one of the undiscovered pleasures of the Northwest Coast. It is neither built up like the Oregon Coast, nor scruffy like much of the accessible Washington Coast. Moreover, within the twenty-eight-mile stretch is a remarkable range of experience: fishing, beachcombing, birdwatching, historical reverie, biking, clamming, or just soaking up the salubrious air amid unspoiled surroundings. A few highlights:

North Jetty—two-miles of mighty boulders stretched out from the southern tip of the Peninsula; fine for fishing or watching the freighters battling across the bar.

Cranguyma Farms—a very large cranberry bog (a lovely sight in itself), with rhododendrons, azaleas, holly and cranberry products for sale; nearby is Clarke Nursery, for more shrubs and particularly heather. (Off Peninsula Road).

Oysterville—one of the state's oldest towns. It commenced in the 1850s, raising the native oysters that are now all but depleted and long ago replaced by Japanese oysters that are much larger and less good. Some Oysterville homes remain in quiet good repair, most of their windows lined with colorful bottles collected from the beaches and older homes.

Leadbetter Point—is an undeveloped park on the northern end of the island: 160 species of birds inhabit this 1400-acre National Wildlife Refuge, along with bear and deer and other animals. It is only accessible by foot, once a poor road deposits you at the entrance. If you want to visit another refuge—this one only accessible by boat—rent a boat at Nahcotta and row over to Long Island, where an old Indian campground makes a picnic base-camp for bird-watchers and fossil-gatherers.

Art—Kenneth Callahan lives on the peninsula, attracted by the remoteness and the flotsam on the beaches; watercolorist Charles Mulvey is another luminary. The one gallery is the Seachest in Seaview.

GRAYLAND

The Dunes ☆

Good seafood cooking is a rarity along the Washington coast, but this place is a notable exception. The house is beautifully nestled amid the dunes; inside, it is sunny and eccentric, with every available inch of wall and ceiling cluttered with an astounding collection of memorabilia and junk.

The same passion for collecting has been expended on the food: the fish is as fresh as can be; the vegetables (gloriously prepared) are gathered from a favored farm forty miles away; soups are delicious; and the desserts are a subject of special pride to Mrs. John Morrison, who bakes them. It's rather like going to grand-mother's house and feasting on country cooking, often with five vegetables laid on in Southern-style lavishness. You can also get excellent breakfasts to prepare you for a day of beachcombing: omelets, say, or pork chops and eggs. Lunches consist of thick sandwiches on homemade bread. The only drawback to this charming, zany, perfectionistic place is the stern outlawing of all liquor.

Route 105, Grayland
Daily, 9-9; closed December and January and also Tues and Wed from
    Sept. 15-December.
Reservations can be negotiated (267-1441)
Moderate
No liquor
No Credit Cards

WESTPORT

Westport Salmon Fishing ☆

If you've come down here to fish—and there's no other reason to—you will probably see enough of the ocean next day; so we recommend staying in the Islander Motel, a smaller place overlooking the fishing boats in the harbor, rather than at the big glossy ones with the ocean view. Ask for a room in the upper two floors and you will have a standard motel room for about $26 a double with a very pretty view (Westhaven Drive, 268-3800, all cards).

Two hundred thousand fishermen a year pass through Westport, so there are plenty of charter boats. Salmon Charters (268-4450) is one to be recommended, for their boats go out earlier than most (6 a.m.) and work hard to find the salmon. You might be advised to bring your own gear or consult with the charters beforehand, since otherwise you will get such heavy tackle as to make catching these great battlers no fight at all. Cost is about $25 a person for the day, with the peak season June-August; the season is closed from November 1 to April 15.

As for eating, Dee's Cafe on South Montesano Street, two miles south of the docks, does a serious job of getting very fresh bass, cod, salmon, and oysters; it's open seven days a week, 7 a.m. to 9 p.m.

OCEAN CITY

Wilms Dinner House ☆

Here's a very encouraging sign: a fairly serious restaurant on the gastronomically blighted Washington coast. The small place (seven tables) only recently opened and had some problems in the early going, but it shows signs of becoming quite a good establishment. The chef, George Andersen, has been cooking for fifty years, and he enjoys doing special dishes for those who call ahead; he is particularly good at creole and French specialties. The manager, Ben Garcia, is a graduate of El Gaucho, which means he knows a lot about service and tableside pyrotechnics.

There are some nice seafood dishes. They do oysters in a light Hollandaise sauce specked with truffles, sole in a cream sauce, and a proper poached salmon. Then there is a special fondness for veal — another most encouraging sign. The chef cuts his own veal, then prepares a stroganoff, a schnitzel, or the inevitable parvenu platter, veal Oscar (with crab legs). There is admirable attention to fresh vegetables, but the wine list is weak so far and the desserts run to baked Alaskas. Since the restaurant is trying to encourage a serious trade, it is advisable to call ahead and inquire what the kitchen is in a mood to do.

Route 109, Ocean City
Dinner only, 5-midnight; closed Tuesday, Wednesday
Reservations: 289-2715
Moderate
No Credit Cards
Full Bar

COPALIS

Iron Springs Resort ☆ ☆

Everybody loves this place, which manages in some mysterious way to epitomize the desired style for resorts in Washington state. It's been here more than twenty years, managed by the charming Olive Little who makes and freezes clam chowder and takes orders for her pies. The cabins are beautifully scattered among trees on a wild bluff looking over a vast spread of beach. One has privacy, a view, peerless clamming (the razor clams are best in February, March, and April), nice kitchens to cook the clams, and a modest heated swimming pool. The rooms are spacious, decorated in Northwest bad taste (lots of aqua walls), and warmed with a fireplace and electric heat. It's enough to evoke everyman's

Northwest dream of a family-filled cabin of his own surrounded by trees and facing right into a roseate Pacific sunset.

The newer cabins are preferable, particularly numbers 14, 15, 16 and 17 which, like 10-A and 10-B, face due west for the sunsets. Prices for the cabins, which easily handle parties of four and more, start at $28. About one month's advance reservation is needed in the summer and this also holds true for the peak of the clamming season in late winter. Off season is magical, as the area is often engulfed in fantastic storms or a heavy fog that is wonderfully melancholy and helps to obscure the dreary towns along the main road.

Despite the tacky look of this stretch of road, there are other resorts quite decent if you are turned away at Iron Springs:

Beachwood Resort, Copalis (289-2177), has a stern ban on pets but is comfortable and small; each of the eighteen units has a fireplace.

Sandpiper, Pacific Beach (276-4580), has a much lower beach than at Iron Springs, as well as a handsome building that descends four stories down the bluff almost to the crashing waves. Rooms 7, 8, 9, and 10 in this building get you close to the water and in a large unit with ceilings up to twenty feet high; cabin 4 is the best of the cabins. What this new resort lacks in trees it makes up in beach access and view.

Ocean Crest Resort, Moclips (276-4465), is prettily constructed into the hillside and features modern units with grand views. It may be a shade too jammed together for your getaway mood, but the resort clearly has the best food for miles: a superior clam chowder and a nice way with fresh fish, some of which is cooked tableside.

Route 109, 3 miles north of Copalis Beach
Year-round; three-day minimum stay, June 10-Labor Day
276-4230
Expensive
Credit Card: BA
Pets allowed

QUINAULT

Lake Quinault Lodge ☆ ☆

Lake Quinault, a lake dammed by a glacial moraine, is carved into a lovely valley in the Olympic Range. The coast-hugging Highway 101 comes inland to the lake at this point affording the traveler the easiest penetration to the interior of the range. You are near a moss-hung rain forest; the fishing for trout and salmon is fine; and the ranger station will provide further advice on hiking or nature-study. The best way to appreciate this region of extraordinary dank fecundity is to hire an Indian to take you, when the river is high enough, 35 miles by hewn cedar-log canoe from the Lake down to the mouth of the Quinault River at the Pacific; the Lodge will make arrangements.

The Lodge is just right—a massive cedar-shingled structure built fifty years ago in a gentle arc around the sweeping lawns that descend to the Lake. The public rooms are nicely done in wicker and antiques. In the huge lobby is a fireplace; the dining room overlooks the lawns, and the rustic bar is lively at night. You can stay in the main building where you will have nice rooms (half with views of the lake) and you may get a bathroom, since there's one for every two rooms. The new, adjoining wing has rooms with views, fireplaces, balconies, and queen-size beds in each modern unit, for which you pay $8 more for a double. The Lodge, a bit too attractive to conventioneers, has a sauna, an indoor heated pool, a putting green, a game room, and a tiny paddle-wheeler for touring the lake. These convention-inspired touches don't really mar the classic feeling of the old lodge, but they have turned the dining room into a familiar medley of items, routinely cooked.

Quinault Rain Forest Road, Quinault
Open year round; dining room hours, 7 a.m.-10 p.m.
Summer reservations needed one month in advance: 288-2520
Expensive
Credit Cards: AE, BA, CB, DC, MC
Pets: $2

KALALOCH

Kalaloch Lodge ☆ ☆

The top attraction here is the beach, wide and wild, with bleached white logs crazily pitched on the slate-gray sand. A few miles north, at Ruby Beach, you can see spectacular rock formations, and there's a short road there leading to "the world's largest cedar tree," a reliquary giant of the species most deeply rooted in the mythology of this area and (since the timber companies don't replant the slow-growing cedar) one probably headed for near-extinction. Another way to learn about the beach is to take one of the guided walks and talks conducted out of the Kalaloch Ranger Station.

The Lodge is quite nice and quite impossible to get into on short notice during the summer: long stays require reservations five months in advance, short ones two months. However, the grand beach makes the resort ideal for off-season respites. There are several kinds of accommodations. Best is in the main lodge, where rooms 1, 6, 7, 8, 10, and 11 have ocean views, and room 11 ($25) has the single fireplace in the lodge. Next best are the suites in the south addition, a kind of motel set among the trees; rooms 406-410 have views, while suites 401, 406, and 410 have fireplaces. Then there are the cabins, which are set out on the bluff and have the best ocean views and the only kitchenettes. The gas heaters used in the winter are wildly fluctuating in temperature, so we disrecommend the cabins at that time, except for the four with fireplaces.

The food in the dining room sometimes matches the splendid ocean view. They get fresh Quinault salmon as well as fresh local oysters; after that, the cooking turns to steaks and plain home-cooking. It tastes fine after a day of salt air and a few belts in the Drift Log Room, admiring the Pacific sunset.

Route 101, Kalaloch
Open year round
962-2271
Moderate
No Credit Cards
Pets in cabins only

FORKS

Slather's Smoke House ☆

A salmon cannery and smoke house are located just behind the restaurant, so the alder-smoked salmon is both wonderful and very well-priced. But they don't just rest on that accomplishment. The smoked turkey sandwich is rich with the taste of hickory. They get fresh cracked crab, turn out notable onion rings, put spicy chunks of smoked salmon in the tossed salad, and make an excellent club sandwich with some new combinations: salmon, crab, and shrimp. The wine list is well chosen (Krug, Mondavi, Wente), and the mixed drinks are big and good. Be sure to save some appetite, since the Italian-style cheese cake, full of ricotta and lightened with lemons, is one of the finest versions of this dessert we know of in the state.

Orders for mailing smoked canned salmon can be placed at the cashier's stand.

Highway 101, quarter-mile north of Forks
Daily, 10 a.m.-midnight; weekends, 10-1 a.m.
Reservations: 374-6258
Moderate
Credit Cards: BA, MC
Full Bar

La Push Ocean Park Motel

The town is a Quileute Indian village noted for its rugged seascapes, fine kite-flying, and Indian fishing by canoe. And that's about it. The eating in the Butts Cafe is poor except for the pies. This motel is quite nice, however, built in a plastic style but situated right on a lovely beach. The rooms all have kitchens that easily solve your eating problems. Four of the cabins have fireplaces, but if you can't get one of them, the rooms on the top floors of each of the two motel buildings are desirable for the nice views. Prices are good, about $20 for a double.

Main (and only) road, Forks
Open year round
374-5267
Moderate
No Credit Cards
Pets Allowed

LAKE CRESCENT

Lake Crescent Lodge ☆

This is the sort of place that displaced easterners — say those accustomed to a few weeks on Lake Winnipesaukee each summer — can go to and feel very happy about. The lodgings are comfortable and well-worn. The main lodge has a grand verandah overlooking the placid, mountain-girt lake, and the cabins also have nice porches. It is well kept up — freshly painted last year — and the service is up to New England standards: eager college kids having a nice summer. Fishing (for a fighting local trout), hiking, tennis and boating are the main activities. The food is merely adequate, but the bar is fine. We recommend staying in the motel rooms or in one of the four cabins with fireplaces; the main lodge is, as they say, "rustic," which means it brings back memories of New England but has no private baths.

Highway 101, Lake Crescent
May 30 to Labor Day only
928-3211
Moderate
No Credit Cards
Pets Allowed

PORT ANGELES

Dupuis Seafood Inn ☆ ☆

This fine institution, forty-four years old, is passionately devoted to a fine tradition: fresh Dungeness crab. The owners go to great lengths to get fresh crab (which is increasingly hard to do), and then they steam it carefully and serve it in a fragrant, lemony sauce. That's the thing to order, although Dupuis does have many other items well worth recommending. The fresh Hood Canal oysters and shrimp are superb, and the Plaskett family can poach a sole with admirable delicacy. The pastries and breads are simply outstanding. They are baked by Fadelma Winters, a local baker whose French wine cakes, fruit cobblers, and lemon pies have earned her a wide reputation and sold quite a few of her cookbooks.

This excellent fare is served up in a surrounding that is a sure reminder that you after all are still on the Peninsula: knotty pine, paper placemats, bad landscapes on the walls.

Route 101, 7 miles east of Port Angeles
Daily, 11-10; closed Tuesdays in fall and winter
Reservations: 457-8033
Moderate
Credit Cards: BA, MC
Full bar

Bayshore Inn

If you're going to stay in this town, you might as well be right on the water, right near the ferry, and in relative luxury. Best rooms are those overlooking the water, where the view out the window can draw the eye away from the standard-issue Northwest-motel decor inside. If you hanker for bigtime nightlife in Port Angeles, head for Aggie's, a big, convention motel, but sleep it off here.

221 North Lincoln Street, Port Angeles
452-9215
Moderate
Credit Cards: AE, BA, CB, DC, MC

DUNGENESS

Three Crabs ☆

The Dungeness crab is one of the major culinary contributions of the Northwest, so how suitable to eat one of the large, sweet, flavorful creatures here at Dungeness. The Three Crabs is a nice family-style place, serving Dungeness crab fresh in season (October to March) and frozen the rest of the time. They also do a good job with other fresh seafood: salmon broiled or steamed, oysters (none on the shell), halibut, even fresh geoduck (a giant local clam). Pies are baked on the premises.

Finding fresh Dungeness crab in a restaurant these days almost requires as much effort as finding the succulent creatures on the beaches. About the only place that really does get them fresh year-round is Dupuis in Port Angeles, which relies on imports from Victoria during the summer. "Fresh," of course, means the crabs have not been frozen after they come in iced from the boats and have been boiled in salt water to prevent them from turning black. A good stand for buying "fresh" crabs for your own dinner or picnic (this crab is terrific served cold with a freshly made mayonnaise) is in the curve of Route 101 around the south end of Discovery Bay.

Dungeness Spit, Dungeness
Daily, 12-12; Sundays, 12-7
683-4264
Moderate
No Cards
Full Bar

SEQUIM

Cedarbrook Herb Farm ☆

Sequim, sunnily positioned in the middle of a rain shadow cast by the mountains, is attractive to retirees and has spawned some touristic attractions. The Lloyd Beebe Olympic Game Farm at nearby Dungeness breeds endangered species and raises a familiar line of beasts for Hollywood; it makes a nice drive-through on winter weekends or summer days.

The Cedarbrook Herb Farm is more unusual. At it, you can observe and buy a vast range of herb plants organically grown, like scented geraniums, tea herbs, and nearly all the kitchen herbs and spices you've ever heard of. In August and September, the French shallots and elephant garlic come to delicious ripeness. The proprietress, Mrs. McReynolds, is a character, and the oddities—like salad bernet, which smells like cucumber and is used to make a cucumber vinegar—are fascinating.

One mile south of the only traffic light in Sequim
April through September, 10-4 daily; closed Sunday
683-4541

PORT TOWNSEND

The Farmhouse ☆ ☆

The setting is probably the finest of any restaurant in the Northwest. An old farmhouse, set among large conifers on a spectacular bluff overlooking the Strait of Juan de Fuca, has been expanded and decorated with excellent taste. It's the sort of restaurant that deserves arriving at a half-hour early, just to stroll among the berry bushes and fields of the wind-swept bluff.

The meal you will consume (for a fixed price of $10) is not to everyone's taste. The owners of the Farmhouse, the Conways, are vastly experienced in the world's cuisines, so much so that dining here gives one a feeling of being at a shrine. The waiters are nervous acolytes. The wine is pointedly withheld until a late course lest anyone numb a palate. And it is no easy matter to get a second portion of some delicious course.

You have no choice on a given night, but over the year the Farmhouse turns out an impressive variety of menus. During the summers one gets fish on Fridays, meat on Saturdays, and fowl on Sundays: normally, the meal consists of excellent soup, a lovely piece of fish (sometimes from the local smoke house), a salad drawn from a vast array of twenty international offerings, a main course that is sometimes nothing more than a glorified pot roast, and a fine dessert.

Off-season, Professor Conway delves into foreign cuisines, with this schedule followed: September, Japanese; October, Italian; November, Hungarian; December, German; January, closed; February, Northern Chinese (a best bet that sometimes carries into March); March, Iranian; April, Northern Indian curries; May, Greek.

The wine is inadequate to the cuisine and the mood is one of enforced reverence, but that aside, the Farmhouse offers the best food on the peninsula.

North Beach (call for directions), Port Townsend
Seatings: Thursday, 6, 9 p.m.; Friday, 6, 9; Saturday, 6, 9; Sunday, 3, 6;
      from Labor Day to June 1, no Thursday seatings, no 3 p.m. Sunday
      seating; closed January.
Reservations required: 385-1411; 523-4625
Moderate
No Credit Cards
Wine

The James House ☆ ☆

Port Townsend was one of those towns that fell for a railroad bubble at the end of last century, overbuilt itself grandly in expectation of the railroad that never came, and then collapsed into decades of lovely somnolence. The rediscovered Victorian homes have now been fixed up by the dozens, and one of the nicest ones, the James House of 1889, has become one of the most pleasant places to stay in the entire state.

Ethel and Bill Eaton have lovingly restored ten units, ranging from $20 to $29. All are beautifully furnished in antiques, but the units in the front of the house have the best views out across the Strait. The main floor has three sumptuous public rooms—a library, a parlor, and a dining room—along with the kitchen where guests partake of delicious continental breakfasts around the big table. Pets, tours, and even children are outlawed. Street noise can be a shade bothersome to light sleepers.

1238 Washington Street, Port Townsend
Weekends only in winter
Reservations: 385-1238
Moderate
No children, no pets
No Credit Cards

Fort Worden ☆

This grandly-situated fort was originally constructed to guard the entrance into Puget Sound, but now the troops are gone and the massive gunmounts on the bluff are only Pompeii-like ruins stripped of their iron. The state parks department now runs the place as a conference center year-round; in the summer, you are likely to find some excellent artists in residence and occasionally performing ballet or chamber music. It's well worth a check to see what may be doing.

The Fort itself also provides a fine place to stay. Thirteen former officers' quarters homes front on the old parade field, and they can be rented. Lodging is in clean, large houses, many with lovely views; the commandant's house with five bedrooms is the choicest spot. Prices start at $7.50 for a single bed and range up to $22 for a full house; children under sixteen can stay for $2 a night if they bring their own sleeping bags. Reservations must be made two weeks in advance, with the first night's charge payable in advance. You'll find excellent walking around the fort grounds as well as a dramatic beach terminating with a romantic lighthouse.

Fort Worden, one mile north of Port Townsend
Reservations: 385-0644
Moderate

PORT LUDLOW

The Admiralty Resort ☆ ☆

This is the one resort in the state that is constructed along Oregon lines of carefully planned luxury. The rooms and suites are in modern condominium units owned by families who rent them out when they are away. Accordingly, you get individually decorated rooms with a kitchen, a porch, a prestolog fireplace, and a spiffy contemporary spacious cedar-shakes style. Since Pope and Talbot, a pioneer timber company now shifting to the land business, expects to found a large recreation and retirement town on this ancestral site, there are plenty of other facilities in place, nicely designed by Naramore Bain Brady and Johanson, architects: squash courts, four good tennis courts, a large pool and a salt-water swimming lagoon, a "teen activity center," a conference center (popular for sales meetings in the winter), and a freshly minted golf course (PNGA rated 72) carved out among old trees and stumps, lakes and creeks. There are a few problems. The food at the Quartermaster is rather standard, except for the notable clam chowder. The site is turned to the east, away from the sunsets and the warming early-evening light, and is a bit skimpy on trees. But for the most part it works very well. Numerous Puget Sound marriages have been saved by weekends here. And the bar is fine.

The best rooms, for views of the water, are in the units called Lopez, Marrowstone, Orcas, and San Juan. New rooms will open this winter, adding 80 rooms to the current 140; these new rooms will have lofts in some of the suites along with other new features.

9 miles north of Hood Canal Bridge, Port Ludlow
Year-round; restaurant hours 8 a.m.-9 p.m.
437-2222
Expensive
Credit Cards: AE, BA, CB, DC, MC
Pets allowed

POULSBO

Poulsbo Inn ☆

Poulsbo is a good stop to keep in mind when heading onto the peninsula for an outing. For one thing, it is a pretty little fishing village. For another, it has several good shops for provisioning for the trip: a bakery (*Bauer's* on Main Street) with notable French bread and Scandinavian products, a seafood store (*Little Norway Seafoods,* on Main Street next door) with a normal line of fish plus some nice pickled Scandinavian items, and a meat store (*Keim's Lemolo Meats* on S. Fourth Street) with excellent beef, sixty-five varieties of sausage, and a very spicy smoked salmon. And—rare for the peninsula—there's a good restaurant.

The best thing about the Poulsbo Inn is the bar, a beautiful imitation of an English pub, with good beer on draft and well-made drinks. The rest of the fixed-up old building carries out the extraordinary attention to detail insisted upon by the owner, Jack Borrodell, an Englishman and an architect. The best place to sit is near the fireplace. The food is ambitious, but we have found the execution uneven: a splendid wilted spinach salad, then a silly veal Oscar overpowered with bleu cheese, then a grand tournedos robed with bordelaise and bearnaise sauces, then a poor wine list, lamentable vegetables, and undistinguished dessert—but all served with marvelous spirit. The menu, incidentally, is becoming more ambitious, with aspirations toward fresh trout, pheasant, frogs legs, etc. The owner is a determined perfectionist, so the place is well worth trying.

The popular Sunday brunches start with excellent drinks and advance into rather substantial meals, again with the same variation from superb to mediocre items. Lunches are comparatively routine.

261 Bond Road, Poulsbo
Lunches, 11-2; dinner 5-10; Sunday brunch only, 12-3; closed Mondays
Reservations: 779-5703
Moderate
Credit Cards: BA, MC
Full Bar (open til midnight, 2 a.m. on Friday and Saturday)

UNION

Alderbrook Inn

Alderbrook is a venerable institution, dating back to 1913. Once it was good, but by now it is under leased management and showing a lot of strain. The food in particular, is just dreadful. The new units that have sprung up are acceptable, but quite short

of the charm necessary to match the nice site on the broad turn of the Hood Canal. The waterfront cottages, with two bedrooms, a fireplace in the living room, kitchen, and porch, have nice views and you can do your own cooking in defense, but the tab of $42 (with no winter-rates) makes one pause. Second-best rooms are in the motel, with the top-floor ones affording the best views.

There's a lot to do and a lot that draws coventions and sales-meetings. The eighteen-hole golf course is picturesquely cut among the trees. There are a couple of tennis courts. The water is fine so there is boating, clamming, water-skiing, and fishing. The lawns and surrounding woodsy acreage are the best things about the resort. It all passes the time and serves to keep you out of the dining room or the bar with its weekend organist.

Route 106, two miles east of Union
Open year round; dinner til 9 p.m.
898-2200
Expensive
Credit Cards: AE, BA, MC
Pets allowed

Puget Sound

FERNDALE

Ferndale ☆

Putting the various reasons together, Ferndale is a good place for an overnight or midday stop: a good restaurant, a good motel, a nice old Swedish farm for the kids.

The restaurant is *Johnson's Fine Food* (at Ferndale-Axton exit from I-5; daily, 6 a.m.-10 p.m.; 384-1601). The food is well-prepared, if only the conventional fare of steaks and seafood, the service is very attentive, and the view from the white country inn is over farmland to Mount Baker.

The motel is *Scottish Lodge* (same Exit 262 as Johnson's; 384-4040; BA, MC; pets allowed). This three-year-old motel had problems under the previous management, but it is now spruced up. The two-story building is half-timber style, concealing a conventional motel within. It may seem too close to the freeway, but insulation is sufficient and half the rooms overlook the nine-hole Riverside Golf Course, where you might even get in a few holes after the day's drive, or there's a heated pool and sauna at the motel. Suite 151 is the single room with a fireplace; doubles are a reasonable $18-20.

The attraction for the children is *Hovander Homestead Park* (open daily in summer, weekends in winter; 384-3855; from Ferndale follow Hovander, Nielsen and River Lea Roads). Whatcom County has restored this 1903 farm homesteaded by Holan Hovander, a Swedish architect. The farm is still working, and kids can pat the animals or inspect the farmhouse or the big barn full of old-fashioned, still-used equipment. There's nice picnicking along the Nooksack and a view of the farmland from atop the water tower.

GLACIER

Graham's ☆

The Mount Baker country is bracing alpine land, wonderful for hiking, cross-country and downhill skiing, climbing, or picnicking—and for building up an enormous appetite. Graham's is the place to ease the appetite and to find robust companionship. Brothers Parker and Gary Graham run this family business with proper concern for good cooking and a genial atmosphere. It is part old-fashioned store (for putting together your picnic), part a collection of old furniture dating back to the store's opening in 1906 or, in the case of the old bar, even farther, and part a jolly restaurant for skiers, natives, and starved tourists en route to or from Mount Baker. A blue-grass band that plays on Saturday nights gets things jumping a bit more.

All the food is homemade, ranging from simple standards to standard fancies. For breakfast there are fine omelets and a good eggs Benedict. For lunch or dinner you can have spaghetti (with a long-simmered meat sauce), French onion soup, or steak cooked with wine and mushrooms. The house fame rests on the Gableburger, a real, quarter-pound, hand-shaped burger named for Clark Gable, who once filmed "Call of the Wild" way up here.

36 miles east of Bellingham, Route 542, Glacier
Summer: 12-12, Sunday 8 a.m.-midnight; Winter: Friday, Saturday, Sunday, Holidays only, 8 a.m.-2 p.m.
No reservations: 599-2833
Moderate
Credit Cards: BA, MC
Beer and Wine

BELLINGHAM

The Oyster Bar ☆ ☆

The cook and the new owner of this little spot are now catching up with its possibilities: a dazzling view out over Samish Bay, nearby supplies of excellent oysters, and happy drivers touring the picturesque Chuckanut Drive. Owner Tom Lee has come a long way from the days when this was no more than a greasy-spoon; he has now attracted a demanding clientele that is even treated to once-monthly $28-per-person gourmet repasts (first Wednesday of each month: advance reservations required).

There is plenty to attract the casual visitor. Seafood omelets are available for lunch, along with a nice platter of fresh oysters from the oyster company a few hundred feet away. Dinners are constructed around seafood. Portions are generous, considering the modest prices. The best dishes are of course the oysters, but you can also find salmon and scampi and scallops. The mushrooms are fresh and delicious, whether in the sauces or atop the good salads. Wines are well-chosen. The best item of all is the cheesecake ($1.75), made by an elderly lady who lives nearby.

The decor is subdued: wood and plants and background guitar-music. Even though the porch has now been enclosed, it is still a small place, with fourteen tables.

Chuckanut Drive (14 miles south of Bellingham)
Open daily, noon-9
766-3305
Moderate
Credit Cards: BA, MC
Beer and Wine

Sudden Valley Country Club Restaurant ☆

Some years ago, this golf-and-condominium project a few miles south of Bellingham was being touted as "the undevelopment." For once, an advertising phrase has some truth to it. The community is lovely, with the buildings designed by Miles Yanick so cannily tucked into trees that you are likely to notice deer grazing unperturbed by the winding road as you drive by. The restaurant is in the handsome lodge overlooking an eighteen-hole golf course; it is a good spot to know about for stop-offs while driving between Seattle and Vancouver.

The food has suffered a decline since it first opened, but there are still some fine items. The Caesar Salad is excellent. The seafood selection is unusually large, and the waiter is likely to inform you what is fresh and worth ordering. Other entrees are likely to be pre-prepared and frozen—never order chicken Kiev at a place like this (or at most places), since it is an invitation to quickie-gourmet cooking. There are elaborate desserts, well worth saving an appetite for. The wine list is adequate. Service is quite good, so the meal can be a pleasant interlude from the drive. (Incidentally, on a slow day you can talk the pro into letting you play the sporting golf course.)

> Lake Whatcom Blvd., 8 miles south of Bellingham (take Lakeway Dr. exit from I-5).
>
> Dinner only, 6-10; closed Mon., Tues. in winter; coffee shop available for breakfast and lunch.
>
> 733-1001; reservations accepted
>
> Moderate
>
> Credit Cards: BA, MC, DC
>
> Full Bar

Leopold Inn

There are more modern places to stay in this old logging town—out on Samish Way where a good Royal Inn is located, for instance; but this combination hotel-motel downtown has more character. The west rooms are particularly desirable, with their fine view of the broad arc of the busy harbor. Rooms are clean and routinely decorated; the staff is friendly; and there are extras like a heated pool and sauna. There are three dining rooms, the most grand being the Chandelier Room, where the gourmet food tops out with steak Diane. This food is quite overlookable, but from the Leopold you can easily walk a few blocks to find better fare.

> 1224 Cornwall Ave. at Chestnut (take State St. exit from I-5)
>
> 733-3500
>
> Moderate (doubles from $12; suites to $36)
>
> Pets allowed
>
> Credit Cards: DC, AE, BA, MC, CB.

Whatcom Museum of History and Art ☆ ☆

This museum is truly spectacular for a city of this size. The handsome old city hall was erected in 1892 and beautifully restored by architect George Bartholick, who blended preservation with modern spaces. The building is surmounted by a dark red Victorian clock tower.

The exhibits rotate frequently and are usually strongest in some imaginatively hung art displays. The regular collection includes good Oriental and Eskimo ivories, Bellingham memorabilia, a collection of area birds, an extensive logging exhibit, and excellent photographs by pioneer lensmen. On occasion, there are some major exhibits of Indian art, some of which is produced by artisans teaching at the museum. Free. The gift shop sells local pottery, art and toys. Some concerts in the Rotunda Room.

121 Prospect Street (downtown)
676-6981
Tues.-Sun., noon-5 p.m.; or by appointment

Chuckanut Drive ☆ ☆

This is one of the loveliest drives in the Northwest, although the numerous turns make it hard for the driver to take in much of the scenery. Heading south, you pick up Route 11 just south of Bellingham, at Fairhaven; the southern outlet is into some lovely Skagit Valley farmland. The best time to take the trip is in the fall, when the leaves provide color and the view out over the San Juans is likely to be clear; in the winter, the road sometimes is closed due to slides.

Cleator Road, milepost 16, is a fairly good dirt road that provides several outstanding views of the Islands as you drive up the hill. At the top is a parking lot and then a short trail that ends with a view of Mt. Baker and the Cascades.

Snow Line Mushroom Farm, at Cook Road, Burlington, gives tours from 9-4 daily. Ira Hagins guides a pleasant tour, complete with a sermon on the value of eating his mushrooms. Not much persuasion is needed. The farm is small but one of the most modern tray farms in the West. His white mushrooms are extraordinarily good; they sell at ninety cents a pound. To find Snow Line, you turn west at Cook Road and look for the big yellow corrugated metal building on the right. (757-7171).

Western Washington State College Architecture ☆

WWSC is a good liberal-arts college to attend and a fine campus to visit. Its handsome architecture provides an encyclopedia of Northwest styles, in particular a humanistic, regional school centering on a few Seattle architects. The features are evident as you walk around this hilly saddle between two tree-blanketed mountains. Brick and other "warm" materials are used, in revolt against more brutal and technological modern media. Certain European, pedestrian-oriented urban forms are echoed, as in Ibsen Nelsen's Red Square, inspired by Danish town squares. Natural surroundings are graciously accepted, most notably in the Ridgeway Dormitories by Fred Bassetti, which recall Italian hillside villages. Finally, there is a sensitive affection for existing older buildings, which fit into the new plan.

Many influences come together under the unobtrusive masterplan: the undulating Matheson and Nash Halls by Henry Klein, for instance, are an elegant echo of Alvar Aalto. Yet there is something approaching a shared style—a modesty, a muting of color that may derive from the landscape, and a human-scaling that springs from the domestic-architecture traditions at which Northwest architects excell. Among the major architects whose works are represented at WWSC: Ibsen Nelsen, Paul Haydon Kirk, Fred Bassetti, A.O. Bumgardner, Paul Thiry, Ralph Anderson, Ted Bower, Henry Klein and George Bartholick, who did the master plan.

Campus security offices have plan-maps; or you can arrange a tour by calling the office of campus planning.

Fairhaven

A California eccentric has found this small old town and set about restoring it along familiar lines: shops, taverns, art galleries, restaurants. The most notable success in this rather odd adventure is a Victorian building now called *The Marketplace* (1200 Harris Ave.). It has four levels of shops around an open interior court. The building is unusually attractive, with some original woodwork and a handblown glass chandelier. The shops are the expected old town variety. The handiest lunch spot is the *European Delicatessen,* whose sandwiches or pies far outdo the bland crepes or soupless onion soup at *La Creperie.* Just about the best thing about the Marketplace is the bordello-esque bathrooms.

There are some other places to inspect nearby. *Dos Padros,* 1111 Harris Ave., serves pretty fair Mexican food, accompanied by a quiet guitar. The *Fairhaven Tavern* has nice lunch sandwiches and better bluegrass music. The hill immediately to the east of Fairhaven contains several interesting Victorian houses, relics of the city's boom-and-bust economy that commenced with the Canadian gold rush of 1858. This hill provides more of the lovely views out over the bay and the San Juans which are characteristic of the town.

NEWHALEM

Skagit Hydroelectric Project Tours ☆

Intriguing tours originate at this pretty company town in a spectacular gorge. Upriver are the dams built from this staging base by a visionary engineer named James Delmage Ross. You ride an inclined railway to Diablo Dam, then go by boat (or better, hike) along the green-water river gorge to Ross Dam, a construction of daring engineering in its time and the source of Seattle's cheap electricity today. Afterward there is a lavish chicken dinner back in Newhalem with the employees (those still around after automation of the dams), and an inspirational walk to the grave of the Rosses and Ladder Creek Falls, with plantings gathered from around the world. Parts of this peculiarly affecting tour can be taken on the spot, but the six-hour grand tour, with food, must be reserved through Seattle City Light (1015 Third Avenue, Seattle; 623-7600). The cost is $6 for adults; these tours are very popular, so reserve well in advance.

Route 20, Newhalem
Daily, Memorial Day to Labor Day.

ANACORTES

Charlie's Restaurant

One block up from the ferry dock is a new restaurant that can console you mightily if you miss the boat, or provide a nice excuse to come up an hour and a half early to get an assured place in line for the Friday night 8 p.m. ferry for the San Juans. The restaurant has a grand view, and inside there is an airy room with hanging plants and oak tables. The cooks are locally trained college students, but the Funks, who own the place, put a premium on getting fresh seafood, not all of which is deep-fried. You can have fresh salmon poached and topped with Hollandaise, for instance, or oysters in a creamy casserole. Steaks are another specialty.

Luncheon specials run to stews, soups, and lasagne, along with conventional sandwiches.

Ferry Terminal Road, Anacortes
Daily, 6 a.m.-2 a.m.
Reservations: 293-7377
Moderate
Credit Cards: BA, MC
Full Bar

LA CONNER

Courtyard Delicatessen ☆

An old building on First Street has been fixed up nicely, and the adjoining courtyard makes a fine spot for lunch on a sunny day. The sandwiches are made from standard fillings, using excellent rolls. The DeLournes bake their own cakes, of which the cheesecake is the best. The Swedish pickled herring is outstanding, and the meal can be rounded out with a Heineken and some freshly ground coffee.

La Conner, a small fishing town on diked delta farmland, is inhabited by important Northwest artists, but there is neither a gallery nor a hangout they favor. If you wish to do a little shopping or pick up local talk, the two best places to start are the La Conner House, a fine old house with an excellent cookware shop managed by Mrs. Bryant Earp, descended from Wyatt (Second Street, 466-3998); and Reynolds Antiques, an emporium with large stock and many great bargains (Morris and First, 466-3209).

First Street, La Conner
Daily, 10:30-5:30; closed Monday in winter
No reservations: 466-3985
Moderate
No Credit Cards
Beer and Wine

SAN JUANS—LOPEZ ISLAND

Betty's Place ☆

Islands attract eccentrics; if you want any proof of this proposition, you will find it at Betty's Place. Betty and B.A. (Smitty) Smith moved to this farmhouse two miles south of the ferry landing five years ago, installed some maple furniture and a few antiques, put twin beds in two rooms upstairs and out in a single cabin, revived a bit of the farm, and then waited for the phone to ring.

What you get when you call is an opportunity to discuss a meal that Smitty, a cook in California once upon a time, might be willing to create. All is negotiable. If you want a breakfast or a lunch, just call ahead and see if the cook is in the mood and what he has. Dinners are more elaborate. You can have a boarding-house meal if you want, but Smitty likes to have orders for stroganoff, or Chinese cuisine, or Mexican food, or Italian, and so on and so forth. Depending on his mood and how well he likes you, the food can be quite good. And the rates are fair enough: from $22-30 a day for two people, which includes a room and two meals.

Visitors should be warned, however, that the experience gets a little bit familiar. The Smiths love to talk, and during your stay you might very well find yourself spending time watching television with the family or even viewing their slides. And a certain mischief-making may set in. One of our visits there produced a delicacy described as Peanuts Ragout. It was not bad, and after we had devoured it, following a day of strenuous hiking, we asked why it had such a name, since we had not found a single peanut. Right on cue, Smitty marched into the kitchen and returned with a snapshot of his pet goat, the late Peanuts.

Ferry and Center Streets, Lopez Island
Open all hours, by reservation only
468-2470
No pets or children under 12 for lodging
No Credit Cards

The Galley ☆

After only a few hours in the Islands, you are bound to hear tales of this restaurant, a half mile south of the Islander Lopez overlooking Fisherman Bay. If you don't mind joining all the fellow tourists at this Mecca, you will have a pleasant meal.

The decor is the expected: driftwood and nets. The menu is nothing out of the ordinary, except that the prices are very good for such large servings. During the season you can get fresh fish, sometimes salmon right off a nearby boat. But the big draw is one of Glen Cushing's mammoth omelets. He makes these only if you have called in advance and if you can assemble a party of four or more. In the huge mound goes ham, cheese, green peppers, and such exotics as pineapple chunks. The adornment is hash browns and a garnish of fruit. For this splendid feed you are charged a mere $3 per person.

The staff is friendly, although hurried during the tourist rush. It's a good place to visit off season, when the locals congregate and the Cushings can easily be talked into cooking a good honest meal. The bar has a nice marine view.

Fisherman Bay, Lopez Island
Open every day, 10 a.m.-2 a.m.
468-2713
Inexpensive
No Credit Cards
Full Bar

The Islander Lopez ☆

Lopez Island is the agricultural island among the San Juans, which means sleepy Lopez is a good one to head for during the peak of the crowded season. While the garish Islander Lopez is not exactly in character with the rural island, it is still the best place to stay—too modern perhaps, but long on conveniences and service.

The lodging is in guest units across the road from the marina and restaurant, so quiet is assured. The units are exceptionally clean and very nicely furnished; the double beds have firm matresses; most of the units have modern electric kitchens. The decor is tasteful Polynesian. The complex boasts many services. A semi-enclosed natatorium complex near the guest units houses a hot Jacuzzi pool, a heated but open-to-the-sky swimming pool, plus an activities room. Across the street is the restaurant and cocktail lounge (with weekend dancing to live music).

You can arrive by boat: Fisherman Bay moorage for fifty boats is just in front of the central lodge. Or seaplane. Or airplane to a strip a few miles south. Or ferry; jitney service is provided from the ferry landing. All this makes the Islander a good spot for a weekend escape. You can even leave the car at Anacortes, take advantage of the lodge's central location on the island and spend the visit exploring the calm countryside by bike: the flatness of the islands makes them ideal for bike-touring.

Fisherman Bay, Lopez Island
468-2233
Moderate
Leashed pets accepted
Credit Cards: BA, MC, AE

SAN JUANS—ORCAS ISLAND

The Chambered Nautilus ☆

The San Juans are becoming one of the last refuges of the international set, in search of dignified retirement somewhere new. This restaurant, in a refurbished strawberry-barreling plant, is a kind of refuge for two young world-travelers who fled the East coast, wandered the world (picking up recipes), and ended up on Orcas. The result is the best food on the Islands, served at very good prices in a restaurant accessible by dock or highway.

Breakfasts consist of nice variations: carefully done blintzes, tacos instead of hashbrowns, corn cakes with pineapple butter. Lunches are sandwiches, fruits, salads, soups, tacos. You cannot Lunches are sandwiches, fruits, salads, soups, tacos. You cannot be sure what dinner will offer. West African items are popular, such as a thick, cayenne-laced peanut sauce with the chicken; but there are also good, fresh seafood dishes and some nice roasts. Prices are great, the wine list is poor, the salads with the meal can be outstanding (picked from the back kitchen-garden), service is casual and hip. You'll be glad you fled your campground, or galley cooking, or the thrice-as-expensive stuff at Rosario.

Olga, Orcas Island
Daily in summers, 8 a.m.-10 p.m.; Mondays, 6-10 p.m.; weekends only
    after Labor Day
Reservations: 376-4606
Moderate
No Credit Cards
Beer and wine

The Bungalow ☆

This is a very nice place to know about. The service is quick and friendly. The room is light and airy, decorated with local art and Indian carvings of good quality, and the room boasts a sweeping view of Eastsound. Two retired schoolteachers keep a matronly eye on quality. Best of all, the menu is arranged to offer modestly priced small portions, just right for a travelling entourage of children and grandmothers. Dinners are admirably priced as well: $2.50-6.75 for a complete dinner. The food is nothing special, but it is precisely prepared by the owners.

Eastsound, Orcas Island
9-9; closed Wednesdays
276-2361
Credit Cards: BA, MC
No liquor

Bartel's Resort Dining Room ☆

A modest, pleasant place with a few distinctive touches, this small, crowded dining room has a splendid view and a traditional menu. But you can get fresh seafood in season, nicely cooked by a young chef with standards unusual for the Islands. He does his own marketing, for instance, and so you are likely to find your steak accompanied by half an acorn squash, dripping with honey and butter, rather than the usual baked potato. The wine list is paltry, but a well-stocked bar is just overhead.

Cayou Road, Eastsound, Orcas Island
Summer, noon-10 daily, winter, Wed., Fri., Sat., Sun., 6-9
376-2242
Credit Cards: BA, MC
Full Bar

Rosario Resort Hotel ☆ ☆

The resort business in Washington has always been spooked by
the short good-weather season and the small population. The
result has been little ambition or, as in the case of Rosario, a
nervous effort to attract every conceivable tourist, honeymooner
or conventioneer.

Rosario invites this kind of excess. One thousand acres surround
the large mansion that Robert Moran (once a Seattle mayor and a
famous shipbuilder) built for himself in 1905. Unfortunately,
owner-manager Gilbert Geiser has chosen to over-develop the site,
adding honeymoon units, a boatel, villas, haciendas, three pools,
etc. On a busy day at Rosario the main entrance can be a noisy
swarm of tourists more reminiscent of the ferry trip to Orcas than
the composure of an exclusive resort. The "haciendas," up on the
hillside away from the main lodge but still overlooking the water,
provide the best chance to avoid the crush. Another warning: only
two tennis courts.

That said, there are some admirable features at the resort. The
staff is professional, the grounds are very well tended, and
everything is spotless. The main lodge is a fascinating outburst of
pomp and display, with marvelous cabinetwork, massive windows
and walls, and parvenu touches like the 26-rank pipe organ in the
music room (still working) or the canoeing lagoon. Somehow the
honeymooners and the affluent retired folk fit in well.

There are several dining rooms, although you really should eat
elsewhere. The amphitheater-like Orcas Room is rather grand for
the mediocre meals served therein, but the view is nice and the
tables are decently spaced. Steak, chicken, and routine fish dishes
fill out the slightly continental menu; the wine list is mostly
domestic, with some good California choices. Nothing matches
the view out into fjord-like Eastsound, rockbound and pristine.

Horseshoe Highway on Cascade Bay, Eastsound, Orcas
376-2222
Restaurant hours: 7 a.m.-11 p.m.
Moderate ($18-46, with three season rates in effect)
Pets in a few units accepted
Credit Cards: BA, AE, MC

Mount Constitution ☆ ☆ ☆

Moran State Park is another splendid legacy from the Moran estate: five thousand acres of trails, good camping (125 sites), a waterfall and four lakes. But the point of it all is the view from the stone-and-timber observation tower atop 2400-foot Mount Constitution. There it all is: islands, mountains, water, Canada, Western Washington and — to recall reality — an ugly television tower sharing one of the world's finest belevederes. The two-hour hike through the secluded woods is much more pleasant than driving to the top.

Darvill's Rare Print Shop ☆

There's more to this modest-seeming shop than the supply of paperbacks, gift items, art supplies and stationery. The Dale Pedersons have an outstanding collection of old prints, kept in a separate room and carefully catalogued. Mrs. Pederson, who will let you see them upon request, is a courteous and expert guide to them. The collection is seventy-five thousand strong, going back to Hogarth. Her husband, who formerly practised law in Eugene, has also assembled a good collection of law books and old legal documents. In all, a fine browse, with tempting prices.

Eastsound, Orcas Island
376-2351

SAN JUANS—SAN JUAN ISLAND

Roche Harbor Resort ☆ ☆

This cozy resort evolved from the company town that John McMillin constructed for his nearby lime deposits. The old Hotel de Haro was built for guests, the most famous of which was Teddy Roosevelt. You really should put your name in the roster along with TR's, for this old-fashioned hotel is fun, nicely refurbished with good furniture, situated on beautiful grounds, and has one of the most inspiring views you'll ever find, out over the yacht-dotted harbor to the islands and the sunset.

The hotel gives a sense of having been glued together with repeated applications of wallpaper, and a few hallway boards give more inches underfoot than one prefers, but if you get an upstairs room (particularly on the north end) opening onto the veranda, you will be well pleased. The beds may sag, but the resort offers numerous compensations: the gorgeous gardens, the large swimming pool, and the general air of cleanliness and old-fashioned comfort. You'll also find many remnants of McMillin's paternalistic imprint on the town he built. The crowning touch is a limestone mausoleum of tall pillars set in the woods, the final resting place for the tycoon and his family.

McMillin's waterside home is the setting for the restaurant, another admirable feature of the resort. The cooking is quite good. This is not the sort of place that will overcook your steamers, or serve them tepid, or stint on the portions. The menu is moderate in range and the wine list is uninspired, but the setting is very homey and the waitresses are as sexy as they are courteous. The bar normally attracts a very jolly gathering of hard-drinking yachtsmen, undeterred by the horrors perpetrated by the resident pianist. All very agreeable, but don't spoil things by falling for the overpriced breakfast buffet next morning.

Roche Harbor, San Juan Island
8 a.m.-10 p.m.; weekends only during off-season
378-2155
Moderate
Full bar
Credit Cards: AE, BA, MC

Mar Vista Resort ☆

Here is a twofold opportunity: to stay cheaply amid spectacular scenery, and to imbibe some more of the Island eccentrism.

The cabins are not much: some paint would help, and the beds sag too much. But they are spaced more than two hundred feet apart, and the extensive surrounding countryside is unbeatable. A meadow slopes down toward a bluff overlooking clean sandy beaches, where shallow water makes for warm swimming as well as good clamming and agate collecting. There is plenty of play equipment for kids. In the evening, when thousands of rabbits come out to play, you may want to retreat to the cabin fireplace or perhaps strike up a conversation with the owners, Milt and Mela Bave, who have strong interests in the arts and maintain (for whenever a guest asks to see it) an oddball collection of animated clockwork figures and hand-carved music boxes.

> False Bay, San Juan Island
> 378-4448
> Moderate ($16, $22)
> No pets
> No credit cards

Lonesome Cove Resort ☆

Remote, hushed, rigorously excluding scuba-divers, tiny—this is the ultimate retreat. It is rather rustic, although each of the seven cottages is very clean, with good beds. Prices are very low. The cabins are set among trees, facing onto fifteen hundred feet of waterfront. Boats are available for rent. Inspired by the solitude of this resort, you might try your hand at the pleasantest way to examine these islands with care: by rowing along their shores.

> 8 miles north of Friday Harbor, San Juan Island
> 378-4477
> Minimum summer stay: 1 week; winter: 2 days.
> Moderate, $9-20.
> Pets $1.
> No credit cards

San Juan Hotel ☆

A very nice restoration, spotlessly clean, attractively decorated and with near-antique furniture, this hotel has genuine appeal. It is tiny, with only two bathrooms for all the guests. The Krabbe family runs the place with the utmost competence, attracting a clientele of some retired folk as well as many young cyclists and back-packers. (It is a good spot for bike-touring, since you are close to the ferry for the next morning's getaway.) Typical of the tidiness is a small garden in the back, perfectly groomed. The back rooms are quieter, overlooking the garden and its old-fashioned glider.

> Spring Street, a block and a half from the ferry dock, San Juan Island
> 378-2070 (reservations required in summer)
> Moderate
> No pets
> Credit cards: BA, MC

Friday Harbor Shops

This fascinating little town of eight hundred has just about the only concentration of shops worth browsing in among the islands. Starting from the water, one finds:

The Old Mill Gift Shop—art, ceramics and tourist-junk, supervised by an interesting artist and conversationalist, Roman Sobinski.

Sweet Tooth Saloon—a genuine soda fountain, along with good sandwiches.

Gourmet's Galley—a bright, clean shop with freshly ground peanut butter, coffee beans, whole spices; one of the few places open on Sunday to sell food.

Ravenhouse Art Gallery Hedda and Ed King are artists who specialize in Northwest Indian design and art. They are worth chatting with, and the gallery is an attractive one.

Little Red Hen Bakery—an old-fashioned bakery worth stocking up at if you're arriving for a weekend of your own cooking.

Boardwalk Bookstore—strong on regional history, and possessing a reasonable stock of paperbacks.

University of Washington Oceanographic Laboratory

These islands have an extraordinary wealth of tidal life, due to the miles of beaches, the nutrients in the Sound from the heavy river runoffs, and the vigorous flushing action of the Sound. Large exposures are available along these beaches, making them ideal for spotting anemones, sea urchins, jellyfish, crabs, kelp, sea plumes, sea cucumbers, chitons, and so on. This teeming life has also drawn University of Washington scientists to the region, and their laboratory gives a short lecture as well as a tour of the tanks and displays feauring local marine life. Regular tours, Wednesday and Saturday afternoons during the summer.

English and American Camp

For some reason probably having something to do with the paucity of local history in the Northwest, the dispute between England and American over ownership of the San Juan Islands from 1859 to 1872 has been elevated to the status of the Boston Tea Party. About the only casualty of the comic-opera faceoff was one English pig. Despite the footnote status of the conflict, the English blockhouse, commissary, garrison, and blacksmith shop can all still be viewed, just south of Roche Harbor. Nearby, adding to the hyperbole, is "the world's largest big leaf maple." American Camp, on the southern shore of the island, has little more than a marker. But the beach here is the real attraction — wholly unhistoric, sandy and vast.

WHIDBEY ISLAND

Coupeville House ☆

Like almost every professor at the University of Washington, Delmond Bennett is a good cook; now he is going to demonstrate it to the public. He and his wife, Shirley, have renovated an old house in Coupeville, and on Saturday and Sunday nights you can drop by and have a meal for around $7 that will consist of excellent professor's-home cooking. A bouillabaisse one night; oysters in clam juice for an appetizer on another; a roast chicken in a cream sauce with cognac and port on a third; simple poached fresh salmon one other time; home made ice cream to finish. These chef's-choice meals are served in two pretty rooms on the first floor of the house, and—except for the current absence of wine—you will dine quite well and quite reasonably.

You can also stay in the house. Three rooms upstairs have been turned into guest rooms, furnished with antiques from the Bennett's antique shop behind the restaurant (it specializes in British antiques). The front room, with a bay window overlooking the harbor and lots of space, is the best one to ask for, a bargain at $18.50.

To get you started in intelligent browsing in Coupeville, you should visit these shops: The Copper Lantern (Main Street), a fine new antique shop with excellent oriental specialties; The Old Town Shop (Front Street), for gifts and cards; and for lunch, Knead and Feed (Front Street), for homemade breads and salads in a congenial atmosphere.

602 North Main Street, Coupeville
Saturday, Sunday, 6-9 p.m.; in summer, Friday also; summer lunches, 11-4
Reservations: 678-4773
Moderate
Credit Cards: BA, MC
No liquor

The Black Swan Cafe ☆

Langley, a pretty little village at the south end of Whidbey Island, is the nicest town on the island—two blocks of fairly interesting shops on a bluff overlooking a bay. Some of these shops are the usual thing, peddling antiques, ice cream, baskets, cookery, etc. But some of them are a cut or two above. Travers LaRue's Virginia Tobacco and Pipe Shoppe is a dandy pipe and tobacco store that takes orders for custom pipes ($40 to $500); Sipapu is an intriguing "black-magic" gallery specializing in "talismans, fetishes, amulets, shrines, and body pieces"; and there's Hellebore, where excellent stained glass is made.

And there is this thoroughly admirable cafe, situated in a small, recycled Spanish-style bank. The owners, young former Seattle school teachers, are devoted to honest, good cooking with a French-cafe accent. For a modest tab, you can have escargots, a big bowl of French onion soup, a lovely bouillabaisse, an outstanding paella, pastas like lasagne or manicotti, a small steak au poivre, ribs (in ginger ale barbecue sauce), or a carbonade. Every detail is well attended to: fresh flowers on the tables, freshly ground coffee of the house's own blend, homemade salad dressings, and a cheesecake made with wine-soaked currants that advances the art of cheesecakery one giant step. The clientele—hips, summerfolk, islandfolk—helps give the restaurant an even nicer feeling.

First and Anthes, Langley, Whidbey Island
Daily, 11 a.m.-8 p.m.; closed Sunday, Monday
Reservations: 321-4818
Moderate
No Cards
Wine license pending

Six Persimmons ☆

This is a one-woman show operated by Rose Chin Brosseau, who is both an instructor in Chinese cooking and a restaurateur. The restaurant is in a fixed-up old grist mill in this pretty little waterfront town. For lunch you can have a delicious won ton soup along with some fried rice or fried noodles. Dinner is chef's choice: normally a soup, some rice, a few vegetables, and a stew, like an Indonesian curry or a Chinese chicken stew. On other nights, Rose will have some of her excellent spring rolls on hand, or she might try something interesting and new like sweet and sour cold vegetables. The cooking is almost always first-rank, the menus are intriguing, and the conversation in the small, cheerful establishment is part of the fun of eating here and being in a close-knit island town.

5 Front Street, Coupeville, Whidbey Island
Saturday, Sunday, noon-8 p.m.; in summers open Thursday and Friday too
No reservations: 678-5444
Moderate
Credit Cards: BA, MC
No liquor

Pancho's

For two reasons, Pancho's is a welcome spot—Mexican food that's any good is hard enough to find in the Northwest, and good food of any sort is welcome on this island.

Both the atmosphere and the food are fairly authentic in a Southwest American way. There's a nice Mexican sweet roll to start things off. The guacamole is freshly made, as are most of the other items except for the tortillas. After the cactus salad dressing, you enter a region of standard favorites, enlivened by the piquant house sauces. Even with a nice bottle of Carta Blanca, you'll have a hard time rolling up a bill higher than $4 a person.

1598 Midway Avenue, Oak Harbor, Whidbey Island
Daily, 11 a.m.-9 p.m. (til 10 in summer)
Reservations: 675-5511
Inexpensive
Credit Cards: BA, MC
Beer and wine

Captain Whidbey Inn ☆

Three miles north of Coupeville, about mid-Whidbey-Island, is an intriguing old inn constructed from madrona logs and dating back to 1907. It's not quite good enough to be charming, but the inn does boast nice service, good prices, satisfactory cooking, and a nice, secluded site nestled among trees on a rise overlooking Penn Cove. It serves well for a quiet weekend and as a base from which to explore the island and nearby Coupeville's shops.

The main building has a pleasant sitting room around the big fireplace, a popular bar, and a sunny dining room that aspires no higher than careful cooking of salmon and prime rib. Upstairs are eight rooms and a communal bathroom. The rooms are small, so you would do well to stay in the single suite, made by combining rooms 1 and 2. Nearby are four cottages, much more capacious and each with a fireplace, a kitchenette, and a bath; cottage 1 is the nicest. A dozen conventional motel units are also being built, across the road.

> Whidbey Inn Road, 3 miles north of Coupeville
> Open year round; dining room, 8-10 a.m., 12-2, 6-9; Sunday, 8-11 a.m., 1-
>   7; one hour longer for each meal in summer.
> Reservations: 678-4097
> Moderate
> Credit Cards: BA, MC
> Pets in cabins only
> Full Bar

EVERETT

Ricardo's ☆

One day not long ago, Richard Heinzen got converted to the pleasures of Mexican cooking.

Ricardo does many things other places long ago forgot to do: he makes his own tamales; he prepares individual tomato sauces for dinner dishes; and when he makes a taco grande, he cooks the shell with the meat stuffing in it. Among the best dishes are a wine marguerita, outstanding flautas with guacamole (Ricardo only makes guacamole when he can get excellent avocados), quesadillas with first-class cheeses, the chili verde, unusually light and fluffy chili rellenos, and a lemony pastry made from a flour tortilla and filled with custard. The room is small and there are no reservations, so it makes sense to go on a slower night. Ricardo welcomes aficionados of Mexican cooking (Southwest U.S. branch), and on evenings when he's not rushed, he loves to talk about the fine points and new variations, and then demonstrate the same.

3201 Rucker Avenue, Everett
Weekdays, 11-11; Saturday, 3-12; Sunday, 3-9
No reservations: 259-1217
Moderate
Credit Card: MC
Wine and Beer; Full bar pending

English's Commitment ☆

"Lunchtime in Everett." The phrase used to produce shudders, unless you were a member of the Everett Golf and Country Club, but now there is at least one place where a mere citizen can get good food. English's Commitment is the creation of two well-to-do Everett housewives with a flair for cooking and a commitment that has held quality firm for two years. The old English's soda fountain in downtown Everett has been restored in proper old-town style with blasted brick, oak tables, and stained glass. The cooks take good products and cook them well.

The soups are particularly good, especially the carrot vichyssoise and Dutch pea soup served with feathery popovers. Daily specials at about $2.50 are fine: a crunchy jambalaya, manicotti, fritattas, lasagne. There are also salads and sandwiches, like the popular avocado, bacon, and tomato to round out the offerings. Save room for Maggie's cheesecake, a delicious custardy version. The hostesses are likely to know what's doing in Milltown, if anything.

1405 Hewitt Avenue, Everett
Monday-Friday, 9 a.m.-4 p.m.
No reservations: 259-6464
Moderate
No Credit Cards
Beer and Wine

Seibold Gallery of Graphic Arts ☆

This handsome gallery, located in a fine 1898 building downtown, features a strong collection of contemporary prints, mostly European but some also from the Middle East, South America, and Japan. Prices, ranging from $60 to $350, are very good, and Beata Seibold is a knowledgeable collector with good New York connections. Multiples by Boni, Piza, and Kazumi are among the strongest. The gallery is open in the afternoons only, but Mrs. Seibold is usually there in the mornings and is glad to open up by appointment. Like most gallery owners, she is also a good source of information about the town.

1616 Hewitt, Everett
Daily, 12:30-4:30 p.m.; closed Thursday, Sunday
252-7376

DUVALL

The Silver Spoon ☆

A funky, fixed-up cafe, the Silver Spoon attracts hips, skiers, hikers, and a few of the local residents in this farming community. The menu consists of big breakfasts, overstuffed sandwiches made with uncommonly good ingredients, hearty soups, outstanding bread made fresh on the premises, some fine pastries, and modest dinners on the weekends. Eggs Goldenrod make a good breakfast; the super and the dagwood deluxe are the two best sandwiches;

and even the bacon-cheeseburger is good enough to make you believe in that idea once more. There's no booze, but the vibrations from this Alice's Restaurant are fine, and the selection of teas is discriminating.

Main Street, Duvall
Daily, 6 a.m.-8 p.m.
No Reservations, no Phone
No Credit Cards
No Alcohol

REDMOND

Marymoor Historical Museum

The real attraction of this museum, in addition to the lovely grounds and park, is its willingness to put on offbeat shows. There's an annual October "collectorama," at which collectors of just about anything rent stalls to peddle wares. Craftsmen are often in action; there's an August Indian encampment; other crafts shows are staged in irregularly. The constant exhibition, housed in the large Clise Mansion, stresses pioneer wares. If the kids are restless, you might do worse than to give the museum a call and see what's doing.

6046 W. Lake Sammamish Parkway NE, on Sammamish Slough, Redmond
Summer, 1-5 p.m., Saturday, Sunday; winter, Tuesday, 10-2; Sunday, 1-5
885-3684
Free

ISSAQUAH

Issaquah Shops ☆

Issaquah is unusual for a suburb, since remnants of a mining village are still visible. Shopkeepers have recognized this and created some nice shops in older buildings that are fun to visit.

Gilman Village is an encouraging blow struck for recyling. It is a small shopping complex made up entirely of old frame homes hauled to the location and nicely spruced up. You can find hand-made quilts, Dior shirts, custom Christmas decorations, unusual children's toys and clothes, antiques, custom-designed stained glass windows, and organic soaps blended to order. Prices reflect suburban affluence, but the architecture reflects an earlier American shingle style.

(Take Front Street exit from I-90; right at Gilman Blvd., left at Juniper.)

The Boarding House for lunch makes a good way to break up the shopping trip at Gilman Village. The home has been nicely redecorated with antiques, while the lunches are carefully prepared by a trio of Bellevue housewives who possess a good way with soups and sandwiches. (Tuesday-Saturday, 10 a.m.-4 p.m.; 392-1100)

Wessex Books—is downtown, in an old brick building. Derek and Felicity Love are serious collectors, specializing in Hardy. The handsome shop contains about four thousand volumes, some of genuine interest to collectors. You can get a lot of books about books, fine bindings, good used books, and an item like a leaf from the French "Book of Hours," c.1470, for a modest $35. (15 N.W. Alder Place, Monday-Saturday, 11-5:30, 392-2333.)

SNOQUALMIE FALLS

Puget Sound Railway Historical Association Museum

The normal routine is to gape at the semi-spectacular, 270-foot Snoqualmie Falls and then have an enormous, semi-good brunch at Snoqualmie Falls Lodge. Well, the quality of those breakfasts has been declining as the crowds have been growing, so unless grandmother insists, we propose an alternative. You can take a steam-locomotive ride to an outdoor museum in the woods, there to view old engines, rolling stock, handcars, streetcars, and donkey engines. Kids will like the outing, particularly the Santa Claus runs the first two Sundays in December, and buffs will like the museum and the bookshop.

> Snoqualmie Falls
> Sundays and holidays, Memorial Day to Labor Day; 11 a.m.-5 p.m.
> 883-0373
> Adults, $1, kids, 50 cents.

NORTH BEND

George's Buttercrust Bakery

Everyone passes through North Bend on the way to Snoqualmie Pass and a day of hiking or skiing. That means this bakery comes into view just about the time you want a second breakfast; it's also a good stop to purchase lunch-fixings. George and Jean Macris have run the place for ten years, during which time they have learned to make thirty-five varieties of bread: French, German rye, Swedish, potato, etc. A fried fruit pie, just out of the kitchen, makes a nice snack with a cup of coffee. For take-out, you might try a Cornish pasty filled with beef, pork and onions, then microwaved hot and put in an insulated bag if you like. The food is good, but if you're going as far as Cle Elum, wait for its bakery.

> 115 Main Street, just east of stoplight, North Bend
> Daily, 8-6; Sunday, 9-3.

VASHON ISLAND

Sound Foods ☆

This restaurant is a mellow place on a rural island in Puget Sound. The food is eclectic and very good, served up in a raw-wood-and-plants kind of room. The new menu contains tempuras, spaghetti with four sauces, a French pastry stuffed with vegetables, Cornish hen glazed with honey and dipped in sesame seeds, oysters, leg of lamb, and a hamburger so stuffed with mushrooms, onions, and things that it weighs in at one pound. The wines are good, too.

Sound Foods is the sort of place that rewards any kind of a drop-in visit, if only for a sandwich or soup at lunch. On Friday and Saturday nights there is some excellent entertainment, often bluegrass, when a large part of the island's young and gently countercultural population comes by.

Main Highway, 2 miles south of Vashon
Daily, 10 a.m.-9 p.m.; closes at 3 p.m., Monday, Tuesday
Reservations: 463-3565
Moderate
No Credit Cards
Beer and Wine

KENT

Caveman Kitchen ☆

Just down the road from the modernistic Boeing Space Center is a small funky restaurant specializing in sandwiches and smoked meats. You get beer across the street at Jackson's, and then you sit in an open-air picnic area, with trucks roaring down the highway thirty feet away. Why are you doing this? Because the smoked meats, the beans, potato salad, and slaw are superb. For $2.65 you can get half a roasted chicken—crisp skin outside, fragrant with hardwood smoke inside—or marvelously pink ribs in a mild sauce, some of the sweetest and tastiest baked beans you've ever had, crusty French bread, and good fresh cole slaw. There are also sausages, ham, smoked salmon, and turkey—as well as Dick Connelly's own version of the pizza, made with French bread, barbecue sauce, sausage, and cheese. There's no place to eat if it rains, but the take-out service is brisk. The hardwood smoker also will smoke your holiday turkey for 30 cents a pound.

807 West Valley Highway, Kent
Every day, 9-9
No reservations: 854-1210
Inexpensive
No Credit Cards
No Alcohol

BLACK DIAMOND

Black Diamond Bakery ☆

This hard-to-find bakery, en route to Mount Rainier, boasts the last wood-fired brick oven in the area. The bread that comes out of it is excellent: raisin, cinnamon, sour rye, potato flour, unbleached flour, pumpernickel, and sourdough French. Big loaves are only 79 cents. The other bakery items are less good than the bread; 1902 brick ovens seem to specialize in bread.

To get there, take Maple Valley exit from I-405; at Black Diamond turn right just before Shell station; at next stop sign veer left; faded, green, wooden bakery is on right in a few seconds.

Black Diamond
Wednesday-Friday, 8-5; Saturday, Sunday, 8-2.
996-2741

TACOMA

RESTAURANTS

Lakewood Terrace ☆ ☆

This very fine restaurant exists to pleasure the wealthy classes of Tacoma, who years ago removed from the city to live around the lakes to the south. The dining room is small, prettily decorated by Roland Terry, and ably served by excellent waitresses. Manager Benny Andersen is a stickler for keeping up the standards, and he has an impressive wine cellar (with, for instance, a good line of 1964 Bordeaux and Burgundies) that he will divulge if you ask him about it.

Our advice for a meal: Start with the homemade lobster bisque. Then by all means have a fish course such as the prawns in a dill sauce, the sole in a sublime sauce Albert, or the Dover sole imported from Holland. The pepper steak or the Chateaubriand make a fine match for the good bottle of red wine you've secured. You might end with fresh fruit. The daily specials are excellent if you wish to spend less.

The place is attractively lacking in pretense—in fact you might even wish to turn around and leave when you confront the coffee shop on your way in—and half of the Lakewood Smart Set finds it agreeable to sneer at this restaurant, but if you give the right signals of desiring good food and don't order three martinis to start, you will dine exceedingly well.

6114 Motor Avenue, Lakewood
Daily, 7 a.m.-11 p.m.; no lunch Sundays
Reservations: 588-5215
Expensive
Credit Cards: AE, BA, CB, DC, MC
Full Bar

Chaplain's Pantry ☆

Jeffrey Smith, formerly the chaplain at University of Puget Sound, offers a wide number of inducements to come to his new parish. His wine selection is very good and nicely displayed. His collection of cooking equipment is one of the most extensive in the state, and therefore well worth the visit in itself. His delicatessen is notable. He offers cooking classes. If you can assemble a group of from twenty to sixty persons, he will open up for dinner and prepare meals of continental, Middle-Eastern, or Chinese provenance. And the good parson is a Bible of information about the religion of good food, as practiced in the Tacoma area.

For your first communion, you should drop by for lunch. It is served amid the church pews and stained glass of the restaurant. Start with an excellent soup, onion or lentil, that comes from a proper stock. Among the good sandwiches is the New Jerusalem, with pastrami and hummus in an Arabian bread. The Saturday special is omelets. The meals, which are very popular, are made more enjoyable by the good wine that can be ordered and the active congregation of cooking converts.

110 Tacoma Avenue North, Tacoma
Daily, 11:30-1:30; Saturday, 11:30-2; shop open 10-5:30; closed Sunday
No Reservations: 627-2213
Moderate
No Credit Cards
Wine

The Tea Leaf ☆

Right across the street from Pacific Lutheran University, a pretty little school, is a tiny Chinese restaurant with minimal decor, that on good nights puts out the best food in the Tacoma area. (It also can have a bad night, typically a jampacked weekend one, when the food is standard dull.) The owner is a hard-working young Korean, Pyong Sun Yi, who has put together a large menu and has gone to moderate lengths to get good ingredients. The cooking ranges far and wide: excellent vegetable dishes (complete with fresh snow peas, year round) or a very popular almond chicken Cantonese style, Mongolian beef cooked in a small wok, Szechuan dishes served very spicy-hot (abalone and pork are recommended), some seafood specialties prepared Mandarin style, and Korean dishes like an exemplary kim chee (cabbage cooked with ginger, garlic, peppers, and sesame seeds).

The place is very small and accepts no reservations except for parties of seven or more, so we advise going on a weekday when you will not have a long wait and the kitchen keeps calm. Start with a hot-and-sour soup to rejuvenate your tastebuds, and then leave the ordering to the genial owner.

520 South Garfield, Parkland
Dinners only, 4 p.m.-midnight; Sunday, 4-10; may open for lunches again
   soon
No reservations: 531-5232
Moderate
Credit Cards: BA, MC
Full Bar

Bimbo's ☆

Bimbo's, fifty years old and still owned by the Rosi family, is the last of its breed. It's an Italian cafe that would be just another place in Brooklyn, or North Beach, but out here it is the only living tie with the Tuscan-style cafes in downtown Tacoma that the early Italian population of railroad-builders used to favor. The standards have fallen quite a bit. The pizza dough is no longer made on the premises. Mission pasta is cooked ahead in frequent batches, so the *al dente* standard is softening, although the spaghetti is still firmer than at other Italian restaurants.

Nonetheless, you can do some serious eating here. The three soups are fine. The daily sautees—rabbit, veal, chicken—come in a dandy sauce that has cooked for hours. They serve a memorable tripe on Thursdays. And the spaghetti is able at least to evoke memories of the real thing: the pasta is cooked firm, and the dark, herbacious, browned meat sauce has simmered since early morning. Then too, the mood is good, enhanced by the joshing waitresses and occasional eruptions from the boisterous Bimbo's baseball team, back in the bar.

> 1516 Pacific Avenue, Tacoma
> Daily, noon-2 a.m.; Sunday, 12-12
> No reservations: 272-6876
> Moderate
> Credit Cards: BA, MC
> Full Bar

The Cloverleaf Tavern

The government crowd is here for lunch. Then around 4 p.m., working men drift in, throwing back beers and the famous pizza. A few nights a week the mayor comes by. Then college kids, followed later by their teachers and coaches. What draws all these people, besides the congenial atmosphere of the big, noisy tavern, are the pizzas made with fresh dough each day, the house's own tomato sauce, good fillings, and proper care in the baking. You may have to wait up to an hour to get one some nights, the pies come only in one size, twelve inches, and they are a shade too oily, but they're worth it. If you ask for the Funk special, named for the manager, Bill Funk, your sausage, onion, and mushroom pizza comes for 25 cents off.

> 6430 Sixth Avenue, Tacoma
> Daily, 10-2 a.m.; Sunday 12-12
> 564-7788
> Moderate
> No Credit Cards
> Beer

Engine House No. 9

The decor of the old firehouse is so attractive you suspect they don't need to care about the food, but they do. Served among the antiques and firefighting memorabilia, you will get good soups, first-class salads, tacos that contain corned beef or assorted cheeses and vegetables and a hot sauce, and brownies or carrot cake for dessert. It's very popular for lunch, and on Sundays they pull in the brunch crowd with quiches. Saturday nights the place jumps to a band, and Sunday afternoons a singer might drop by.

611 North Pine, Tacoma
Daily, 11:30-2 a.m.; Sunday, 11:30-10 p.m.
Reservations: 272-5837
Moderate
No Credit Cards
Beer and Wine

El Toro

Fort Lewis, an enormous Army base south of Tacoma inhabited by 25,000 soldiers or so, naturally has quite a few dedicated fans of Mexican cooking. The best place that has sprung up to serve such aficionados is the funky El Toro in Ponders, a nice quick stop for dinner on the freeway if you're passing through. The cook has been here for eleven years, and he's figured out how to do good Mexican cooking of a Chicano sort. The combination dinner and the chili rellenos are good bets, but the best item is a green chili burrito, enchilada style — not on the menu, but well worth begging the chef to make.

12914 Pacific Highway, Ponders
Daily, 5-11 p.m.; Sunday, 4-9 p.m.
No reservations: 588-5888
Inexpensive
No Credit Cards, No Checks
Beer

Harbor Lights

Seafood places in Washington cities are generally pretty poor, but this one, on a dock along Tacoma's waterfront and all done up in the obligatory nautical decor, has several redeeming virtues. They do try to get fresh fish, so you can normally have a nice grilled salmon, some fresh halibut, and some raw Willapa oysters (not on the shell, however). For $5.75 you can get a huge bucket of excellent steamers — four and one-half pounds, to be precise. The fish and chips aren't bad, either: good halibut dipped in a special batter and served with fries they cut themselves — then dunked in one of those restaurant-supply oils. The waitresses may have been around too long, but it is comforting to know that the same owner has minded the store here for eighteen years.

2761 Ruston Way, Tacoma
Weekdays, 11-11; Friday, Saturday, 11-1 a.m.; Sunday, 2-9
Reservations: 752-8600
Moderate
Credit Cards: AE, BA, MC
Full Bar

LODGING

Lakewood Motor Inn ☆

Tacoma is sorely lacking in good lodgings: the downtown is bereft, and the two big motels on the Freeway are too close to the road. The Lakewood Motor Inn is your best bet. It is in the heart of a small shopping complex created by Norton Clapp about forty years ago — the Duke of Weyerhaeuser taking care of his executive aristocracy. While not luxurious, the motel is nicely done, is a distinct bargain, and is consistently well managed. It has a heated pool and most of the rooms are air conditioned. The view from the rear rooms reveals some lovely oak trees, and the view from the front exposes an inspiring vista: the Lakewood Terrace restaurant, where you can have a splendid dinner.

To get here, take the "McChord-Lakewood" exit from Interstate 5 and follow the signs to Lakewood Center, a mile and a half northwest of the freeway.

6125 Motor Avenue S.W., Lakewood
584-2212
Moderate
Credit Cards: AE, BA, CB, DC, MC
Pets limited

TOURISM

Tacoma Tourism

Despite the close-in, smoky industry and despite the long period of decline downtown, Tacoma is still a city with splendid topography, marvelous views, and many stately mansions. Particularly the North End, that long peninsula stretching up to Point Defiance Park, has a settled, mature dignity that many cities in the Northwest have yet to attain. Some things to see:

Old City Hall, Seventh Avenue and Pacific Avenue, is a dazzling bit of Italian Renaissance architecture, now turned into a shopping arcade.

State Historical Museum, 315 Stadium Way, has a good display of Indian artifacts, old photographs, and American silver.

Point Defiance Park has in its 640 acres virgin forests, a good aquarium and zoo, a reconstructed logging camp, a part of Fort Nisqually (moved and rebuilt in 1934), and a good spot for a seafood lunch, the Boathouse Grill. The city's other fine park is Wright Park (Division and I Street), with an arboretum and a conservatory.

Weyerhaeuser Mansion, North 43rd and Stevens, is a suitable reminder of Tacoma's company-town status—first railroads, then the Weyerhaeusers. The Tudor mansion was built for J.P. Weyerhaeuser in 1923 and has since become a theological seminary.

Culture in Tacoma

Visual Arts. The Tacoma Art Museum is right downtown (South 12th at Pacific) and it is worth a visit for its Japanese prints, modern American multiples, and a children's gallery. The Silver Image Gallery (727 Commerce Street: 572-4410) is a serious gallery devoted to fine photography; it is open afternoons only.

Music. Pacific Luthern University puts on free concerts during the year at which its own orchestra offers intriguing premieres of modern works, some of them specially commissioned for this adventurous program (531-6900 for information).

GIG HARBOR

The Tides Tavern ☆

Gig Harbor has a postcard-pretty harbor just made for fishing boats and tourists. The shops, almost entirely owned by women, have not been distinguished in past years, but recently a wave of quality has washed up onto the shore. There are two good places to visit for starters and for advice on new arrivals. One is Mary Bonneville's Gallery and Loom Room (3102 Harborview Drive), where there are excellent wall-hangings, weavings, and apparel, plus the state's most complete line of loom equipment and materials. The second is Carol Chalk's White Whale Gallery (7811 Pioneer Way), where you will find an uncommonly broad collection of arts and crafts by Northwest artists.

Many of the other attractions are undergoing new ownership. Scandia Gaard, a complex of shops, a museum, and a restaurant atop the hill overlooking the harbor, is currently in transition, while its former manager has opened a rival Scandinavian restaurant, Tall Pines, out on Highway 16—a good spot for brunch. But the Tides Tavern is a solid place for assured good eating. It's very popular, offering good food, good vibes, and a good view from the deck overlooking the dock. There are homemade soups, good pastrami sandwiches, a dandy salad of mushrooms, peppers, sprouts, mozzarella and provolone cheeses, and shrimp for $3.25, and best of all, the overstuffed pizzas made from dough freshly rolled out and piled so high as to resemble a deep-dish pie.

3000 Harborview Drive, Gig Harbor
11-2 a.m. daily; 12-12 Sunday
858-3982
Moderate
No Credit Cards
Beer and Wine

EATONVILLE

Northwest Trek ☆

Thanks to the gift of a 600-acre tract of land, the Tacoma park district has been able to create a modern zoo: the animals roam "free" and the people are caged inside small propane buses which tour the grounds. The five-mile tour of this controlled wilderness is well-narrated and takes about an hour, passing by a large collection of the animals of the Northwest.

After the Trek Tramride, you can hike for miles on trails, picnic, or inspect the small animal exhibit. When in Eatonville, too, you should sample the local specialty, wild mountain black-berry pie, made from a delicious berry with small seeds that abounds locally. The Mountain View Cafe, downtown, makes a nice pie, and Barney's (three miles east of Eatonville on Route 161) offers 85-cent slices from pies made fresh daily year-round. Just before the Nisqually entrance to Mount Rainier is another cafe specializing in the pie, Copper Creek Inn.

Route 161, Eatonville
Daily, 10 a.m.-one hour before sunset; November-April, closed Monday
   and Tuesday
832-6116
$3 for adults

MOUNT RAINIER

Mount Rainier ☆ ☆

It might be nice if Mount Rainier had a small volcanic erup-tion, just enough to wipe away the inept efforts at developing her into a worthy tourist attraction so we could start over again. As things now stand, the tourists stream in for a few months in the summer, jamming the main east and south-face roads and the campgrounds; then the heavy winter snows discourage the

National Park Service from erecting a decent mountain inn as at Mount Hood. But of course the enormous cloud-wrapped bulk of the mountain abides our coming. And if you go in early June or early September you might find some solitude.

One unusual opportunity to learn a new skill and to escape the hordes is to climb the 14,440 monster. It's easier than you may think, not without some danger but requiring no previous experience at climbing. You sign up with Rainier Mountaineering Inc. (run by Lou Whittaker, brother of Jim) at Paradise, take a mandatory, quite enjoyable, one-day climbing-school course — where you can find out whether you're in shape for the climb — and then embark on a two-day, 9,000-foot ascent of the glacier-clad peak. The guide-led climb, in parties of up to two dozen, stops at 10,000-foot Camp Muir first night, where the evening meal is a skimpy portion of lousy freeze-dried food, then heads for the summit and returns to Paradise next day. Climb, $55; school, $15; half-price rainchecks given out for the 25 percent or so of the climbs that fall short of the top due to bad weather. (Mid-May to mid-September; 569-2227; reservations should be made a month in advance.)

Paradise Inn is a modest attempt at creating a real lodge, with the obligatory beams in the lobby, stone fireplace, and Indian rugs on the walls. The rooms have their own baths and have been improved recently. There's a bar and a dining room that serves a standard beef, chicken, and salmon menu, passably good. Nearest good food is at Copper Creek Inn, just outside the Nisqually (southwest) entrance.

Paradise Lodge, an ugly-duckling of a tourist center, has some interesting exhibits if you can elbow your way through the masses to them. The famous ice-caves up-mountain from Paradise have been unreachable since the heavy snows of 1971, but wildflowers still come out normally (best in late July and early August).

Paradise Inn
20 miles east of Longmire entrance, Paradise
June 15-Labor Day only; dining hours, 7-9, 12-2, 6-8.
Reservations: 569-2291
Moderate
Credit Cards: BA, MC
Full Bar

OLYMPIA

Tumwater Valley Inn ☆ ☆

Food in Olympia is a special breed of cooking: lobbyist cuisine. That means mediocre steaks combined with either Olympia oysters or a few tired crab legs. There is, however, one place to escape this fate, the pleasant Tumwater Valley Inn overlooking a golf course which the nearby Olympia Brewery reclaimed from some lowland. The club itself is worth keeping in mind, too, since its golf course, pool, and four tennis courts are all open to the public. This oasis on the Deschutes River makes a nice stop for breakfast and for lunch; the latter features two specials each day, fashioned from such things as fresh, pan-fried fish, Mexican items, roasts, and sometimes crepes.

But the real attraction comes from the continental dinners, nicely fashioned by a conscientious chef, Arnold Ball, who knows enough to make his own stocks carefully and not to overload the cooks with too many fancy specials. A meal might start with some small oysters in a delicate wine and cream sauce, fragrant with delicate herbs. For a main course, we would recommend the meticulously soaked and de-membraned sweetbreads, the duck a l'orange, and the tournedos adorned with a superior sauce made from veal stock and brandy. The sauces with all of these dishes are very well bred.

The meal will not be perfect. The wine list is weak, the side vegetables can be a grave disappointment, and the desserts are not much. But the service is agreeable, the prices are bargains, and the chef enjoys meeting a serious dinner party and dispensing helpful advice.

Tumwater Valley Drive just off Capitol Boulevard, Olympia
Tuesday-Saturday, 7 a.m.-10 p.m.; closes Sunday at 8 p.m.; no dinner
  Monday.
Reservations: 943-9620
Moderate
Credit Cards: BA, MC
Full Bar

The Old Brown Derby ☆

This spot, small and hard to squeeze into at lunch, is a block off the Capitol campus, so you might want to leave the legislative hearing early, before the crush. It's been here for 35 years. The sandwiches are fine, but the real treats are the soups—such as the homemade chicken noodle, thick with noodles and big hunks of chicken—and the pies. There are only 20 seats, and you may get pushed around a bit by the clientele.

Tenth and Capitol Way, Olympia
357-7527

The Greenwood Inn ☆

Olympia is another one of those Puget Sound cities with a dramatic topography of hills overlooking lovely bays of water—and a rather dreary little city, resolutely turning its back on those advantages. The Greenwood Inn, overlooking Capitol Lake, is one place that does take advantage of such a view, and it offers seclusion and quiet as a bonus. The rooms are larger than other motels in town can offer, so it's the best place to stay, even if the food and the service are nothing special.

2300 Evergreen Park Drive, off Route 101, Olympia
943-4000
Moderate
Credit Cards: AE, BA, CB, DC, MC
Small pets allowed

Olympia Tourism

The Capitol. The masonry dome, completed in 1928, is the fourth highest in the world. The walk up the 287 steps to a viewing lantern atop was closed by an earthquake in 1965, but is due to be allowed again soon, so it is worth inquiring of the guide service in the Capitol if you can ascend. The interior of the Capitol is sumptuous, and there are the usual civics-book tours given free in the summer. The grounds are lovely, especially in the spring when the Japanese cherry trees bloom. The State Library Building has some good art works by Kenneth Callahan and other Northwest notables. The State Capitol Museum (211 West 21st Street) has a meager display in a nice old mansion.

The Brewery. The proud Schmidt family have created a spotless brewery with an excellent tour (45 minutes, ending up with a chance to quaff some freshly-made brew), and outside, the Tumwater Valley has been turned into a pretty park with spectacular blooms. There are modest historical reminders that this is the oldest town on Puget Sound (1845).

Nightlife. The legislators and the bureaucrats adjourn at 5 p.m., usually to The Melting Pot (11th and Capitol Way); later at night, the bar where you can overhear the best state secrets is at the Tyee (5 miles south on Interstate 5).

CHEHALIS

Mary McCrank's Dinner House ☆

Mary McCrank's, in business for forty years, is now on the old main road, but it is still the nicest stop you can make along the freeway corridor from Seattle to Portland. The restaurant is a large home, with fireplaces in some of the dining rooms, a nice window overlooking the garden, and armchairs scattered around amid bookshelves crammed with Reader's Digest Condensed Books. The food is all homemade and unbeatably priced: a full dinner runs up to $5 a person.

The meal usually starts with a visit from the outspoken Mrs. McCrank, who is quite likely to tell you once again about the time Charles Laughton ate here. Then you get relishes; an outstanding tray of watermelon pickles, cucumbers with onions, corn relish, and the homemade jams for the homemade breads. The dinner offerings include: fried chicken, chicken with dumplings, pork roast, fresh trout, crab curries, and other country fixings. You end with such glorious pies as a sourcream raisin. The cooking is always good, and it is a delight to have delicious plain fare with all the Chehalis folks.

Old 99, four miles south of Chehalis
Dinner only, 5-8:30; Sunday, 12:30-5
Reservations: 748-3662
Inexpensive
No Credit Cards
No Alcohol

LONGVIEW

Henri's ☆

Although it has French decor and a few French items, they call it "Henry's" around here and the menu contains a lot of steaks and prime rib. Still, reliable continental cooking does come out of the kitchen—the shrimp bisque made each Wednesday and the lobster bisque on Saturday, the rack of lamb served with a decent bearnaise, and some good wine. For lunch, the crab or shrimp sandwiches are recommended.

4545 Ocean Beach Highway, Longview
Daily, 11-11; Saturday, 4:30-12; closed Sunday
Reservations: 425-7970
Moderate
Credit Cards: AE, BA, DC, MC
Full Bar

VANCOUVER

Inn at the Quay ☆

Facing each other across the Columbia, just west of the Interstate 5 bridge, are two gaudy, large motels run by the Thunderbird Inns chain. The one in Vancouver is preferable for its less flamboyant decor and for its proximity to the old part of Vancouver. The rooms are routinely plush, some with views of the river. The dining room and bar are done up in an impressive imitation of a square-rigger, so it's a good enough spot for breakfast or a drink. Both Portland and the Portland airport are easy, twenty-minute drives from the motel. Fort Vancouver (East Evergreen Boulevard) is a 160-acre historical site where pieces of the mid-nineteenth-century trading outpost are gradually being reassembled and simulated.

Columbia Street and the Columbia River, Vancouver
694-8341
Expensive
Credit Cards: AE, BA, CB, DC, MC

Edelweiss

They do some nice German cooking here, cutting their own veal for the wiener schnitzel, making their own sauerkraut for the smoked pork loin, and preparing their own pickled red cabbage for sauerbraten. There's only one German beer, but there are plenty of good German wines. You'll eat in a large inn with a Bavarian atmosphere replete with accordionists and singing waitresses, but if that doesn't offend your sensibility, you will be fairly well pleased with the fare.

8800 Northeast Highway 99, 2 miles north of Vancouver
Weekday lunches, 11-2; dinners, 5-10; Sunday, 2-9 p.m.
Reservations: 696-4649
Moderate
Credit Cards: BA, MC
Full Bar

Eastern Washington

RESTAURANTS

Peking Garden ☆ ☆

It's not likely your taxi driver will have heard of the place — way out east of town on East Sprague, an ugly stretch of drive-ins — but for our money this is the best place in town for food. The Lo and Liu families came here recently from Formosa via Los Angeles, and they do very skillful Mandarin cooking.

There are several superior hot-spiced dishes, like the hot curried chicken with cashews, or a hot and sour soup that is spiced right to your sweating point, or a fiery shrimp dish made with garlic, ginger, and peppers. These are always worth ordering, both for their rarity and because they will wake up your palate for the duration of the meal. For the rest, the menu is very wide-ranging. The duck is always good (with a Peking duck available with a day's notice), the chicken dishes work well with hot sauces, and the soups and shrimp dishes are among the top items. The cook on duty is always willing to do your ordering for you. One nice touch is when he comes out after you've had a few bites of the first really spicy dish, asks if that is too hot, and then cooks the rest of the meal accordingly.

The room is decorated in standard Chinese-restaurant style, perhaps a bit nicer; the service is excellent; prices are very fair,

198

considering that this kind of cooking necessitates numerous trips up to Vancouver to get authentic spices; and it stays open til 3 a.m.

> 3420 East Sprague, Spokane
> Daily, 11:30 a.m.-3 a.m.; Saturday, 4 p.m.-3 a.m.; Sunday, 4-10 p.m.;
>   closed Tuesday
> Reservations: KE 4-2525
> Moderate
> Credit Cards: BA, MC
> Full Bar

Longhorn Barbecue ☆☆

Twenty years ago, five Lehnertz brothers plus one cousin transported their finest Texas tradition, barbecueing, to Spokane. The popular place they founded has held up remarkably well over the years, and they still dispense the best barbecue we know of in these states.

The ribs are cooked over a Texas-style pit, brick-lined and fired with apple, alder, and birch wood. The meats are basted in a secret sauce, and the facility is constructed so that ample smoke surrounds the operation like a fine incense. They do ribs, of course, and also chicken, roast beef (unbasted), ham, and polish sausage. For $3.95 you get a full, messy dinner of meat, potato, barbecued beans, bread, and a beverage (lots of beer is also at hand). Top it off with home-made ice cream. The Longhorn is situated in a big red building resembling a barn, and it's open for breakfast (nothing special) and lunch as well as for a popular take-out trade. Go early for dinner, and ask for any extra roast-beef ends.

> Sunset Highway 2, near the airport, Spokane
> Daily, 7 a.m.-11 p.m.; closed Sunday, Monday
> Reservations for lunch only: 838-8372
> Moderate
> Credit Cards: BA, MC
> Full Bar

Spokane House ☆

For years this was the best place in Spokane to dine and the best place to hear great rock bands in the lounge after dinner. The fifty-five rooms in the motel may be a shade compact, but it is a small motel with good food.

Whether the food is still good is difficult to say, since the indispensable owner-manager, Guy Miesch, died last year. Presumably the flock of devotees will keep the standards up, but the specialities—like lobster flown in and poached in vermouth, or bluepoint oysters—will probably vanish. It's probably still worth trying; the dining rooms are elegantly appointed, and the view back to the city is quite good.

Sunset Boulevard, 3 miles west of Spokane
Restaurant hours, daily 11:30-2; 5-10:30 p.m.
838-1471
Moderate
Credit Cards: AE, BA, CB, DC, MC
Full Bar

Strobel's ☆

Snooty travelers will immediately detect the provenance of this place, with its fern-filled decor, its Vanessi-inspired menu, and its numerous allusions to Seattle's Boondock's, San Francisco's McArthur Park, and Los Angeles' The Greenhouse. But the important point lies unadvertised: the cook, John Simonds, is a dedicated practitioner of his trade. Your sauteed vegetables, your omelets, your steaks, your heavily laden specialties of meats-with-vegetables - with - cheese - with - eggs - with - sprouts - with - sauce - Mornay, will all come out surprisingly good, assuming Simonds is in the kitchen. The bar, a laid-back place with cushions on the floor, is a popular spot for the singles, and it serves good drinks. All in all, a distinguished practitioner of a slick genre.

North 118 Stevens, Spokane
Daily, 11-2 a.m.; closed Sunday
Reservations: 456-8988
Moderate
Credit Cards: BA, MC
Full Bar

Clinkerdagger, Bickerstaff and Pett's Public House Bar ☆

The food in the restaurant is carefully portion-controlled and good enough in a conventional way, but we prefer the bar. The view out over the boiling basaltic gorge of the Spokane Falls is one major plus. A nice Pimm's Cup, not the easiest summer drink to find, is another. A third is the decor, which is very well done, if laid on in a thick, merrie way.

This pub is part of a handsome old flour mill that has been restored to house shops and offices, so you might set the rest of the family browsing while you recover in the bar.

West 621 Mallon, Spokane
Daily, 11:30-9 p.m.; til 10:30 on weekends; Sunday brunch, 9:30-1:30
Reservations: 328-5965
Moderate
Credit Cards: BA, MC

Sweet Swiss Bakery ☆

This very congenial little spot, off the lobby of the Paulsen Building, is just the place for a nice breakfast, particularly if you drop in on a Friday morning right after the chefs have made their outstandingly good croissants and brioches. For about 50 cents, you can have a continental breakfast that really is. The other baked goods, leaving aside the unexceptional breads, are also very fine, as prepared by a German and an Austrian chef. There are cookies, small French pastries, small tortes and cakes beautifully decorated, lacy Florentine cookies, and tiny cones filled with a luscious semi-bitter chocolate. A small shelf with chocolates and other Swiss goodies completes this stop for picnic goods, a house gift, or munching food for the drive out into the desert.

Riverside and Stevens Streets, Spokane
Monday-Friday, 7:30-5:30; closed weekends
838-1730

LODGING

Davenport Hotel ☆ ☆

When the Davenport opened in 1914, named for a famous restaurateur of the town and designed by the city's famous architect, Kirkland Cutter, Spokane was quite a town. Its wealth, made from Idaho mineral rushes two generations before, had composed itself into a kind of dignified ostentation that once prompted an English writer to remark that Spokane was the only

city in America, outside New York, where gentlemen looked comfortable in formal clothes. Opera was presented on a huge stage. Louis Davenport's oysters arrived in iced railcars from both coasts. And it all revolved around the splendid Davenport, its lobby filled crazily with hundreds of caged birds, and its change made in coin that emerged dazzling from chemical baths.

The hotel, after surviving a series of near-bankruptcies, is once more solvent. The birds are back in the lobby (in a modest flock), the public rooms have been air-conditioned, and the Dallas-based management has even taken some steps to improve the execrable food. For $20 a night for a double you can stay in the grandest of the remaining old hotels of the Northwest. The small rooms can be rather dreary, but there are nice suites; the rooms ending in 21 or 22 are pleasant and they face north toward the river. The top suites (312, 927, 1405) are decorated in regal excess and can run up to $105 a night. The public rooms are marvelously ornate.

West 807 Sprague, Spokane
MA 4-2121
Moderate, with expensive suites
Credit Cards: AE, BA, CB, DC, MC

Sheraton Spokane Hotel

All during EXPO this hotel was being built, smack in the middle of the amusement park. EXPO's gone—no tears are necessary—and a splendid riverfront park may someday take its place. And the Sheraton is finally completed, nicely situated to overlook the river and the Opera House. It's a very standard kind of a hotel: plastic lobby, a continental dining room, middle-of-the-road shows in the lounge, and an open-air, flower-filled coffee shop. The best river views are in the north and west wings, the higher up the better (and the more expensive). Double start at $21 and top off in suite 1502-4 at $75. The four-hundred-room hotel is aimed at conventions, in case that matters.

Spokane Falls Court, Spokane
455-9600
Moderate, with expensive suites
Credit Cards: AE, BA, CB, DC, MC
Pets negotiable

TOURISM

Golfing ☆ ☆

An inspirational documentary the Chamber of Commerce loves to show makes much over the contentment of the local laboring class. This dogma is regularly reinforced in Spokane by the construction of yet another splendid public golf course to pleasure the local workers and content them for foregone wage increases. No fewer than ten courses are open to the public in the area, six of them municipal or county courses.

Indian Canyon, west of Spokane, off Sunset Highway, is the best. It is immaculately groomed and lush; its location on a challenging hillside overlooking the city means all but the most hearty should rent a cart. Some have called it the most beautiful public course in America.

Hangman Valley, ten miles south of Spokane, off Palouse highway, is another gem set in a picturesque country meadow traversed by winding Hangman Creek.

Lou Lou Custom Ski Service ☆ ☆

Spokane is hardly the capital of Northwest skiing, despite its drier snow. Schweitzer Basin has nice facilities, but its long, gentle slopes make it best for family skiing. 49 Degrees North, at Chewelah, is best for beginners. Mount Spokane is very challenging (lift no. 4's runs are as steep as any at Alpental), but its facilities are only fair.

Nonetheless, here is a ski shop which for repairs and expert advice is one of the best on the whole West Coast. Louis Kneubuhler, the owner, used to be a companion-in-training with Jean-Claud Killy for the French international racing team, and somehow he ended up in Spokane. His shop can handle the most complicated custom alteration or repair problem. Kneubuhler will also select skis for individuals with great care—although he carries only Rossignol—or custom-fit boots. Good prices, too.

East 428 Pacific, Spokane
Daily, 11-7 p.m.; closed Sunday
624-9994
Credit Cards: BA, MC

Pacific Northwest Indian Center ☆

This teepee-shaped museum contains one of the most comprehensive collections of Indian artifacts and archives in the country. The scholarly section houses thousands of manuscripts and books, while the four-story museum contains good representative displays of Northwest and Western Indian arts, crafts, clothing, and assorted historical items. The museum has had its share of controversy and it has managed to alienate a lot of Indians. The exhibits are rather overwhelming and are not very informatively or carefully displayed, but individual items like the baskets and the costumes are among the best you'll ever see. The gift shop is routine.

There are two other museums of merit in this history-rich town:

Campbell House, West 2316 First Street, is a grand, half-timbered house in Brown's Addition, restored to the original magnificence desired by Amas Basaliel Campbell, who made his pile in mining; upstairs, suitably, are minerals from the Coeur d'Alene country. The adjoining Cheney Cowles Museum, named for a member of the current first family (timber, media and downtown property barons), has a good collection of relics and Indian artifacts.

Crosbyana Room, at Gonzaga University's Crosby Museum (donated by the crooner-alumnus), is a nice exercise in campy tourism: gold records, an Oscar, autographed photos—the whole bit.

East 200 Cataldo, on river just south of Gonzaga University, Spokane
Monday-Saturday, 9-6; Sunday, noon-8 p.m.
326-4550
Adults: $1

SANDPOINT

The Pasta House ☆

This Italian restaurant is good enough to make us stretch our imposed boundary forty miles into northern Idaho. Should you find yourself weary of Spokane food, you would do well to drive the ninety miles to this charming little town on Lake Pend Oreille.

The restaurant serves dinner only and the range is not wide. There might be a freshly made manicotti, fragrant and herbacious; or a meltingly tender veal cutlet with onions, mushrooms, fresh basil and parmesan; and then an exemplary, crunchy cannoli for dessert. The wine list is feeble, but the rest of the place in a gracious old home exhibits such care for the lost art of Italian cooking in America that such a slight lapse is easily forgiven.

> 521 North Fourth Street, Sandpoint, Idaho
> Dinner only, daily, 5:30-10 p.m.
> Reservations: 263-6722
> Moderate
> Credit cards: BA, MC
> Beer (Coors) and wine

MOSCOW

Allino's

Moscow, with its own state university, is a kind of twin city to Pullman. The drinking age is lower in Idaho, however, and so the food is better, or at least better enough to justify the seven-mile drive across the border.

Allino's is an Italian restaurant that is starting off slowly, with mediocre hoagies, poor wines and a very nice homemade lasagne. But owner Al Deskowitz wants to do much better. He's building a patio to accommodate al fresco diners and expanding the menu to include some carefully made pastas and veal dishes. It should be worth a call to the owner (long distance from Pullman!) to see if he's ready for any tifosos.

308 W. Sixth Street, Moscow
Weekdays, 11-10; Friday, Saturday, open til midnight; Sunday, 4-10 p.m.
No reservations: 882-4545
Moderate
Credit Cards: BA, MC
Beer and Wine

The New Idaho Hotel

"New" is scarcely the word for this hotel, in YMCA-level of repair, but there are some new ideas in the food department. *The Gourmet Owl* is a small dining room, open Thursday, Friday, and Saturday nights only, seating twenty-two persons, and custom-cooking an ambitious menu. You can get a coquille, frogs legs, tournedos Rossini, chicken breasts flamed in apricot brandy, and an anise souffle. The economics of such an operation are shaky, so you should call the chef, Barbara Crossler, to see if she's been able to keep the Owl alive.

Another downstairs room of the hotel has become a wine and fondue establishment, called *The Winery*. It is a popular spot for college kids, featuring a dull wine card, passable cheese, beef and chocolate fondues, and excellent folksinging.

124 North Main Street, Moscow
Owl dinners, 6-10 p.m., Thursday-Saturday
Reservations: 882-4529
Moderate
Credit Cards: AE, BA, MC
Full Bar

PULLMAN

The Seasons ☆

One step inside this house restaurant and you'll know you're in a college town. The waitresses are college-hip; the menu is eclectic, unpredictable, and vaguely healthy. The owner-chef, John Bonnier, is an experienced cook whose experiments are well worth trying. Each night he selects two specialties from among his repertoire: fifteen different chicken dishes, beef carbonades, Greek meatballs, lasagnes, and so on. The prices are very good, either $3.75 or $4.25 for the complete meal, which also includes a salad with a nice yoghurt-bleu dressing, rice, and a good dessert such as yoghurt cake. Inglenook wines are served. For lunch you have your choice of sandwiches on homemade bread and salads.

The mood is mellow, but there is one maddening feature. The Seasons orders food conservatively, so on many nights they exhaust the day's provisions early and simply turn away later arrivals.

Southeast 215 Paradise, Pullman
Daily, 11:30-1; 5:30-8:30; closed Sunday, Monday
No Reservations: 564-9711
Moderate
No Credit Cards
Wine

Hilltop Motel

Motels in this attractive town are nothing much, so we recommend staying in this twenty-year-old one, with nice views of the valley, and bargain prices (doubles start at $10). The rooms are quiet, decently decorated and even fitted out with color television. Another benefit from this tidy operation is the adjoining steakhouse, also with a good view; it boasts well-aged Yakima beef.

Colfax Highway, Pullman
564-1195
Restaurant just serves dinner, 5-10 p.m.; 5-11 on weekends; closed Sunday
Inexpensive
Credit Cards: AE, BA, MC

WALLA WALLA

Blue Mountain Tavern

A stab is being made here at recreating an old-fashioned tavern, complete with a card room, beer steins, wall decorations of faint historic interest, and hanging 1880s lamps. We like the beer prices better than the decor — 35 cents for a 15-ounce schooner — and the sandwiches aren't bad: you can get a generous openface polish-sausage-and-cheese sandwich for $1.60. Takeout, too.

2005 Isaacs, Walla Walla
Monday-Saturday, 10 a.m.-2 a.m.; Sunday, 2-10 p.m.
529-3950
Inexpensive

Klicker Berry Stand

This pleasing hodge-podge is a good stand for assembling a picnic. The fruit is good, and they carry excellent sausages (from Bavarian Meats and Torino Sausage Co.) as well as a pretty fair line of cheese. Half the place is a showroom for mediocre antiques. It's a friendly sort of stand, hence a good spot for picking up advice on local doings. Summer only.

East Isaacs Street (Route 4), Walla Walla
Every day, from June 1 to September 15, 9 a.m.-8 p.m.
525-8650
No Credit Cards

Royal Motor Inn

Walla Walla was at one time an oasis for the pioneers who struggled in from the savage landscape to the east. The surrounding scenery is still idyllic, with its groomed, rolling wheatland, but the town's no oasis for the traveler any more.

The old downtown hotel, the Marcus Whitman, has been ruined by a restoration project, so you are best advised to stay at this motel, with decent rooms overlooking an inner courtyard with a nice pool. It's near the campus of Whitman College where you can take a nice stroll. The dining room should be avoided at dinner, but you can get hot biscuits with cream gravy for breakfast and some nicely made fresh soups for lunch.

325 East Main Street, Walla Walla
529-4360
Moderate
Credit Cards: BA, MC

Walla Walla Tourism

The attractions in this pretty town aren't much individually, but by adding up a number of things you can put together a satisfying short visit.

Old Houses — They are best viewed on South Palouse and South Catherine Streets, where the mature trees lend a New England aspect to the nineteenth-century mansions.

Culture — The Whitman campus, lovely to look at itself, normally has a play, a concert, or a film series during weekends; the Carnegie Center for the Arts (109 South Palouse) is the local center for arts and crafts exhibitions; the Whitman library is strong in Northwest materials.

Eating — The best products are Walla Walla sweet onions which you can buy from Japanese truck farmers who set up stands at the west end of town; the onions, so sweet you can eat them raw, are normally sold only in fifty-pound sacks; if they are not in season, the other vegetables are also splendid. Andy's Market, in the Seventh Day Adventist town of College Place, is a terrific vegetarian store. In the absence of good restaurants, you might visit the Pastime Cafe on West Main Street for an honest plate of lasagne.

Historical Reverie—The Whitman Mission, uninspiringly commemorated, is seven miles west; Fort Walla Walla Park has a pioneer village; Pioneer Park has a bandstand with Saturday and Sunday afternoon music, nicely suited to this relic of small-town Americana.

RICHLAND

Le Petit Restaurant

Being so far from New York you might have a hankering for a French restaurant that treats you like a worm. This tiny, ugly spot will oblige, dishing out insults and mostly bad dishes along with a few that are quite good. In a way, it's rather fun being so treated, and besides it's much less expensive than eating mock-gourmet cooking at the fancy motels. The fruit pies can be very good; sweetbreads and chicken dishes are worth risking for a main course.

> 3892 W. Van Gieser, West Richland
> Tuesday-Friday, noon-2; Tuesday-Saturday, 5-9 p.m.
> Reservations: 967-2905
> Moderate
> No Cards
> Beer and Wine

Hanford House ☆

In order to win a contract managing a part of the Hanford plutonium works, ARCO had to lend a hand to diversification in this area, so they built this large motel alongside the Columbia River and spawned a convention business. The complex, never administered with full enthusiasm, has recently been bought by Thunderbird Inns, who will probably jazz it up some but maybe not too much.

The rooms are large, expensive, and tastefully furnished. The best ones are in the section overlooking the river (169-187 and 269-87, odd numbers only); otherwise, to avoid a view of the parking lots, ask for a room on the courtyard (any even-numbered room). The courtyard is pretty, with a putting green, a small pool, and shuffleboard. Extending in both directions from the motel complex are lush riverside parks, and just across the levee the Columbia hisses by in silky strength.

There is a tiered dining room, decorated incongruously to look like a ski lodge in the middle of a broiling desert. It serves an ambitious menu, well beyond the capacity of local suppliers or cooks.

802 George Washington Way, Richland
946-7611
Expensive

Meadow Springs Country Club ☆

Nearly everything worth doing in the Tri Cities is outside: fishing, renting a boat for waterskiing (Metz Marina, Kennewick) picnicking or bird-watching or even snake-watching in one of the splendid Corps of Engineers parks along the dammed-up river, swimming in the warm lagoons, hunting, sunbathing. Venture inside to something like the Hanford Science Center, to learn about the plutonium industry that created Richland, and you will regret it: the museum is woefully uninspired. Again you're better off outside, driving ten miles north to inspect a reactor under construction (obtain permission from the Washington Public Power Supply System office, Richland).

The best way to enjoy the Arizona-style landscape and weather is to play golf at Meadow Springs. It is a very difficult course—second only to Seattle's brutal Sahalee—with forty-six traps and eleven holes with water coming into play. The seventeenth hole, for instance, plays 245 yards, par three from the championship tee, almost entirely over water. The grass is in terrific condition, and all around are a handsome, growing residential development and the sagebrush landscape. Fees are $7.50 on weekends, $6.50 on weekdays. In another few years, when the club membership is filled out, the course will be closed to the public. On slower days you can probably have lunch or dinner in the private clubhouse, thus solving the serious problem of how to get good food in the Tri Cities.

Take Route 12 west from Kennewick, take Leslie Road left, follow signs
783-8165
Open All Year

OTHELLO

Freddie's ☆

Othello is in the middle of splendid duck-hunting country, and fortunately for the practitioners of this sport, the town has a cafe where one can get some distinguished cooking after a day thinking about delicious dinners. Fred Eng has operated this cafe for two decades, serving primarily American food for lunch in the coffee-shop up front, and then shifting to Cantonese cooking in the evenings for the dining rooms to the rear. The cooking is first-class Cantonese fare: sweet-and-sours, excellent prawns, sugar pea pods, a good almond chicken, and the usual chop sueys and family-style combinations. If you get to know the chef and are willing to pay more, he will do more ambitious Chinese specials— such as a duck—and perhaps even invite his own family to join your party in this feast. The regular cooking and the daily specials are perfectly good, but if you want to end a day of shooting in proper style, you might do well to call Mr. Eng in advance and see what he might be willing to do.

67 South First Street, Othello
Daily, 11 a.m.-midnight; closed Sunday
Reservations: 488-2704
Moderate
Credit Cards: BA, MC
Full Bar

CRESTON

Deb Cobenhaver's Cafe ☆

Deb was a world-champion rodeo-rider back in the mid-1950s, and after he retired he set up this cafe, about as authentic a model as we know. Outside there is a wooden porch, just like a stage-set saloon. Inside the place is strewn with trophies, photos, and saddles. Cowboy-hatted men and women shoot pool in the bar. In the back room the town gathers to square dance on Thursday night or to grill steaks and enjoy Western music on Saturday night.

In the main cafe Clara Simonson is in formidable command. You can get a farm breakfast as early as 6 a.m., a few sandwiches for lunch, and then for dinner mostly steaks. There are some nice touches like the fries, which are cut in the kitchen and carefully cooked. The "home-made pies" haven't been for years, but if you josh the cook a bit you'll get good, honest cooking. Best of all is the warm sense of community in this town gathering-place, a robust sociability that normally leaves us in high spirits all during the next two hours of monotonous driving.

Route 2, Creston
Daily, 6 a.m.-10 p.m.; open Saturday til 1:30 a.m.
636-9231
Inexpensive
Credit Cards: BA, MC
Full Bar

GRAND COULEE

Grand Coulee ☆ ☆

It is not easy to appreciate the boggling grandeur of this region. The dam itself is as tall as a forty-six story building, its spillway twice the height of Niagra, and its length that of a dozen city blocks. But the scale of things in this part of the country is so outsized that the dam can seem to be just another ordinary dam tucked into the cliffs. A good way to comprehend the enormity is to drive down on Route 155 into the Grand Coulee itself where, fifty thousand years ago, the Columbia coursed in a flow of glacier-fed water greater than any river known on earth, slicing down through lava plateaus until a valley was created as wide as five miles and as deep as five hundred feet. (The ice-dam that diverted the Columbia to this course was located where the concrete-dam now stands.) The prehistoric wonder of this vast "lost" river is best evoked at Dry Falls, where the torrential river crashed over falls three miles wide and four hundred feet high. Down in the Coulee there are lakes for soaking up the sun or camping; the magical time comes when the sun gets low and the glints of mineral-color come out of the brooding, slag-like cliffs.

One can stay at a passable motel in Coulee Dam, the Ponderosa, but you are much better off renting a boat and camping on the shore of 150-mile-long Roosevelt Lake, backed up by the dam; you can boat into campgrounds inaccessible by car.

SOAP LAKE

Don's ☆

The decor is modestly western, and fortunately the cooking is not pseudo-gourmet but just what you hope for over here: good red meat. They cut their own steaks and then age them for about three weeks. The delicious meat comes without tenderizers but just a dash of seasoning salt. The portions are large: a sixteen-ounce New York strip goes for $10. If you want some fries with this dinner, you will get potatoes that have been peeled and cut on the premises. The other dishes show the same dedication to good ingredients: the veal is cut in the kitchen, and they will even leave it unbreaded if you are an effete type who prefers veal cutlets that way; the hams and turkeys are cooked up fresh; and the lamb chop is cut double-thick.

119 Third Street, Soap Lake
Daily, 4 p.m.-midnight; closed Sunday
Reservations: 246-3511
Moderate
Credit Cards: BA, MC
Full Bar

LAKE CHELAN

Lake Chelan ☆

The lake, a deep, narrow shaft thrusting fifty-five miles into the heart of the North Cascades, provides an easy way far into the back country. You can board a modest steamer at 8:30 in the morning and, after cruising between the narrowing mountain walls, be at the head of the lake, Stehekin, four and a half hours later. The boat returns in just an hour, but you can stay longer by booking a room at North Cascades Lodge (no phone; write Stehekin 98852), and from this acceptable alpine lodge you can go on a rubber raft trip down a river, do some fishing, or head farther into the mountains.

The southern end of the lake is rather tacky and tourist-trampled by comparison, but the swimming can be nice during the boiling days, and the wind is strong for sailors. The best place to stay is in the new wing of Campbell's Lodge (682-9561), but prices are high. For a decent steak, go to Murphy's (dinner only, 4 p.m.-midnight: 682-2431; closed Tuesdays).

Lake Chelan Boat Company
Daily summer trips; October-May 15, Monday, Wednesday, Friday only
$8 adults
682-2224

WINTHROP

Sun Mountain Lodge ☆ ☆

Perched and cantilevered fifteen hundred feet above the gorgeous Methow Valley, this resort offers splendid views into the North Cascades almost everywhere one looks. The lodge is handsomely designed by Roland Terry, Seattle's establishment architect, and the rooms, while a shade small, are done with Terry's usual good taste. Best rooms are suites 101 and 201, about $40 each, the only ones with fireplaces.

The lodge is a fine place for a weekend getaway, particularly if you go a bit before or after the summer season. Among the things to do are riding trails, taking pack trips, swimming, playing tennis (the four courts get badly overcrowded in a busy weekend), or attending a communal cookout; in the winter you can ice-skate, ski downhill (at Loup Loup, thirty miles away), or cross-country, or go on horse-drawn sleigh rides.

The food is conventional but well-prepared and served in a room with another grand outlook. There are steaks, of course, but also a nicely fried trout, a few grills, and fowl. It is virtually the only decent place to eat in the entire valley, so the restaurant can get badly crowded, requiring waits of up to two hours some weekends. The lodge was unfortunately built too small for the resort, so it makes sense to come when crowds are down even though there are only fifty units in the complex. Summer has posed another disadvantage that might be remedied by this time: no air conditioning.

Follow signs off Highway 20, a few miles east of Winthrop
Closed November, December
996-2211
Expensive
Credit Cards: AE, BA, MC

ENTIAT

Candlelight Restaurant ☆

Confronted with a name like this, a town like this, and a plug-ugly facade like this, you would be quite justified in whizzing right past this new restaurant on the road between Chelan and Wenatchee. Nonetheless, inside there is a good, widely experienced Danish chef preparing a French menu for moderate prices.

You sit in a pleasantly decorated, homey room. The meal commences with excellent French bread and perhaps some snails. The soup course is particularly good, with daily specials like Danish apple augmenting a hearty French onion. For the main course the seafood dishes are the best bet — baked crab, scallops in a creamy casserole, a proper poached salmon with an admirable Hollandaise, even a good bouillabaisse this far from the sea. Beef courses consist of brochette Wellington, a filet, and a peppercorn steak. You will finish with peach flambe or some Danish desserts. There is a small, sound wine list.

Prices are very good, topping out at $7.95 for the most expensive complete dinner. Chef Jan Kuchta, having cooked in many major cities, is a master of good sauces. He knows what he's doing — as one had better to open a French restaurant in such a place.

> Highway 97, Entiat
> Dinners only, 5:30-10:30; closed Monday, Tuesday in winter
> Reservations: 784-1412
> Moderate
> No credit cards
> Wine and beer

WENATCHEE

The Windmill ☆ ☆

Wenatchee is one of those small, heavily-moteled cities where you might suffer a passing temptation to have a "gourmet" meal, served up by a bumbling maitre d' in a snazzy new motel. It would be a bad mistake. The best food in this town is at a tiny steakhouse where everything is superbly selected and cooked, the atmosphere is infectiously sociable, and the only problem is that it is so popular with the locals that it is hard to get in.

The Windmill has been an institution in this town for forty-five years; for the past twenty-two the preservation of this tradition has been in the capable hands of Larry and Willie Lewin, a charming couple who know everybody and keep things humming. It's a fairly simple dinner. You start with breadsticks, a good salad, and a bottle of wine from a decent wine list (ask for the red to be served un-chilled). Then come steaks of excellent Yakima beef, unblemished by tenderizers; they are thick and cooked exactly to order. The baked potato or the unfrozen French fries are equally good. You finish with one of Willie's magnificent pies, baked fresh daily.

Reservations are taken only for parties of six. The place has just eleven booths — it really is no larger than the base of a windmill — plus eight stools at the front counter (the jolliest place to sit). On weekends, you'll wait if you come between 6 and 9 p.m. But the company is splendid and the dandy waitresses move things along smartly. In sum: the Windmill comes close to being the perfect steakhouse.

1501 N. Wenatchee Avenue, Wenatchee
Tuesday-Saturday, 5-9:30 p.m.
No reservations: 663-3478
Moderate
Credit Cards: BA, MC
Beer and Wine

The Chieftain Motel ☆

The motels in Wenatchee are nearly all in an uninspiring row along Wenatchee Avenue. This one has a stable tradition behind it since 1928, a smaller pool but bigger rooms than at the new, gaudy Thunderbird, and a predominance of locals in the dining room. The rooms in the new wing, the "executive rooms" (numbers 127-154 and 227-254), cost only a dollar more per night but are considerably larger and nicer than the rest. The decor is subdued. The restaurant is nothing much, except for the popular prime rib.

> 1005 North Wenatchee Avenue, Wenatchee
> 663-8141
> Moderate
> Credit Cards: AE, BA, CB, DC, MC

Ohme Gardens ☆

Forty-three years ago, orchardist Herman Ohme started transforming a 600-foot high promontory on his land into an edenic retreat for the family after a day in the broiling orchards below. The lovely gardens are open to the public in the summer, and they are worth visiting both for the view of the Columbia and for the fastidiously created small ecosystems of rain forest, alpine meadows, desert, etc.

> Highway 97, four miles north of Wenatchee
> April-October, 8 a.m.-sunset
> $1.25

LEAVENWORTH

Der Ritterhof Motor Inn ☆

All very nice: a small, clean motel, with nice views of the spectacular mountains all around, quiet decor, big beds, a pleasant owner who's been here four years, good prices (starting at $18), a heated pool, groomed grounds. During the summer, you need to book weekend rooms about two weeks in advance. Best room is 220.

Highway 2, just west of Leavenworth
548-5845
Moderate
Credit Cards: AE, BA, MC

Leavenworth Shops

Leavenworth is tucked into one of the most beautiful parts of the Northwest, the cascading Tumwater Valley of the Wenatchee River. The little town decided ten years ago, when it had almost expired, to adopt a Bavarian motif and redecorate its fading old main street. The false fronts have now been placed in front of the false fronts, and a couple dozen shops have moved in, along with three German restaurants that never seem to have any wiener schnitzel, to oblige the weekend tourist trade. Our advice is a quick look-see followed by a long picnic out in the dazzling country, say up Icicle Creek. A couple of shops will take care of your picnic needs, and two others can provide you with a gift you needn't be embarrassed about.

Hansel and Gretel, 816 Front Street (across from the bandstand), makes fine sandwiches from Bavarian meats' sausages (an excellent Seattle supplier) and adds a redolent homemade kraut laced with apples and juniper berries and smellable clear across the street. They also carry five-ounce packets of nicely ripened Brie de Meaux.

Petit Vineyard, 819 Front (downstairs), is the place to go for the alcoholic part of the picnic. James Gullard has assembled an interesting line of California rarities and some decent German wines; his selection of fourteen imported beers is topped off with the peerless Czech beer, Pilsner Urquell.

The Strawberry Patch, next to the wineshop, has unusual handcrafted gifts in good taste including, if you must, carved apple-core faces.

The Wood Shop, 833 Front Street (downstairs), makes on the premises some fine wooden toys, puppets, cooking tools, and looms.

Basic hours of the shops are 10-6 on weekdays and 10-8 on weekends.

ELLENSBURG

Hi-Way Grille ☆

Ellensburg, poised in the middle of the state astride major expressways, is difficult to avoid eating in. Accordingly, the food served up at the freewayside eateries is about what you'd expect captive diners to get. The trick is to drive into the town a mile or so and eat where travelers used to eat and Ellensburgers dine today. The Hi-Way Grille, here for thirty-five years, was formerly at the intersection of the main roads to Yakima, Spokane, and Seattle. Now most of the tourists are gone, so the little place with polished pine ceilings and counters serves good country cooking: chicken, real mashed potatoes (better than the frozen fries), well-priced, delicious steaks, chicken-fried steaks, and suchlike. The mood is mellow.

111 West Eighth, Ellensburg (junction of highways 10 and 97)
Daily, 6 a.m.-11 p.m.; Sundays closed at 10 p.m.
962-9977
Moderate
Credit Cards: BA, MC
Full Bar

Goofy's

Ellensburg is a college town primarily—except for the week each Labor Day when it's a rodeo town. A good place for lunch or supper or a little night music is Goofy's, a tavern particularly popular with the college students. Another attraction of the large, two-story establishment is that it is located right downtown, so you will have a chance to inspect the nicely restored western storefronts along the main streets. The sandwiches are good, if you avoid the frozen steak sandwich they microwave. If you want company, you can sit at the friendly bar for lunch. In the evening, you can cook your own steak on a gas grill, play pool, or go upstairs to hear the jazz or rock.

107 West 4th, Ellensburg
Daily, 11:30-2 a.m.; Sunday, 4 p.m.-midnight
925-3236
Moderate
Credit Cards: BA
Full Bar

CLE ELUM

Cle Elum Bakery ☆ ☆

This bakery, one of the best in the state if not *the* best, has been here since 1906. The locals seem to appreciate it fully, for on most days a big crowd can be found in the white brick building that houses the busy bakery and the shop. Just about everything owner-baker Ivan Osmonivich turns out is superb. The fried pies are crunchy and filled with perfectly seasoned apples. The cake donuts have a splendid texture and are cooked with careful attention to the grease. The French bread (57 cents a loaf) is better than any we've found in Seattle. There are lots of other breads of course, so that we normally buy whatever is freshest from the ovens. Cookies can be magnificent. Just promising a stop at this place should be enough to keep a camperful of children in well-behaved anticipation clear from Seattle. Unfortunately it's not open on Sundays, and there's no coffee served in the shop.

First and Peoh, Cle Elum
Monday-Friday, 8-5:30; open Saturday til 6 p.m.
674-2233

VANTAGE

Ginkgo Gem Shop ☆

The area around Vantage, on the Columbia River, contains a vast amount of petrified wood. These sometimes-beautiful specimens were formed millions of years ago when silica from a lava crust seeped into buried logs and replaced the fiber with rock, textured like wood and bright with mineral coloring. A polished collection is on view at the Interpretive Center of the Ginkgo Petrified Forest State Park, just north of Vantage and I-90, but this tourist-jammed museum is better for its splendid view and picnic tables under shade than for getting close to the petrified wood. For that, you should go to the Ginkgo Gem Shop, where you can pick up modest bargains, heft the "wood," and also poke around in the rock yard in the back for uncut examples at 50 cents a pound. Bill and Dee Rose, the owners, will tell you where you might take the family to do some prospecting for logs of your own (a good one will sell for $1 a pound at the Gem Shop).

Half mile north of Interstate 90, Vantage
856-2225
Museum hours: daily 10-5; closed Monday, Tuesday

YAKIMA

Gasperetti's Gourmet Restaurant ☆ ☆

If we say that this is the best dining in Eastern Washington, we hope you won't take that to be unnecessarily faint praise. Perhaps we should also add that right now it's the best Italian cooking in the state.

The restaurant is decorated to resemble a country dining room of the Victorian era. Antiques are scattered throughout; dried weeds and fresh flowers abound. You'll probably have to wait for a table, but you sit in a pretty room on white wicker chairs and then enter an intimate dining room with more flowers atop yellow checkered tablecloths.

The food is prepared by a French-trained chef, Brad Patterson, but since the restaurant is the last remaining good one of the distinguished cooking family of Gasperetti's, the focus is Italian food, Florentine style. Specialities vary according to the season. If fresh clams are on hand, for instance, there will be linguine, imported from Italy and cooked *al dente*. The kitchen makes its own fennel-laced pork sausage, its own ravioli, its own delicious sauces, and its famous french-fried onion rings, served as a snack while you wait for a table. Desserts are quite up to the glorious Italian traditions. The wine list is small and good. Service is admirable. It is open only for dinner, alas.

1013 North First Street, Yakima
Tuesday-Saturday, 5:45 p.m.-10:30 p.m.; closed January and July
Reservations for larger parties only: 248-4410
Credit Cards: BA, MC
Moderate
Beer and Wine

Keoki's Oriental Restaurant ☆

Yakima is not exactly the town where you expect to find a Hawaiian-owned restaurant, but why knock it? Keoki's is a pleasant place with expert, cheerful service and a nice array of Chinese and Japanese specialties. For lunch you might select beef or chicken yakitori, marinated chunks lightly grilled on a skewer; or donburi, a splendid broth with perfectly cooked noodles, barbecued meat, egg, and scallions; or maybe some mediocre bow, sausage-stuffed dumplings. At dinnertime you will see why a place like this belongs in Yakima's cattle-raising country. Keoki's has a teppanyaki table, a square wooden counter surrounding the cooking island where the chef will grill fastidiously a beautiful teriyaki steak, cut by himself from lovely local beef. It's a great way to enjoy the steak you came to Yakima to find.

During weekends, when no reservations are taken and locals crowd to the place, you'll have to wait in the bar a while.

Lincoln Center, Yakima
Tuesday-Friday, 11-10; Saturday, 4-midnight; Sunday, 12-10
No weekend reservations: 453-2401
Moderate
Credit Cards:
Full Bar

Cosmopolitan Chinook Motel ☆

Yakima is an interesting town, with tree-lined streets and a certain settled, prosperous look about the architecture. This mid-rise hotel in downtown Yakima gives you a nice view of it.

You can get up as high as the eleventh floor. The corner rooms have nice window alcoves, and those on the south side have the best views. The rooms are a shade small for families, but the prices are fair. Room 1107 is the best choice. Public rooms are ugly, but the pool is agreeable; you can even have a buffet around the pool for lunch, if you don't mind sun-melted salads. You will be located near a nicely done Nordstrom store, the Yakima downtown mall, and some of the better old buildings.

Fourth Street and E. Yakima Avenue, Yakima
452-8533
Credit Cards: AE, BA, CB, DC, MC
Moderate

ZILLAH

El Ranchito ☆ ☆

You would hope to find a great Mexican restaurant here, in the heart of the hops and fruit-growing country where numerous Mexican families and migrant workers live. Your hopes are rewarded.

El Ranchito has been in business in Zillah for twenty-five years, and by now it has grown into a virtual conglomerate. There is a busy tortilla factory in the rear; if you buy some tortillas, as you should, be sure to get them in a freezer in short order, for otherwise they will spoil. The store — a bursting, colorful Mexican general store — specializes in a huge array of herbs, beans, canned goods and baked goods of true Mexican style. There are also some nice gifts and cookingware.

But the real treat is the food, served up hot for you to carry into a flower-festooned patio crowded with Mexican and Indian families. All the food is marvelous, rich and creamy and fresh in a way that most American versions of this neglected cuisine never attain. Our recommendation for a first visit is the combination plate of tacos, enchiladas, tamales and the wonderful refried beans; with maybe an unbeatable, smooth burrito on the side. There are also exotic items like tripe and hominy in chili soup. Prices are great.

There is no beer for sale, so you might remember to pick up some at a nearby store. When the waitress asks you if you want the sauce mild, medium or hot, you should remember that "medium" translates into very hot.

First Avenue (Route 12), Zillah
8-7 every day
829-5880
Moderate
No Credit Cards
No Liquor

GOLDENDALE

Maryhill Museum

Sam Hill, a wealthy son-in-law of James J. Hill, was sufficiently enamored of Europe to perceive that the Columbia Gorge was as splendid a spot for castles as the Rhine. So he built one (the only one) filled it up with the flotsam of European royalty, and eventually turned it into a museum. There are twenty-two galleries, containing lesser works by Rembrandt and Renoir (no less), as well as Indian artifacts, Greek pottery, coronation clothes, etc. All very odd and well worth visiting. Just east is another Hill indulgence: a scale model of Stonehenge, meant as a war memorial and not quite ruined by graffiti yet.

North thirteen miles is the town of Goldendale, a charming village with a dandy county historical museum (May-October; Tuesday-Sunday, 10-5; 773-4303).

> Route 14, 13 miles south of Goldendale
> Daily, 9-5:30 ; closed November 15-March 15
> 75 cents

COLUMBIA GORGE

Columbia Gorge ☆ ☆

There are advantages in going up the Gorge on the Washington side: the nice views across river to the Oregon waterfalls, the far fewer tourists, and some interesting attractions.

Washougal. Here is the one good place to eat, Parker's Landing, and the one nice motel, The Brass Lamp, to be found for most of the route. The main attraction, however, is the Pendleton Woolen Mills, which operates a "seconds" store that offers greater bargains than you can find even at the main mill at Pendleton, Oregon.

Beacon Rock. A three-quarter-mile path switchbacks up the enormous monolith, at the end of which you have a dazzling view east into the Gorge and west to the tidal part of the magnificent river.

White Salmon. Fine berry country, with huckleberries best in September.

Oregon

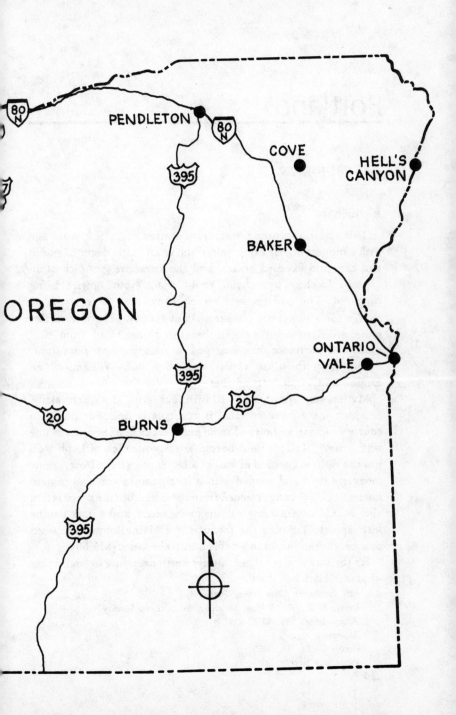

Portland

RESTAURANTS

L'Omelette ☆ ☆ ☆

This small, downtown restaurant started off a few years ago with a modest offering of omelets, the usual rustic decor of stucco and tiles and exposed beams, and the attractive gimmick of an exposed kitchen where you could watch your omelet being prepared. The omelets were merely okay, and there was a $6 charge for a stoneware pitcher of Paul Masson. There were also some ordinary non-omelet dishes for dinner, and from that modest department has emerged a distinguished restaurant, dating from the time a year ago when Bob Williamson, an Englishman, signed on as chef.

Matters start simply and well with four soups and seven salads, of which the mushroom salad is particularly fine. For the main course you have a choice of some excellent casseroles, such as one with oysters, scallops, and bacon, a gorgeous rack of lamb with just the right suggestion of garlic, a Dover sole (from Dover) done meuniere style and topped with a lovely mushroom and tomato sauce, duck a l'orange rescued from the cliche by fine preparation and the addition of a few walnuts to the sauce, and a pork flambe with apples. Topping the menu is live Maine lobster prepared broiled, thermidor, or in a noble bordelaise sauce ($15.50).

It's the sort of place that is always worth dropping by and trying what the chef has discovered.

815 Southwest Alder Street, Portland
Daily, 11-3, 5-10; Friday, Saturday, 5-11; closed Sunday
Reservations: 248-9661
Expensive
Credit Cards: BA, MC
Wine and Beer

Lu Yen ☆☆☆

John Yu is a young cook from Taiwan via San Francisco whose cooking of Szechuan specialties is extremely refined and delicious. On some nights, when the small place is full of happy people and the kitchen is in top form, this plain-looking restaurant serves up the best food in the city.

Lu Yen has only twelve tables, making it difficult to get into on weekends, but the menu is extensive. There are wonderful soups to begin with: the obligatory hot and sour, a sizzling rice, and then milder soups you might want to order toward the close of the meal like seafood or abalone. Next comes a choice of spicy beef, pork, and chicken dishes. Among the best is twice-cooked pork and Kung Tao chicken with peanuts, a dish made fiery by the usual Szechuan spicing with ginger, garlic and hot peppers. After this dish, you should calm your tastebuds with a shrimp and abalone combination; then warm up again with spicy duck (Peking duck is available with a day's notice) or a braised whole fish with black bean sauce. For dessert there are candy-cooked bananas and apples.

This style of cooking is splendid for your winter sinuses and, as Yu does it, a fine version of Chinese cooking with simple natural sauces unclouded by overdoses of cornstarch and MSG.

14 Northwest 28th Avenue, at Burnside, Portland
Daily, 11-9:30; open til 10:30 Friday, Saturday; closed Sunday
Weekend reservations only: 235-1911
Moderate
No Credit Cards
No alcohol

R. House ☆☆☆

Our praise is high for this place not because of the decor, tacky and home-made, or the service, amateur but eager, or the location, baffling even to taxi-drivers, or the room, too hot in the summer. It is a simple thing: the food is fresh, skillfully prepared, and the menus are intelligent and innovative.

Chef Christopher Renaud has a special way with chicken,

having constructed a special oven and ordered his birds from Arkansas to get the right amount of fat. He can take an old restaurant standard, prawns, and get such fresh specimens and robe them in such a nice remoulade sauce that you might actually order the things eagerly once again. The bread will be exceptional. A simple thing like a chicken consomme can come out dark and incredibly rich. The waiter may inform you that some nice mushrooms are on hand, so how about an omelette? (You'll regret saying no.) Surpassing even these dishes are the desserts, elegant, delicate, and flavorful.

It is a rather strange place to describe. The young chef has merely built himself a dream kitchen and started turning out home cooking of the sort that the best home cook you know can do. If it's on the menu, it will be startlingly good.

> 1239 SW Washington, Portland
> Lunches, 11:30-2:30; Dinners, Tuesday-Saturday, 5-10 p.m.; coffee and pastries, weekends, 10-midnight.
> Reservations: 223-4484
> No credit cards
> No liquor

Yung An ☆ ☆

One of the more encouraging topics of debate in Portland is whether Yung An or the nearby Lu Yen is currently doing the better northern Chinese cooking. Both are fine, and the chef here, Paul Chang, has more experience and a wider range. His Szechuan dishes account for only about 20 percent of the menu and tend to be conventional offerings of crispy duck and spicy beef. The Mandarin menu is the better one, with Mandarin chicken (deep fried to crispness and vibrant with ginger), the sizzling rice soup, and the shrimp in wine sauce among the finest offerings. Another difference is in the atmosphere: Yung An is a bit larger, a lot more formal, closer to shopping at Lloyd Center, and less of a family-style restaurant than its rival. The chef, incidentally, used to cook at the very successful Pot Sticker and

Sizzling Rice, and before that at the Olympic Hotel and Peking in Seattle.

2016 Northeast Sandy Boulevard, Portland
Daily, 11-10; Sunday, 5-9
Reservations: 235-6529
Moderate
Credit Cards: BA, MC
No alcohol

The Genoa ☆ ☆

Like other restaurants in Michael Vidor's chain (L'Auburge, The Woodstove), The Genoa is located in an unprepossessing building in an odd neighborhood. This one is in Southeast Portland near Reed College, whence comes most of the help. Like the others, it has a skillful decor and a prix-fixe meal that varies bi-weekly. A new owner should improve its consistency.

When the first team is cooking, the meal can be terrific: a lively antipasto (normally a bagna cauda for dipping vegetables); a well-made soup (sometimes an impeccable zuppa pavese); a tasty, small pasta course; a few butter clams in a delicate veloute; a medallion of pork sauteed in oil and herbs; a few fresh vegetables prepared in an original manner (spinach with raisins and pine-nuts, for instance); and then a selection of glorious desserts.

Unfortunately things do not go this well all the time. We have had evenings when the kitchen resembles a college cooking course. The soup may come out too salty to eat, the pork dry yet served with a splendid mustard sauce, the prawns cooked just right but tough and dull. The poor wine list is being remedied. The Genoa nonetheless is quite worth the risk, considering the rarity of good Italian cuisine in the Northwest.

2832 SE Belmont, Portland
Tuesday-Saturday, 6-10 p.m.
Reservations essential: 238-1464
Moderate
No credit cards
Wine

Indigine ☆ ☆

Two former teachers, Millie Howe (the cook) and Howard Waskow (the brunchmaker), have opened the kind of restaurant we all dream about starting: it serves a maximum of sixteen people, is open for dinner only two nights a week, offers the guests no choice in what they eat, and is so popular that the reservations list is now backed up three months.

The routine is fixed. You arrive for one of two sittings, 6 or 8:30, and then are presented with a prix fixe meal at $8 per person. First: a glass of refreshing apple cider. Second: a platter of exquisite raw vegetables with two dips (like guacamole and garlic mayonnaise), plus, oddly, cheeses and fresh-baked bagels with a chicken-liver pate. Third: an individual souffle, often made with spinach. Fourth: the entree, such as salmon Hollandaise on Friday or Cornish hen on Saturday. Fifth: a choice of five desserts, best of which are the home made fruit ice cream and the carrot chiffon cake. The food is excellent—carefully gathered ingredients cooked according to an exacting schedule under ideal conditions. The only problems are the absence of wine, the minimal decor, and the fact that you can't get in.

One way you can get in is for Sunday brunch. The fare consists of omelets, sourdough items like the waffles, cinnamon rolls, and bagels with chopped chicken livers. It adds up to the best brunch in brunch-crazy Portland.

3725 Southeast Division, Portland
Friday, Saturday, 6, 8:30; Sunday, 9-2
Reservations: 238-1470
Moderate
No Credit Cards
No alcohol

L'Ecurie ☆ ☆

French restaurants run by French restaurateurs are a relative
rarity in Portland, except for L'Odeon and this new establishment. The chef proprietor, Gregory Balough, has fixed up the
handsome restaurant with wooden panels and stucco to look like a
rustic inn, plus some motifs from the stable, as the name suggests.
Prices are held in tight rein by the limited menu, and even the
wines only range up to a $12 Nuits St. George. This style of
cooking permits few hints of Balough's origins in Tours, but the
freshness and care in each dish show an encouraging French
manner.

Lunches normally cost less than $3, with the selection including
omelets, crepes of spinach, chicken or ham, quiches, a mushroom
tart, and homemade soup. For dinner, at around $7 per person,
there is a no-choice first course—a vegetable dish or a cocotte—
and then a choice of a veal fricasse, chicken in red wine, poached
salmon, or peppercorn steak. The wines are quite well chosen,
and dessert might be a pear tart. The restaurant, seating only
thirty-eight, is small enough so that you can be assured of a
precisely cooked meal and a short chat with the chef.

12386 Southwest Main Street, Tigard
Weekday lunches, 11:30-3; dinner, 6-10; closed Sunday
Reservations: 620-5101
Moderate
Credit Card: BA
Wine and Beer

Pettygrove House ☆ ☆

Here's another Portland-style restaurant in a Victorian house:
small, antique-y, middle-Julia-Child cooking, classical
background music, inconsistent. It can be exquisite when things
click—a slow, pleasant dinner with subtle seasoning of seasonal
ingredients. But on other nights you might be bothered by routine
cooking, the rickety tables, the absence of wine, the tiny portions,
and the glacial service.

You start with bread and a well-dressed small salad. The

sauteed mushrooms and the French onion soup are both fine for the next course. Entrees tend to be too small and seasoned with a very light touch. Nor are the dishes very unusual: peppercorn steak, prawns in lemon butter and so on. The vegetables are lovely. The desserts also would make Julia proud: you can have a classic flan or a glorified chocolate sundae.

2287 Northwest Pettygrove Street, Portland
Dinners only, 6-10; Friday, Saturday, 6-12; closed Sunday-Tuesday
Reservations: 223-6025
Moderate
No Credit Cards
No alcohol

Sweet Tibby Dunbar ☆ ☆

A California restaurant chain, Farwest Services, has taken an old golf clubhouse, the former Ireland's restaurant, and converted it into a very successful restaurant experience located one block from Lloyd Center. The lounge has a proper British pub feel, with a large fireplace dividing it into two convivial rooms. The dining takes place in a great hall, a flower-filled greenhouse, and an upstairs room — all of which are thick with antiques, stained glass, golf trophies and enough Scottishisms to justify the name of the place, taken from a Robert Burns' song, "Tibbie Dunbar."

What distinguishes this restaurant from another slick effort at instant atmosphere is the superior cooking. You really can get fresh fish each day. The dinner salads will have capers in them, a nice touch to a nice serving. That's a decent, freshly made mornay sauce that goes atop the shrimp, ham, and asparagus in the omelet. And until the price hit $7.25 a pound wholesale, Sweet Tibby turned out a wonderful plate of properly cooked abalone. All this means you can get a very satisfying lunch here, choosing from inventive sandwiches (tuna, avocado, and bacon), omelets, fine salads, and well-prepared fish; or a dinner that runs to prime rib, steak with artichoke and crab and bearnaise, bouillabaisse, and duck in a mandarin orange sauce. The food will be fine, the room most attractive, the bar congenial, and the wait very long if you haven't booked ahead.

718 Northeast 12th Avenue, Portland
Weekdays, 11-11; Saturday, 5-12; Sunday 4-10
Reservations: 232-1801
Moderate
Credit Cards: BA, MC
Full Bar

Canlis ☆ ☆

Peter Canlis is not right upstairs to keep as sharp an eye on things as at the Seattle version, but most of the Canlis touches are in evidence: tasteful Northwest decor, a splendid view from the twenty-third floor of the Hilton, expert service, great ingredients, unfancy cooking well brought off, and steep prices. Menu details are included in Seattle review, page 90. The bar is a good late-night spot.

921 Southwest Sixth, Hilton Hotel, Portland
Dinners only, 5:30-11:30; closed Sunday
Reservations: 228-7475
Expensive
Credit cards: AE, BA, CB, MC
Full Bar

Trader Vic's ☆ ☆

A slightly less grand version of the chain than usual, this Trader's is in the bowels of the Benson, and it is a better bet for dinner and drinks than the more famous London Grill. The menu and experience replicate the Seattle restaurant, page 88.

309 Southwest Broadway, Benson Hotel, Portland
Dinners, 5:30-10:45; closed Sunday
Reservations: 228-9611
Expensive
Credit cards: AE, BA, CB, DC, MC
Full Bar

The Original Pancake House ☆

To be precise, the *original* original pancake house opened in 1953 a mile north of here, but the same folks are still in charge, and despite the thorough degradation of the idea of pancake houses since that time, this spot still keeps up the standards admirably. The traditions have by now frozen into place. You first wait in the lobby outside, appetites raging. You then have a choice of seven juices (including fresh-squeezed orange), eleven kinds of fruit, oatmeal, eggs, and of course the pancakes. The basic pancake is a buttermilk one, but owner Les Highet doesn't stop there—he has French, Swedish, Mandarin, Hawaiian, Palestinian, wheat germ, banana, pecan, apple. . .They are all so good and so meticulously prepared that no recommendations are needed, but if you insist, we would rank them in this order: first the "Dutch Baby," a pancake made with so many eggs it puffs up to the size of a bowl in the oven and served with lemon juice and powdered sugar; second, the French pancake served with a conserve of whole strawberries and then doused with a triple sec sauce; third, the green-apple waffle; and fourth, the Swedish pancakes with lingonberry butter. It's a joy equal to the pleasure of the food to see a restaurant so well run.

> 8600 Southwest Barbur Boulevard
> Tuesday-Saturday, 7 a.m.-6 p.m.; Sunday, 7-3; closed Monday
> No reservations: 246-9007
> Inexpensive
> No credit cards
> No liquor

Jake's Crawfish ☆

Jake's has been a Portland landmark for nearly seventy years, during which time its fortunes have been variable. At its best it's one of the finest seafood restaurants in the Northwest, serving delicious crayfish with liederkranz or an unbeatable bouillabaisse. But then its management or its cooks change once more, and it is only a step above a Fisherman's Wharf tourist trap. The bouillabaisse and the salmon are almost always reliable, as are the simpler fish dishes and the crab louis. The fancy dishes tend to be too rich. The old place is one of the handsomest in the city, with a particularly fine bar where generations of brewery workers have stood.

Southwest 12th and Stark, Portland
Daily, 5-11; Friday, Saturday, 5-12; Sunday, 5-10
Reservations: 226-1419
Moderate
Credit Cards: AE, BA, MC
Full bar

Poor Shoes ☆

If anyone were ever to open up a really fine Mexican restaurant in a Northwest city, he or she would probably get very rich very fast: the cuisine is notably ill-served here, as any expatriot Californian will attest. Portland has made a decent stab at it, however, in Poor Shoes. Now in a new location after its birth in Tigard, the restaurant has one more dining room than before but the same menu. The familiar classics are here, along with an area of intriguing originality: the enchiladas. One nice new idea is a pinenut, beef, and olive enchilada, with sour cream and scallions on the side. Northwesterners should first try the salmon enchilada, specked with black olives and also served with the sour cream.

11041 Southwest Barbur Boulevard, Portland
Daily, 11:30-11:30; Saturday, Sunday, 5-11:30
Reservations: 246-0023
Moderate
No Credit Cards
Beer and Wine

Fernwood Inn ☆

It ought to be a lot better than it is, since this handsome stone mansion high on a hill is one of the few restaurants in the city with a view of the Willamette. Things start well: a boy parks your car when you enter, and inside there is an intriguing maze of rooms, lots of friendly waiters, and an ambitious Swiss menu. But the food is a disappointment—tasteless soups, poor bread, and entrees that take excellent cuts of meat and somehow fail to do them full justice. Beef Wellington, for instance, turns out to be filet with a dull pate and an individual balloon of dough. The wine list matches the rest of the food. Service, despite all the people, gets slow.

Still, the view of the river is most consoling, and the grand old house makes for a pleasant long dinner if you need to take out some clients and obviously spend a lot on them. Our advice would be to dine defensively, perhaps with the famous bouillabaisse from the recipe of the previous chef, Ernest Aebi, or a simpler preparation of the well-aged steaks.

> 2311 Sixth Avenue, Milwaukie
> Every night, 5-11
> Reservations: 659-1735
> Expensive
> Credit Cards: AE, BA, MC
> Full Bar

The Woodstove ☆

Another Vidor restaurant experience, The Woodstove is a sort of fantasia of early Americana, mixing pioneer austerity (e.g., a superb cornbread), Brahmin affluence (a Bourbon filet), and Great Plains abundance (spit-roasted meats). Like the other Vidor restaurants, this one is located in a forsaken neighborhood, is charmingly decorated and well run, features a multi-course prix fixe meal with a choice of main dish, and ends strong with terrific desserts. (The roasted meats form part of a banquet that must be ordered a day in advance.)

The meal starts with good breads and dull salad. You then choose among the day's casserole, which can be a great bargain, things like a simply grilled salmon or an excellent Dungeness crab curry, chicken and dumplings, and the beef dishes. Wines are most interesting, including some of the marvelous Eyrie Vineyards wines from western Oregon. This Bicentennial year you might as well end the feast with strawberry shortcake, good enough here for any year.

Lunches are another reason for venturing out to this blue-collar district. There are open-faced sandwiches, meat salads, deep-dish pizzas, and salades Nicoises. Not very American, this last? Then top it off with homemade apple pie.

2601 Northwest Vaughn Street, Portland
Weekday lunches, 11:30-2; dinners, 6-10; closed Sunday
Reservations needed: 227-6956
Moderate
No credit cards
Beer and Wine

La Bonne Crepe ☆

There is practically only one kind of French restaurant in this country that can serve food at low cost and that's a creperie, where small portions are compensated for by careful preparation and a smattering of classic items like a slice of quiche or a cup of onion gratinee. Portland's example of the genre is a most respectable entry. The restaurant located far south of town in a snazzy boutique complex called John's Landing, is elegantly appointed, boasts impeccable service, and offers good value. Since the location is popular and La Bonne Crepe takes no reservations, you had better be prepared to wait.

The fillings are carefully made, whether ratatouille, coquilles, sherried crab, or spinach in sauce Mornay. The side dishes—soup, salads, quiche—are all worth ordering; and the wine list is unusually good for such a place. Dessert crepes are also delicious, particularly one with dates and walnuts, topped with sour cream. The final plus is quite rare for creperies: the prices are very good.

5331 Southwest Macadam, Portland
Weekdays, 11:30-3, 5-1 a.m.; Saturday, Sunday, 11:30 a.m.-1 a.m.
No reservations: 248-9300
Inexpensive
Credit Cards: AE, BA, MC
Beer and Wine

Goldberg's ☆

Unlike Seattle, Portland has a substantial Jewish population, and here, after the lamentable decline of Rose's, is the best place to eat Jewish food. The cafeteria is quite uneven, with steam-table lunches and mediocre desserts (a marshmallowy cheesecake, for instance), but all is forgiven when you order a sandwich. The corned beef is sliced to order—thick—and served on New York Jewish rye with just the right Russian dressing and slaw. Even better is the reuben. You also can get authentic chopped chicken liver. The crowds should not deter you: when at Lloyd Center go here for lunch.

> 1329 Lloyd Center, Portland
> Daily, 11-7:30; Friday, Saturday, 11-8:30; closed Sunday
> No reservations: 284-5351
> Inexpensive
> No Credit Cards
> Beer

The London Grill ☆

This restaurant, so beloved of Holiday Award-givers, is of a piece with the rest of the Benson Hotel. At first glance it seems the model of a deluxe Continental hotel dining room—warm and rich and low and thick with supercilious waiters. The wine cellar is outstanding and many vintages have unbelievably low prices. It's rather like first driving up to and walking into the Benson: you think you've arrived.

But you need to be cautious. The hors d'oeuvres will still be lullingly good: marinated artichoke hearts with prosciutto, a delicate spinach puree on the oysters Rockefeller, a crusty French bread to compensate for the bland escargots. But after this, instant defrosted gourmet delights start obtruding into the meal. The menu overpromises, and the execution gets shaky; things like roast duckling masquerade their problems beneath a honey glaze, Japanese peaches, chestnuts, and almonds. Nor will the desserts salvage the meal. Still, the place does have its good nights, and by concentrating on a nice hors d'oeuvres, a filet, and a good wine, you will be well pleased.

Sunday mornings feature a famous brunch which, if you can get into it, is a delight — ample, with a huge array of foods, plenty of champagne, glorious fruits. If the Grill is so busy that they send you up to the bar for a cut-down version of the brunch — come back another day.

Broadway and S.W. Oak, Portland
Daily, 5:30 p.m.-11 p.m.; Sunday brunch, 9-2
228-9611
Expensive
Credit Cards: AE, BA, CB, DC, MC
Full Bar

L'Auberge ☆

When it opened six years ago, L'Auberge was nearly the first restaurant in Portland with a quiet ambience bespeaking dedication to dining as a fine art. There were plain wood tables and hard chairs in a narrow room adorned with iron cookware. The menu was quite idiosyncratic. Then the founding chef departed, and the meals have become chancy, dependent on whoever is in the kitchen.

A typical prix-fixe meal will start with a dull liver pate. The soups can be good, the salads indifferent; then comes a house stunt, a mushroom meringue that ranges from inedible to just plain silly. Entrees might be chicken en papillote, salmon with sauce mousseline, or beef tenderloin, each of which can be very good. The side vegetables vary in quality. Desserts are generally poor, the wine list is good.

2180 West Burnside, Portland
Tuesday-Saturday, 6-10 p.m.
Reservations essential: 223-3302
Moderate
No credit cards
Wine

Pot Sticker and Sizzling Rice ☆

A Northern Chinese restaurant in Old Town done in contemporary design (scraped brick, black director's chairs, hanging ferns), this restaurant makes an unbeatable combination. Adding to the attractions of the room is an open kitchen, where you can observe the cooking of your pot stickers (pan-fried won-tons stuffed with pork, ginger, and scallions and then eaten with vinegar). A stir-fried meat-and-vegetable dish for lunch makes a light and delicious meal. In the evenings, the menu enlarges to a full range of Mandarin specialties, but the former chef has just opened his own restaurant, Yung An, so we do not know whether his high standards will remain.

> 228 Northwest Davis, Portland
> Daily, 11:30-2:30, 5:30-9; closed Sunday
> Reservations: 248-9231
> Moderate
> No Credit Cards
> No alcohol

Crepe Faire ☆

The decor is something out of Gaudi — bent cedar slats wrapped sinuously around pipe — but the cooking demonstrates a straightforward concentration on doing a few simple things well. The flavorful home-made soups. The limited number of crepes with carefully made fillings. The quiches. A few fresh salads. And finally, six or seven luscious dessert crepes. In short, this is just about perfect for a quick lunch when in Old Town: honest food done with some flair at fair prices, and with a little decor thrown in for when the conversation falters.

> 117 Northwest Second, Portland
> Lunches, Monday-Saturday, 11:30-2:30; dinners, Wednesday-Saturday, 6-
>   10; closed Sunday
> No reservations: 227-3365
> Moderate
> No Credit Cards
> Wine and Beer

Victoria's Nephew ☆

Particularly on sunny days when you can sit out on the sidewalk, this mellow little restaurant is a fine spot for a down-town lunch. Everything is carefully made and home made. In the summer the soups are delicious cold ones such as gaspacho or cucumber; in the winter you can get hearty chowders or smooth creams. There are sweet fruit breads baked daily and outstanding baked goods, like the creamy cheesecake, which go well with the good coffee and the fine line of English teas. Two good sand-wiches are the Captain Cook, of lox, onion rings, avocado, and lettuce on rye, and the George II, of cream cheese, shrimp, and avocado on Middle eastern bread.

It is close to downtown or Old Town shopping, but far enough away so that your table companions will not be tourists but more likely staffers from the nearby *Willamette Week*.

212 Southwest Stark Street, Portland
Monday-Friday, 7:30-4; closed Saturday, Sunday
No reservations: 223-7299
Inexpensive
No Credit Cards
No alcohol

Dan and Louis Oyster Bar ☆

The neighborhood around this institution has unfortunately upgraded smartly, bringing on the tourists and commercializing the food until it is now not much better than Fisherman's Wharf. The restaurant still looks as good: the low, varnished, beamed ceilings like the hold of a sailing ship, panelled walls covered with old fish platters, and commemorations of the St. Louis Ex-position. But about the only dish to have survived the past twenty years is the oyster stew, a superb, simple dish with nothing but milk, salt, pepper, butter, and the meaty Yaquina Bay oysters still brought in from the restaurant's own beds. Further voyaging in the menu is likely to yield greasy pan-fried items. And no booze.

208 SW Ankeny, Portland
Daily, 11-11
No reservations, long lines: 227-5906
Moderate
Credit Cards: AE, BA, CB, DC, MC
No Liquor

L'Odeon ☆

This French restaurant actually has a French chef, Roger Lextrait, but otherwise it is similar to other Portland restaurants that aspire to good cooking in a small and tasteful restaurant. It is located in an 1895 building in suburban Lake Oswego, and the small upstairs restaurant is decorated country-style with provincial wallpaper and lace curtains. It is all very charming, but on hot days one gets uncomfortably warm.

A modest lunch menu specializes in crepes, but for dinner there are some adventurous plates. The chef does a fine filet en croute, rich with a liver pate and a few specks of truffles. The rabbit stew is nicely marinated and cooked in a rich, well-seasoned sauce. Such a meal is augmented with an appetizer of hearts-of-palm dressed with an unusual vichyssoise-based sauce, wine from the limited but interesting list, and then an exemplary creme caramel for dessert. Not bad at all.

On the other hand, the meal might work out much less well: a flabby vegetable soup, a coarse and garlicky pate, a steak au poivre sadly lacking in pepper and sauced with a kind of country cream gravy, a watery salad, and a chocolate mousse marred by the use of sweet chocolate. But recent reports stress the improvements.

Second and B Streets, Lake Oswego
Lunches, 11:30-2; dinners, 6-10; closed Sunday, Monday
Reservations: 636-0808
Moderate
No Credit Cards
Wine

Four Seasons ☆

This is a pleasant restaurant in a typical Portland mode. The green-and-white house dates back to 1915; the antiques within give it a bit more age. The food is relatively simple, but it is all cooked to order with care. The prices are very reasonable, the wine list modest. The single room has ten tables, and the service is fine.

In ten years, the chef and co-owner Gene Boom has refined the menu until the dinners are very reliable. The home-baked bread, usually white, is delicious. Steaks and seafood follow, with the latter the more interesting. Among the best dishes are baked scallops in a wine sauce, poached fresh Chinook salmon with a proper Hollandaise, and sauteed jumbo prawns flamed at the table. The lovely potato has been baked once, then mixed with butter and spices and rebaked. Vegetables are frozen peas, blanched so delicately they almost taste fresh. Grapes jubilee makes a good, novel dessert.

2820 Southeast Park Avenue, Milwaukie
Lunches, Tuesday-Friday, 11:30-2; dinners, 6-9; closed Sunday and
    Monday
Reservations: 654-0337
Moderate
Credit Cards: AE, BA
Wine and Beer

Huber's

Located under the stained-glass skylight of the Oregon Pioneer Building, this restaurant is a pioneer itself, dating from 1879. It was once the snazziest saloon in town; during Prohibition it sported potted palms and a tea-room air as the most public speakeasy for miles. Beyond the decor and the setting however, there's not a lot to recommend. The specialty is turkey and ham, served in sandwiches or for dinner and justly esteemed. Adequate results come from careful picking through the rest of the menu.

411 S.W. Third, Portland
Daily, 9-9; closed Sunday
Dinner reservations only: 228-5686
Moderate
Credit Cards: BA, MC
Full Bar

LODGING

The Benson Hotel ☆ ☆

Simon Benson was a philanthropic lumber baron who, in 1913, built the Benson with orders to spare no expense. He created a very noble building with thirteen stories of brick and marble (now with a lovely pale-green patina) and put in the lovely lobby extensive panels of richly carved Circassian walnut. The effect is very tasteful, particularly fine in that the scale of the hotel is so modest: like a doll-house Plaza. One step into the lobby and you know you are in the smartest spot in Portland.

Your next step might be a bad mistake. The rooms in the original, 200-room section are very disappointing: small, many of them overlooking noisy Broadway (where, of all things, thousands of kids still drag on the weekends), jammed with furniture, and often fitted out with a bathroom that has been inserted into a former closet. So be sure to ask for a room in the newer (1959) section called the South Wing, preferably one overlooking the court. These rooms, while decorated in standard Western International Hotels unoffensive modern, are at least quiet and moderately spacious. You will then be able to enjoy the hotel's discreet bar, its Trader Vic's branch or the London Grill, without spending too much time wondering what ever happened to Simon Benson's standards of staffing, or the grand pianos that once graced each corner room, or the complimentary hot clam nectar once proffered each morning to fend off the Oregon damp.

309 South Broadway, Portland
228-9611
Expensive
Credit Cards: AE, BA, CB, DC, MC

Ramada Inn ☆ ☆

The southern portion of Portland's downtown has one of the few attractive urban renewal projects in America: handsome apartment towers by Skidmore-Owings-Merrill set amid the sensitive landscaping and fountains of Lawrence Halprin. This motel enables you to stay just next to these projects and also be an easy walk through them to the Civic Auditorium. The rooms are standard but tasteful, and they look out into an attractively landscaped central courtyard with a pool. The public rooms are somewhat tacky, but the sleeping rooms of the motel manage by the use of brick to avoid the usual glossy plastic look. The freeway is a few blocks away.

310 Southwest Lincoln Street, Portland
221-0450
Moderate
Credit Cards: AE, BA, CB, DC, MC

The New Congress Hotel ☆

Hotels in Portland are often divided according to which candidates stay where for the quadrennial presidential primaries. A Kennedy, of course, would stay at the Benson; this economical, friendly, family hotel boasts Eugene McCarthy. Other than that, it makes few pretensions to class at all. It's convenient to down-town shopping or the Civic Auditorium six blocks away. The rooms are plain, somewhat worn, reasonably furnished, and priced fairly. Ask for a room away from noisy Sixth Avenue. Touring ballet troupes and musical organizations usually stay here, so you might chat with Martha Graham in the elevator, in case McCarthy isn't running this year.

> 1024 S.W. Sixth Avenue, Portland
> 228-0181
> Moderate
> Credit Cards: AE, BA, CB, DC, MC
> Pets allowed

Rose Manor Motel ☆

Here is a most unusual place to stay near Reed College. The complex sprawls over many acres, with one and two-story white frame buildings set among beautifully landscaped grounds. The furnishings match the same odd, home-made quality of the place. The prices are unbeatable, ranging from $16 bargains in the rooms called "hotels," up to a full house that takes six or more people for a mere $31. The best rooms are those with queen size beds in them, but all look out on the placid lawns, lovely gardens, and the numerous hanging baskets of flowers dotting this little village.

> 4546 S.E. McLoughlin Boulevard, Portland
> 236-4175
> Moderate
> No pets
> Credit Cards: AE, BA, MC

Mallory Hotel ☆

This pleasant, clean, older hotel out by the Civic Theater is one of the best bargains in the city. The rooms are relatively spacious, the area is quiet yet close to the downtown, the air conditioning works adequately, parking is not a problem, the staff is agreeable, check-out is not til 3 p.m., and the old building with its funny stairways is not without character. Doubles start at the amazing price of $11, so you may want to splurge and get a $19 suite with a living room and a fine view either out over the river or up into the residential hills to the west.

Southwest 15th and Yamhill, Portland
223-6311
Moderate
No Credit Cards
Pets allowed

Roosevelt Hotel ☆

One of Portland's most charming features is the downtown row of greenery called the Park Blocks, a recreation in linear form of the village green in English towns. The Blocks make for fine strolling, and some of the city's best architecture borders their edges. This small hotel one block from the Art Museum enables you to stay overlooking the Park Blocks, which puts you in a secluded section just a couple of blocks from the downtown. Rooms start at $11.50, where they are a bit musty, but the $16 doubles are fine bargains in a friendly, clean hotel. Free parking is provided two blocks away.

Southwest Park Avenue at Salmon Street, Portland
223-7141
Moderate
Credit Cards: AE, BA, MC
Pets limited

TOURISM

Portland Parks ☆ ☆ ☆

With 138 parks covering 7000 acres, Portland is a remarkable city for parks, ranging from small downtown patches to an eight-square-mile wilderness park.

Park Blocks. These sixteen blocks stretching north from Portland State pass by many of the downtown museums and institutions.

Pittock Mansion. The French Renaissance mansion built seventy years ago by the founder of the *Oregonian* is a beautiful house to tour, and the surrounding park is full of birds and splendid views back over the city.

West Hills Parks. Beautiful Washington Park has the famous rose gardens and tennis courts where you can play amid wild roses on the fences. A feature of the lovely Japanese Gardens is the sand garden. The Zoo is famous for its elephants and its train rides through the grounds. Hoyt Arboretum has seven miles of trails and 500 types of trees among some virgin stands. The Oregon Museum of Science and Industry features excellent displays: a walk-in heart, a mechanical cow, a planetarium (4015 Southwest Canyon Road, 224-9500, $1.50 adults).

Forest Park. This enormous park of native conifer trees is reserved in the summer for hikers and equestrians (stables at 7575 Northwest Thompson Street).

American Rhododendron Test Gardens. These gardens near Reed College have five thousand rhododendrons on display, and the setting on an island makes for great duck-feeding (Southeast Woodstock and Southeast 28th Avenue).

Sauvie Island. This fabulous wild island at the confluence of the Willamette and the Columbia is the best park for bird-watching or picnicking or just getting away. A fine way to explore it is by canoe, rented at Brown's Landing, Scappoose (take Route 30 ten miles northwest of Portland).

Portland Antique Shops ☆ ☆

Oregon quite rightly thinks of itself as the part of the Northwest with some history to speak of, and its residents are fond of collecting antiques. There are several strong shops to get you started on your rounds.

Marneff Antiques, 6515 North Interstate Avenue (289-2645), has a collection that is of museum quality, with particular strengths in eighteenth century and European pieces.

McDuffee-Mongeon Galleries, 115 Southwest Ash (223-9093), is a focal point for collectors since Jack Mongeon is one of the main appraisers of estates in the city. He has some of the oldest pieces you'll find in the state: colonial American, oil paintings, glass, silver, furniture. The building itself is notable as one of the best cast-iron structures in Old Town.

George Root Jr., 2381 Northwest Flanders (223-7834), is not always easy to find open, but the collection of brass, furniture, and some oriental pieces is very fine.

Arthur W. Erickson, 630 Southwest 12th (227-4710), is the place for early Indian and pre-Columbian artifacts.

Old Oregon Bookstore, 610 Southwest 12th (227-2742), has 150,000 titles and collections of considerable interest to scholars. The emphasis is on Northwest history, of course, a Portland specialty. The town also has a peculiar fondness for comic books: Apache Books (631 Southeast Morriston) and Old Weird Herald's (6804 Northeast Broadway) each have thousands of back titles.

Portland Nightlife ☆ ☆

Sociable city that Portland is, there is a thriving tavern and coffeehouse culture here. Some suggestions:

Coffeehouses: Mountain Moving Cafe (523 Southeast 39th) has music and poetry and is open exclusively for women on Wednesday nights. Arbuckle Flat (16th and Southwest Morrison) is for dancing and good snacks. The Veritable Quandary (122 Southwest First) is a good place for talking.

Taverns: Goose Hollow Inn (1927 Southwest Jefferson) is a place with good pizza and sandwiches, and it used to be a hangout for media types. Henry's Pizzeria (1981 Southwest Fourth) is a PSU spot with superior pizza. Rock Creek Tavern (Old Cornelius Pass Road) is the top place for music. Pretty Boy Floyd's (Southwest Washington and 14th Southwest) has good food and a hip clientele. Euphoria (315 Southeast Third) has loud music for dancing.

Bars: Sweet Tibby Dunbar (718 Northeast 12th) has the nicest room. Jake's (401 Southwest 12th) is an elegant old bar, now devoted to the singles. Canlis and Trader Vic's would be the two reliable hotel watering holes.

Portland Architecture ☆ ☆

With its small blocks, downtown parks, and modest scale, Portland is architecturally one of the most satisfying American cities. Except for a few sore thumbs like the finned and flared First National Bank building, Portland's downtown has a harmonious, civilized collection of buildings, many of which possess considerable architectural interest.

The Old Town section, centering on First and Burnside, has the largest number of cast-iron facade buildings outside of New York; tours are sometimes given of this fascinating region, with details available at the Oregon Historical Museum.

Next in historical interest are the classicist buildings of A.E. Doyle, whose works give the Broadway section of town around the Benson (by Doyle) its special urbanity. The stately U.S. National Bank, main branch (Stark and Southwest Sixth) and the Multnomah County library (Taylor and Southwest 10th) are two fine examples. Pietro Belluschi, who worked in Doyle's office, became a major American architect and the founder of a Northwest style based on weathered cedar boards and simplified, self-effacing design. His Portland Art Museum (1219 Southwest Park) is a daring exercise in austere monumentalism from 1932; the Commonwealth Building (Southwest Sixth and Washington) was one of the first curtain-wall buildings in the country, and it is still very much in fashion.

Among contemporary works are buildings by John Storrs, a prolific designer carrying on the humanistic, regionalist style at projects like the Portland Garden Club (1132 Southwest Vista), Salishan, and the Water Tower shopping complex (5920 Southwest Macadam). Finally, there is the popular waterfall fountain by Lawrence Halprin just in front of the Civic Auditorium, a marvelous splash of nature in the urban core.

Portland Specialty Shopping ☆ ☆

Portland excells in generating centers with small, smart shops:
Old Town. Best time to go is Saturday morning, when a street market is held. Some of the better shops, to get you started, are:

Quintana's Indian Arts, 139 Northwest Second, with excellent turquoise jewelry and fine Southwest American Indian art; Patricia Green Imports, 133 Northwest Second, offering fine baskets and batiks; Daisy Kingdom, 217 Northwest Davis, the Cuckoo's Nest, 217 Northwest Second, and Couch Street Outfitters, 213 Northwest Couch—among the best of the unusual casual clothes shops.

Morgan's Alley, Southwest Broadway and Southwest Alder, is a dandy collection of shops along with several good restaurants. Eat at Rian's, and start your shopping at Oregon Products (just what it means), Nova Express or Omer's for women's wear, the latter featuring imports from Turkey. Two blocks south is more good shopping for women's (and men's) casual wear: the Clothes Horse, Charles F. Berg, and Nordstrom. The best women's wear store in the city, incidentally, is Helen's Of Course, 9875 Beaverton Hillsdale Highway, a very chic shop with a formidable owner.

The Water Tower, 5920 Southwest Macadam, is a handsome complex of specialty shops and restaurants in a recycled warehouse, with a stress on women's clothes, crafts, and food stores. La Bonne Crepe is the best place to eat.

Galleria, Southwest Tenth and Southwest Alder, is the most recent of these complexes, due to open around Christmas 1975 in a 1905 building right downtown. The development will revive an old style of shopping: a large atrium, marble, and tile floors. The shops will sell imported items, antiques, clothing, records; one of the welcome possible revivals will be a genuine oyster bar.

Anderson's Delicatessen ☆

For years, Vern Anderson has been a major figure in Portland gastronomy, starting when he ran his store in the Farmer's Market and continuing even when he deserted to the western suburbs. His well-stocked delicatessen is one of the best in the area and an obligatory stop if you are heading out to tour the villages, the vineyards, the covered bridges, and the coastal routes to the west.

The cheese selection is one of the strongest you will find, with enough volume so that you can get ripe Brie for a picnic. The wine inventory is also extensive, with particularly good California,

Oregon, and French wines. The deli is large, but except for the salads and the cheese cake, not distinguished. The selection of spices is notable for its specialization in Indian spices.

9525 Southwest Beaverton-Hillsdale Highway, Beaverton
Daily, 9-6; closed Sunday
643-5415
No Credit Cards

Culture in Portland ☆

Visual Arts. Outstanding for Portland or for any other city is the Portland Center for the Visual Arts (117 Northwest Fifth; 222-7107). Located just north of downtown and on the unfashionable side of Burnside, PCVA's third-floor loft presents ambitious, month-long shows of the finest contemporary artists on the national scene. The time schedule varies but it is usually open daily from noon to 4 p.m.; it normally closes for the summer. The Portland Art Museum (1219 Southwest Park) presents some interesting touring shows, but only its exceptional assembly of Northwest Indian art stands out in the permanent collection. The city is not a strong collector's town; for the best in multiples, try Original Graphics Gallery (917 Southwest Alder) or The Image Gallery (242 Southwest Ankeny) for ethnic and Northwest art.

Music. Principal interest is the Portland Opera, run by the quirky but very talented Stefan Minde. Its four annual productions emphasize the musical side of the art almost to the exclusion of the theatrical, but smart casting from the European opera houses brings frequent discoveries. The Oregon Symphony under Lawrence Smith is presentable but not exceptional; the local hot ticket is Norman Leyden's "pops" concerts. Of special interest in the summer are the chamber music concerts sponsored by Reed College and Portland State University: usually sold out far in advance. The Youth Symphony is extraordinary.

Theater. Portland theater is still the far side of Equity. Its strongest offerings are mounted by the Portland Civic Theater (1530 Southwest Yamhill) which though technically a community theater, offers the most professional operation in town.

Sports in Oregon ☆ ☆

Golf—In the Portland area is the ranking course of the state, the fine old Portland Golf Club: tight, well-treed, and with lots of water. Royal Oaks in Vancouver is another testing course with plenty of water; wide open Waverly is the best of the Columbia River links; and the venerable public course near Reed College, Eastmoreland, makes for a fine round. On the coast the only first-rate course is Astoria Golf Club, a genuine Scottish style course along the seaside and a killer when the wind is blowing. Down the Willamette there is Illahee at Salem for demanding play; the extremely tough Eugene Country Club, long and narrow; and Rogue Valley Country Club in Medford, always in fine condition. Two good mountain courses are Black Butte near Sisters, a course requiring accuracy amid distractingly gorgeous scenery, and Tokatee at Blue River on the McKenzie, a new, long course that will be a great one.

Skiing—The two best ski areas are Mount Bachelor, 22 miles west of Bend, with the finest family skiing in the Northwest owing to good variety and excellent accommodations nearby; and Mount Hood Meadows on the north slope of Mount Hood, for a long season and a well-maintained facility. Otherwise, Mount Ashland is an evolving area with the best terrain in the state and numerous slopes for advanced skiers; Mount Hood has high-altitude novelty skiing until mid July; and Anthony Lakes Ski Area, 36 miles from Baker, has fine powder over mediocre terrain.

Outdoors—Camping in Oregon is extremely popular, so you should be sure to have reservations for most state-owned campgrounds, arranged through the State Parks and Recreation Section of the Oregon State Highway Division, Salem. Salmon, steelhead, bass, and trout are the chief game fish of the state; deer, elk, and game birds also abound for the hunter. There are two good outfitting shops in Portland where you can get the latest advice: Norman Thompson Outfitters, 1805 Northwest Thurman (221-0764), with marvelous fly-fishing equipment and fine British clothing for shooting or fishing expeditions; the other is Oregon Mountain Community, 222 Southwest Main (227-1038), for mountaineering, backpacking, and skiing equipment of the latest advanced design.

Spectator sports—Bill Walton is a disappointment, but the Trailblazers are still a contender in the National Basketball Association, playing at the Coliseum. The Timbers are a first-rate team in the North American Soccer League. For the rest it is minor league stuff: the Buckaroos of the Pacific Coast Hockey League, the Beavers of the Pacific Coast Baseball League; horse racing at Portland Meadows, and greyhound races at Fairview Park; so-so college football at Portland, Corvallis, and Eugene.

Oregon Coast

Anton Josephson's Salmon Smokehouse ☆ ☆

The salmon here is salted and cured in the old way, much like a ham, so it comes out on the salty side. But this makes it ideal for shipping, whether in the moist, medium, or dry-smoked form, since the six to eight percent sale content retards spoilage. The salmon is cured in brine for three weeks each August, then repacked in salt for another three weeks; afterward the fish are smoked very slowly over alder logs cut in the spring. The results are delicious, if fairly expensive. While you are in the shop you should munch on some sweet pickled salmon, and if things aren't too busy, Mrs. Avis Josephson, who manages this half-century-old family business, might agree to show you around the aromatic smokehouse.

106 Marine Drive, Astoria
Daily, 10-5; closed Sundays in winter
325-2190
Credit Cards: BA, MC

The Ship Inn ☆

The seafood is fresh and delicious at this converted tavern. It comes with chowder, salad, and ice cream, and at prices that rarely top $5.50. But the real treat at this smallish restaurant is the fish and chips. The owners, Jill and Fenton Stokeld, are

English expatriots who have mastered the British art of cooking this dish: they take nice halibut, cut it themselves, dip it in a thin, delicate, seasoned batter, and use the right potatoes for chips. To complete the authenticity, they offer Guinness stout. If you wish, there are also cod, prawns, scallops, and oysters for the deep-frying.

12 Marine Drive, Astoria
Daily, 11:30-10:30; closed Monday
Reservations: 325-0033
Moderate
Credit Card: BA
Beer and Wine

Columbia River Maritime Museum ☆ ☆

Founded only a dozen years ago, this well-backed showplace of Columbia River nautical artifacts is the best maritime museum in the Northwest. Objects are thoughtfully chosen for their representative value and are clearly explained. Scrimshaw, ship models, marine art, charts, hardware, whaling equipment, and Indian dugout canoes are among the top items; nearby is the old Columbia lightship.

If this puts you in a mood for history, there are some other attractions nearby. Clatsop County Historical Museum (441 Eighth Street) is a fine gingerbread mansion, housing a mediocre collection. Ten miles west is Fort Stevens, built in the 1860s and massively rearmed in 1917. The stripped bunkers make for satisfying walks, and the beach in the adjoining park has a melancholy wreck from 1906 washed up on the sands; the dunes themselves are an unusual example of a stabilized coastal ecology. Six miles southwest of Astoria is Fort Clatsop, at the site where Lewis and Clark spent a miserable winter in 1805-06. The fort is entirely a modern reconstruction, based on drawings in Clark's notebooks, but the large park, with trails to the beach and other historical spots, gives a nice feeling for where the Northwest began—in a perpetual downpour that gave it forever its damp reputation.

16th and Exchange Streets, Astoria
Daily, 10:30-5; closed Monday in winter
Adults, 50 cents
325-2323

GEARHART

Tillamook House ☆

Gearhart was once the center of genteel Oregon's summer homes; now the center of Gearhart is a new six-story condominium. Its ninety-six units are owned, but many of them can be rented by transients. The setting is splendid, looking out over a bay toward the mighty Tillamook Head. The decor is a trifle gaudy, the interiors clean and quiet, and the routine furnishings no match at all for the view. The Surfside restaurant, behind the hotel, offers a pretentious menu, mediocre food, and an off-key cocktail organist fond of singing oldies.

Marion Avenue At E Street
738-8331
Expensive
Pets accepted
Credit Cards: BA, AE

SEASIDE

The Crab Broiler ☆ ☆

The Daggatt family has owned and operated this place for thirty years, and by now it has become an Oregon institution, attracting a steady stream of visitors who have discovered this unassuming highway restaurant serves top-quality food at moderate prices. The ugly decor once was part of the charm but the place is now remodeled: still the people jam into the large restaurant and order up old favorites.

The stock in trade is, of course, the crab, which comes fresh, succulent and delicious. You can get it cracked, served with a spicy barbecue sauce, in crab cakes, in casserole or in almost any guise; the crab cocktail is almost an entire meal. But don't limit yourself to the specialty. The Broiler has oysters, and naturally they're the very best: Kumamotos from Bay City. When you come back for your fourth visit, you might venture into the steaks, stews or chowders—the same high standards pertain. The wine list is unimpressive. You can finish the festivities with pastry, made on the premises and admirable. Best bet for lunch is a seafood salad.

> Highway 101, 4 miles south of Seaside at Rte. 26.
> 11:30 a.m.-9 p.m. daily (open til 10 July and August)
> 738-5313
> Moderate
> Credit Cards: BA, MC
> Full Bar

Par-Tee Room ☆

A restaurant located overlooking a public golf course is not a logical spot for good food, but here's an exception. The steaks are as tasty as the seafood, and even that usual invitation to indigestion—the Captain's plate—is good here. Prices are very reasonable. It is not a pretentious place, but if you go in for that sort of thing, you can order one of the Polynesian dishes.

> 451 Avenue U, Seaside
> 5:30-11:30 p.m.; closed Mondays
> 738-7241 (reservations accepted)
> Moderate
> Credit Cards: BA, MC
> Full Bar

The Ginkgo Tree Gallery ☆

The Oregon Coast professes a serious concern for the arts, but aside from Salishan there isn't much to substantiate the claim. This gallery, with its distinguished collection of Northwest artists, is a major exception. The art is well selected, and it comes from a wide range of media: batiks, calligraphy, drawings, jewelry, photography, prints, pottery, sculpture, stained glass, weaving and plain old painting. A fine browse and an oasis for information about other spots en route.

409 Broadway, Seaside
738-6285
Summer hours: 10-5; open till 6 on Friday and Saturday

CANNON BEACH

Surfsand ☆ ☆

This is a model motel. The rooms are large, with oversized beds and ample dressing rooms. There's lots of free firewood, and a fire is laid each day. In the morning a copy of the *Oregonian* is placed in front of your door. The staff pampers you after a frazzling week. The heated pool, the Jacuzzi, or the ocean, just outside the balcony, take care of the rest. No other frills: just everything in its proper place. Ask for rooms in the beachfront building.

Division St., Cannon Beach
436-2274
Moderate
Pets Allowed
Credit Cards: AE, BA, CB, DC, MC

Tolovana Inn ☆

A good, nothing-special motel in a town that has more going for it than most on the Coast since it is becoming a year-round home for young people, artists and retired folk. The Inn has superb ocean views and good low-bank beach access. The rooms are clean, the service is good, and the family clientele is pleasant (a good thing, since the walls are somewhat thin). There are an enclosed swimming pool, fireplaces, sauna and a rec room. The restaurant is serviceable, and it puts on a nice champagne brunch on Sundays, featuring clam skievers.

Warren Way, one-quarter mile west of 101, Cannon Beach
436-1111
Moderate
Pets accepted
Credit Cards: BA, MC

MANZANITA

Father's ☆

Nelson and April Souza underwent a religious conversion a few years ago, and one of the results is this restaurant, together with the band of converts who have made the handsome furniture and glass in the small room. It is a chef's-choice restaurant, and the skilled chef is likely to offer chicken, salmon, a curry, veal Marengo or things like that. The vegetables are almost always fresh and lovely. The breads are made by the collective, and they are very good. Best of all are the desserts.

You really never quite know what the Souzas are going to be doing. For a while last year, they were experimenting with a $10 fixed-price meal; then they decided to let each customer pay what he or she thought they could afford and the meal was worth. The menu changes a lot too, so it is well to call before and inquire. Father's is also open on Sundays for a day-long brunch. It's a very mellow place — and a certain way to get off the well-beaten tourist tracks.

Laneda St., Manzanita
368-6110
Moderate
No Credit Cards
Wine

NEHALEM

Nehalem Bay Wine Co.

Oregon is famous for its fruit—so why not fruit wine? One taste and you may agree with us that there are good reasons why not; but a tour of this winery, with its rustic tasting room and enthusiastic spiel by owner Pat McCoy, is well worth doing and quite educational. At the end, you may find yourself disarmed and ready to purchase a bottle each of the peach, plum and apricot.

One-half mile east of Nehalem, on Highway 53
Open daily 12-6 p.m.
368-5009

GARIBALDI

Edmonds Crabs ☆

What any coast like this one badly needs is a good seafood store: here it is. There are always good fresh fish and crabs; the smoked smelt and smoked tuna are superb; and to cap the catch they carry Petite Point oysters, in jars or fresh.

Highway 101, just north of Garibaldi
Daily, 9-6
322-3410

TILLAMOOK

Petite Point Oyster Company ☆ ☆ ☆ ☆

The finest oysters we have located on the Northwest Coast are the small ones grown by the Hayes family in Bay City, about four miles north of Tillamook. These oysters are small enough to resemble the nearly depleted native oysters (called Olympias), but they are really a delicate Japanese transplant. They are smaller and much more delicate in taste than all other Japanese (or Pacific) oysters, and the deeply cupped shells are of exquisite beauty. These magnificent bivalves are rarely available in the shell, so be sure to buy some here, perhaps to eat on the beach. You can also get jars of these "Kumamotos" to take home to envious friends. Each year the Hayes family thinks of quitting its arduous calling, so give them all the encouragement you can — no difficult task after one swallow of a raw Kumamoto on the half shell.

Bay City, four miles north of Tillamook
Daily, 8-4; weekends, 10-4
377-2210

Pioneer Museum ☆ ☆

An excellent museum, authentically recreating the pioneer past. It occupies three floors of the 1905 county courthouse, and the rooms are stuffed with good things: an 1850 handhewn cradle, carved beeswax washed ashore from a Spanish treasure ship of two hundred years ago, a pioneer home and barn, old cars, campaign memorabilia, and assorted oddities discovered on local beaches. The wildlife department is first-rate, with probably the best such exhibits in the state.

Second St. at Pacific, Tillamook
Daily, 9-5; Sunday 1-5; closed Monday in winter
Free

Tillamook County Creamery

Daily tours of this mammoth processing plant are offered, at the end of which you can buy some of the famous Tillamook cheddar. Then take it home and age it for at least six months.

Two miles north of Tillamook on U.S. 101
Daily, 9-5
Free

Clamming in Netart's Bay ☆ ☆

Clamming is a great sport on the Oregon Coast. There are eight species of clams (plus mussels) available from uncontaminated waters year-round without a license. Netart's Bay south of Tillamook is our choice for the best bed: extreme low tides often empty the small saltwater bay, making the clams very accessible on foot.

LINCOLN CITY

The Smokehouse ☆ ☆

David Wu, owner and chef of this small restaurant overlooking the ocean, understands well how to provide fresh seafood for his menu. Accordingly he breaks the menu down into three classes. The regular one might have a fresh fish like tuna if one happens to be available, but also offers filet mignon in mushroom sauce and such frozen specialties as sturgeon. A one-day's-notice menu has continental specialties: a rack of veal, scallopine, sweetbreads provencal, and fish dishes like a bouillabaisse or shad roe Baltimore style (the chef's earlier experience was in Washington, D.C.). A two-day's notice menu proffers such sumptuous dishes as a chateaubriand in lobster sauce, paella, and a whole fresh salmon stuffed with lobster, shrimp, and ham. It's the sort of dedicated restaurant that invites discussions with the chef a day or so beforehand. If he can get some good Kumamoto oysters, he might stuff and broil them. If he knows of some splendid whitefish that he can poach with herbs (as he did for an impressed James Beard a few years ago), he might suggest that when you call.

The result is some of the best dining on the coast, nicely served in a small room finished with native woods. Indicative of the personal touch at The Smokehouse is the fact that Mr. Wu not only has assembled a good wine cellar; he blends his own house wine. He will treat serious diners with the same attention.

> Route 101, five miles south of Salishan, at Boiler Bay
> Dinners only, 5-11; Sunday, 4-11; closed Monday, Tuesday; closed November 1-April 1
> Reservations: 765-2224
> Expensive
> No Credit Cards
> Wine and Beer

Salishan Lodge ☆ ☆ ☆

This famous resort, the dream of Portland industrialist John Gray, has many wonderful features — and several jarring notes. The setting is sensitively handled. The eightplex units are spread around the lush fairways of the Robert-Trent-Jones-designed golf course, and the use of indigenous building materials is simple and elegant. As several critics have noted, Salishan has an almost Japanese attention to the placement of rocks and trees and walkways. This care extends inside as well. Handwoven rugs, dashes of some excellent modern regional art, and attractive fieldstone complete the effect. And the units have large rooms, with oversized beds and attractive furniture. Additionally, the ten-year-old Salishan has an excellent array of sporting facilities: the golf course ($9 greens fees), three *indoor* tennis courts ($4-6 for 75 minutes of play), a pool, a gym, game rooms, hiking trails into a private 750-acre forest, three miles of beach. While there are conferences held at the outstanding facilities, drawing executives from all over the nation, the resort is not a crowded condominium: there are just 126 units.

The resort is located across Route 101 from Siletz Bay, so you might find yourself more distant from the ocean than you hoped; on the other hand, staying at the lodge gets you an electronic pass to the private, long beach along Salishan Peninsula fronting the homes in Salishan Properties, and the beach is celebrated for its driftwood accumulations. Another cause for disappointment can be the main dining room, a place called *The Gourmet Room*. Surely the setting is lovely: outside the wide windows one can admire the work of a talented landscape designer, Barbara Fealy, who has artfully arranged salal and Oregon grape in the foreground of the view from the three-level room. The maitre d', Phil DeVito, has a supplemental wine list that is extraordinary— such as a half dozen bottlings of 1961 Bordeaux, with prices up to $125. But the food is no match, despite the florid menu descriptions of the continental fare. Our recommendations: chicken diable (in a delicate mustard sauce) and bananas Foster for dessert, along with a good wine and a trip to the splendid bar overhead for an after-dinner drink.

Thus warned, you can have a marvelous stay at Salishan. The rates are very reasonable for the rooms, and if you get one in either Spruce or Fairway units, you will have a nice view, away from the parking lots.

Highway 101, five miles south of Lincoln City
764-2371
Gourmet Room open for dinner only (6-11); coffee shop for other meals
Pets accepted
Expensive
Credit Card: MC

Inn at Spanish Head ☆ ☆

This is one of the McMillan Inns, pioneers in the concept of selling condominiums in such a way that the owners can rent out their apartments to the general public and keep 60 percent of the rent. There are many fine features. The 125-room structure drops down the side of a cliff for ten stories, thus getting close to a nice stretch of ocean while at the same time not blocking the view from Highway 101 above. the beach is well worth being near. The suites are attractively decorated in Moorish-modern motif; and all have kitchens and all face the magnificent view.

We have also found some demerits. The staff is not especially cooperative. The Inn caters to the business-conference crowd, handling conventions up to 250 people. The restaurant is nothing special; parking and highway access are awkward, due to the site.

4009 S. Highway 101, Lincoln City
966-2161
Expensive
No pets
Credit Cards: AE, BC, MC, DC

Mossy Creek Pottery ☆ ☆

Inevitably, you will be looking for some gifts along the Coast. This shop features high-fired stoneware designed and produced by Bob Richardson. The quality is superb, and there is a good selection at a wide range of prices.

Immonen Road, just north of Salishan, on 101
996-2415

NEWPORT

Mo's Restaurant ☆ ☆

Don't be misled: the service is bad, the atmosphere is loud, the place is jammed with family-style diners, and the prices look suspiciously low. But the food is exceptionally fine. If you get in, you are likely to have a meal of wonderful chowder (clam or oyster and not to be missed), a small shrimp salad (made from local shrimp), the day's specials—oysters, sole, salmon, trout—and a cup of coffee. All for less than $3.50. Finish up with a slice of delicious pie.

Mo's success has spawned other branches. The main restaurant (named for Indian owner Mohava Nimie) features fried fish. Mo's Annex, kitty-corner from the genesis, has a better view and is less crowded; their specialties are casseroles and barbecued oysters. Mo's West, out at Otter Rock, adds beer and wine to the basic fare, and it also has some dandy open-faced sandwiches of shrimp or sausage. Then there are also Mo's at Seaside and Taft, but these have drifted a bit too far from the magnetic field to keep up the superior standards at Main Mo's.

622 S.W. Bay Boulevard, Old Newport
Daily, 11 a.m.-9 p.m.; Annex: 11-3.
265-2979; no reservations
Inexpensive
No credit cards
No liquor (except at Mo's West)

The Centre ☆

This is one of the nicest places we know on the coast for lunch. Owner-manager Ed Doyle has fixed up an old bakery into a European cafe. For lunch you can have a cheese and fruit platter, hot or cold sandwiches made with homemade bread, oddities like Cornish pasties or Scotch eggs, and to wash it down, herb tea or Italian or Yugoslav sodas. Dinners can also be interesting: steak cooked the French way in a pan, shepherd's pie, or perhaps a well-cooked rainbow trout. The atmosphere is agreeable and the service is expert. The home-baked pastries are marvelous.

Canyon Way, Newport (take Herbert Exit, marked To Bayfront).
Winter hours, 10-6 Mon-Fri; 10-10 on Sat.' summers, open two hours
   longer.
265-8319
Moderate

Pizza Works

You probably didn't drive all the way to the Coast for a pizza, but you might want to sample these. The pies are made from whole wheat crusts—well worth trying—and the conventional toppings are quite good.

Highway 101, middle of Newport
265-5652

Inn at Otter Crest ☆ ☆ ☆

To our mind, this four-year-old McMillan Inn is the best resort on the coast.

The Inn does not try to imitate a Miami Beach or an Hawaiian palace; rather it genuinely fits into the landscape and celebrates the natural life of the Northwest. For openers, you leave your car a half-mile from the units. The car is parked by an attendant (in a lot camouflaged by trees) while you are taken first by shuttle cart and then by inclined tramway to your suite. The suites are located in fourplex and eightplex units that have been carefully constructed so as to preserve as much of the ecology as seems humanly possible. Pilings, rather than foundations, support the buildings; the units are placed around the major clumps of trees; during construction, the heavy cranes rested on platforms built on pilings — another measure to avoid disturbing the undergrowth. Finally, development was confined to the sloping hillside; down at the fragile region where the bluff meets the ocean, the natural grassy promontory is largely retained, while at the base of the bluff the management is endeavoring to preserve a state marine garden.

The architecture is a match for the landscape. Wood siding is used extensively, and the condominium-motel units have a random, contoured fit to the hillside that recalls Italian villages. The rooms are spacious; all suites have an ocean view and balconies. The decor varies a little, depending on who is the permanent owner of the unit you have rented, but it is all very tasteful. Finally, the support facilities are good, too. The dining room, called the Flying Dutchman Room, has fair continental cuisine, with such touchstones as an outstanding bouillabaisse, fresh-baked breads, milkfed eastern veal, salmon stuffed with oysters, and scrumptious desserts baked daily. There is plenty of sports equipment — pool, saunas, two tennis courts, putting green, volleyball and badminton — and it doesn't cost to use it, as it does at Salishan.

Perhaps the only warning necessary is that the Inn books conventions in the winter to take up the slack. The service is outstanding, however, and a call ahead will get an answer about the expected clientele that weekend.

Otter Crest, five miles north of Newport
765-2111
Expensive
Pets allowed
Credit Cards: BA, AE, DC

Embarcadero ☆ ☆

This is a rather unusual condominium-motel, located in Yaquina Bay harbor, near Old Town Newport. The chief attraction of the development is the boat moorage, and most of the units face the little harbor. The setting is handsome, and the units are nicely designed with cedar-shingle exteriors and rather lavish interiors. The allure of the Embarcadero is that it offers a lot to do for those who get bored just gazing at the ocean: boating, fishing, a heated and protected pool, a walk to the nearby fishing piers or shops, children's play areas, an exercise complex and (eventually) a quality restaurant. Nearly all units come with kitchens and fireplaces, as well as a semi-enclosed viewing deck cut into the sloped roof. Quarters may seem a little crowded and active for a getaway weekend, but to some tastes this resort happily combines luxury with bustle, especially now in its partially developed state.

1000 S.E. Bay Boulevard, Newport
265-8521
Expensive
No pets
Credit Cards: AE, BA, MC

OreAqua Fishing

This project, adjacent to the Oregon State Marine Science Center, provides an enjoyable followup to the displays at the OSU Center. OreAqua is a seafarm raising salmon and trout from broodstock through hatchery. You can angle for the year-old, market-size fish in the saltwater rearing ponds overlooking Yaquina Bay. Attendants lend a hand to youngsters and other non-fishermen. Then your catch is cleaned and ice-packed. It's the ideal way for easily bored fishermen to catch a delicious dinner: no license, no gear needed, no limit.

Marine Science Drive, Newport
867-6931

Depoe Bay Aquarium Shell Shop ☆ ☆

The aquarium has the usual displays and a seal show, but the shell shop—crowded, littered and dank—is probably the best shell shop in the Northwest. Its shells run up to $100 for the rarities, but these prices are fair, and the quality is extremely high. Collectors come from afar, making it really a collectors' shop. Another good shell shop is nearby, just south at The Lookout on Cape Foulweather.

> U.S. 101 at Bay Drive, Depoe Bay, ten miles north of Newport
> Daily, 10 a.m.-8 p.m.

YACHATS

Adobe Motel ☆ ☆

This motel, pleasantly perched above a craggy beach, is a popular spot for families and silver smelt fishermen. It is handsomely decorated, with a charming lounge and public rooms furnished in fine antiques (most for sale). The rooms in the older, adobe-style section of the complex are preferred for their individual fireplaces, stained glass, handmade adobe bricks, beamed ceilings and natural wood.

The associated amenities keep up the standard. Surf casting is handy from the motel beach; there's a pitch-and-putt course as well as shuffleboard. Best of all, the restaurant is quite good, serving admirable continental dishes and offering a well-stocked wine cellar to boot. Since there's free coffee in the rooms, one night you might call up Leo Bucko at Yachats Cottages (LI 7-3518) and order one of his pies to go, especially the unbeatable strawberry rhubarb.

> Highway 101, half-mile north of Yachats
> 547-3141
> Moderate
> No pets
> Credit Cards: BA, MC, DC, AE

FLORENCE

Bearfoot Plaza ☆

Owner-chef George Stiglinski, who opened this cafe in 1968 after retiring from the military, prepares food from the many places he has visited or lived in. Each day, as the mood takes him, he might cook up Chinese, Japanese, German, Mexican, or Yugoslavian specialities. The Mexican food is so good it has made it onto the regular, daily menu, where it comes with a very hot salsa. You can also order good, big sandwiches or steaks cut to big-eater proportions by the chef. The clientele is strictly local. No booze.

> Highway 101, 1 mile south of Florence
> Daily, 11-7:30; closes 6:30, Sunday-Tuesday; closed Wednesday
> 997-3889
> Inexpensive
> Credit Cards
> No Liquor

Driftwood Shores Surfside Resort Inn ☆

One of the attractive features of this resort is that it is one of the few places in the southcentral coast where you can stay right on the beach—101 swings a few miles inland in this stretch. The building is large, five stories, an intruder in the sand. But the spacious units are tastefully furnished. All have ocean views and balconies; some have kitchens; a few have fireplaces. You can range all the way up to a suite with three bedrooms, a living room, and two baths, for around $70. It started as a condominium-motel but now is a pure motel with aspirations to get into the convention trade.

> Hecata Beach Road, 3 miles north of Florence
> Year round
> 997-8263
> Pets $1
> Moderate
> Credit Cards: AE, BA, MC

The Toy Factory ☆

Vacationing with kids normally means there aren't enough toys along, so here's a spot for replenishment. Nearly all of the toys are handmade of sturdy woods: doll cribs, hobby horses, doll houses and furniture, trucks, cars, trains, and machinery—and of course logging trucks with logs. The owner Jim Noel, a refugee from East Coast federal bureaucracies, has a shop in the back where he makes the toys and gives short tours. His wife Sue is a former schoolteacher with sage advice.

Toys not made locally come from craftsmen in Vermont and the Appalachias. A catalog is available for mail-order, and you can also get custom-made items.

Highway 101, five miles north of Florence
Daily 11-5; closed Wednesdays
997-8604

Quilts ☆

It isn't exactly a shop. You walk through a cluttered kitchen to the living room where Mrs. Kathleen Ware makes quilts to supplement her income. The craftsmanship is outstanding, and the prices are extremely low: a double-bed quilt sells for about $60. You can also buy quilt tops, pillows, stuffed toys, and potholders. The patterns are mostly traditional, with some original designs in tasteful colors. Special orders are also taken.

South side of Highway 36, Walton
935-1470

CHARLESTON

Holiday House ☆

Coos Bay folks enjoy driving eight miles over to the small boat-basin town of Charleston in order to eat good seafood. The catch comes from local fishermen, which means you can get sole, snapper, salmon, oysters, clams and crabs. The oyster stew is well prepared. Servings are large and prices are good. The accompaniments, such as superb homemade potato salad, bread and pies, are just as good as the fish.

Small Boat Basin, Charleston
Summers, daily 8 a.m.-11 p.m.; winters, daily 11-11; closed December
Moderate
Credit Cards: BA, MC
Full Bar

GOLD BEACH

The Captain's Table

There's a view of the ocean — strangely hard to find in this town. The breakfasts are good, except for the frozen hash-browns. The prices are reasonable. They get fresh shrimp and salmon and grill the latter nicely. And that's about it.

Highway 101, Gold Beach
Daily, 7 a.m.-10 p.m.; closed November 15-March 1
Moderate
No Credit Cards
No Liquor

Rod 'n Reel

The dining room is viewless and the waitresses are overworked, but this honest restaurant serves better seafood than most. We suggest starting with one of the excellent soups, then the day's special fresh seafood. Steer clear of the expensive Italian dinners.

Just north of the Rogue River, Gold Beach
Daily, 5-10 p.m.
247-6823
Moderate
Credit Cards: AE, BA, CB, DC, MC
Beer and Wine

Ireland's Rustic Lodges ☆ ☆

Corabelle Ireland has run this place for thirty-eight years, and she hopes to retire soon to Portland to be near her family, who recently sold the Ireland's restaurants, Portland landmarks for ages. It's unlikely you'll ever find a place like the Rustic Lodges again, once they're sold.

The lodges are real log bungalows, all but one of which have large stone fireplaces. Each of the eight lodges is different, with the largest accommodating a family of five, but they are all kept in immaculate condition. The decor is a mixture of 1950s overstuffed middle-class furniture and intricate needlework executed by the proprietress. The beach is just a few yards away, and the lodges are set amid extensive lawns and flower gardens. Cedar and Spruce Lodge have the best ocean views; Redwood and Pine have no views.

The feature that has made Ireland's a coast institution is dinner. Miss Ireland and her assistant cook the dinners (there are no kitchens in the lodges) and then serve them to you at your own lodge by the fire. If you splurge and order steak, it would cost you $6 for this meal. Breakfasts are cooked at the main lodge, which doubles as the Ireland home, and eaten there.

The prices for the lodges are unbelievable, starting at $16 for a double. Such prices will never survive the coming change in ownership, but how much else will is impossible to predict.

Highway 101, south of Gold Beach
Closed November 15-February 15
247-7718
Moderate
No Credit Cards
Pets Allowed

Inn of the Beachcomber ☆

The name may be evocative, but the place is just a good, standard beachfront hotel. One nice touch is the reservation of the lower building, farthest from the road, for adults only. These rooms are also closest to the beach, so you'll be able to fall asleep with the sound of the ocean, not the whirr of the air-conditioner. Large, heated pool; sauna; motelish decor.

Highway 101, south of Gold Beach
247-6691
Moderate
Credit Cards: AE, BA, CB, DC, MC

Willamette Valley

Oregon Winegrowers ☆ ☆

Some of the finest wine in the Northwest is grown in western
Oregon, in a relatively adverse climate that actually is much closer
to the variable conditions in France than is the weather in
California or Eastern Washington. These Oregon wines, while still
in their early stages of development and inconsistent from year to
year, have their own characteristics, are full of flavor, and are
very well made by dedicated, experienced professionals who have
moved here from California. The small wineries are run by
proprietors who are often willing to show around interested
parties. Since output and distribution is limited, stopping by these
wineries is sometimes the only way to get the wines. A tour of a
winery, followed by a picnic overlooking the Willamette with a
few bottles of the local white wine, can make a glorious outing.

The best are a short drive west and south from Portland.

Charles Coury Vineyards, Forest Grove; daily tours, 1-5 p.m.,
with vines also for sale. Coury's best wines are the pinot noir, the
gewurtztraminer, the riesling, and the dry rose (357-7602).

Eyrie Vineyards, 935 East Tenth Street, McMinnville. David
Lett is the knowledgeable owner, and his winery is open to the
public on Saturdays only. His white wines are outstanding,
especially the 1973 pinot gris, the "spring wine," and the very dry
rieslings (864-2410).

Tualatin Vineyards, Forest Grove. Bill Fuller's place is open
only by appointment; his best wine is an intriguing experiment, a
dry Muscat (357-5005).

Erath Vineyards, Worden Hill Road, Dundee, requires advance reservations with owner Richard Erath; best are his riesling and pinot (538-3318).

Hillcrest Vineyards, Elgarose Road, Roseburg. This vineyard, open daily from 10-5, was started by the pioneer varietal grower in Oregon, Richard Sommer. The riesling is his best wine (673-3709).

ZIG ZAG

Salazar's ☆

Here is a nice place to stop for dinner on your way back from Mount Hood. The 85-person dining room is attractively decorated with antiques collected during the past twenty years by chef Al Salazar. During the winter, the upstairs room has a magical view out over the snowscape. The food is interesting too: some New Orleans-style preparations of oysters and prawns, a roast duck in a savory natural sauce, an Italianate treatment of chicken with vegetables and white sauce, and even a tasty way of dressing up swiss steak with sour cream. There are steaks and some simple fish dishes, as well as a passable wine list. Salazar's is popular with doctors and lawyers who motor out for dinner or are coming back from the slopes, so be sure to reserve in advance.

Route 26, one mile east of Zig Zag
Dinners only, 5-11; Sunday, 4-8:30; closed Tuesday
Reservations: 622-3775
Moderate
Credit Cards: BA, MC
Wine and Beer

MOUNT HOOD

Timberline Lodge ☆ ☆

A dramatic, massive structure, Timberline lodge is also an interesting product of the Depression and testimonial to American crafts. The WPA project employed many skilled craftsmen, whose work is evident in the tooled metal, the carved beams, the strap metal furniture, the rugs, and the murals. The main lobby, with its gargantuan wooden beams flying overhead in an intricate octagonal pattern, is a magnificent space. The rooms are quite comfortable if you are willing to spend above $25 (in season) and get one with a view or a fireplace. During the summer, rates drop about $3 per room.

Food in the lodge is standard American fare and the bar entertainment is staid, but there are many fine attractions in the area. Skiing is moderately good, with the novelty of summer skiing at about 9,000 feet through transportation by snow cat. The best skiing is to the east, at Mount Hood Meadows. A huge heated pool is open year round. In the summer you can climb the mountain, hike the alpine meadows, and fish for trout.

> Six miles north of Route 26, Timberline
> 272-3311
> Expensive
> Credit Cards: AE, BA, MC
> Pets Limited

OREGON CITY

Oregon City ☆

The first incorporated town west of the Missouri, Oregon City was settled in 1829 and later was the home of Dr. John McLoughlin, the famous friend of the Indians and the early settlers in the valley. The town is a curious one, built on three terraces above the falls; an elevator lifts pedestrians between two of the levels. As you would expect in history-conscious Oregon, much has been preserved. Best are McLoughlin's 1845 house (713 Center Street, $1), filled with old furniture; and Mountain View Cemetery (Hilda Street), where many famous early figures are buried and the views are inspiring.

Across the river is the West Linn Inn, a famous old hotel now closed to lodgers but a nice spot for lunch or dinner (500 Mill Street, 656-2613, full bar); a walk from the inn leads to the 103-year-old locks on the river, another picturesque place.

MOUNT ANGEL

Mount Angel Abbey ☆ ☆

The Abbey is a Benedictine monastery established here in 1884. The view of the river valley is so fine that one can understand why the Indians considered this hill to be a holy place. Another reason for your pilgrimage is the architecture, particularly the library and reading room by Alvar Aalto, the great Finnish architect who has here created one of the finest works of architecture in the Northwest.

> Church Street, Mount Angel
> 845-3030
> Library hours, 9-12; 1-5; 7-11

SALEM

The Other Place ☆

This new restaurant, opening just this fall, will combine a tried-and-true menu—prime rib, veal Oscar, salmon, steak and lobster—with a formula for decor that is also proven many times over in Neo-New England Oregon: antiques everywhere. The quality of the cooking remains to be shown, but the recycled pizza house is uncommonly handsome inside. Old buffets hold the serving trays, and wood paneling and a half-circle bar enhance the lounge. The kitchen will turn out a day's soup as well as quiches, stews, and crepes for lunch. A fancy espresso machine is on hand for elaborate coffee drinks. Small and steeped in instant history, this establishment should be a nice stopover for travelers up and down the freeway.

Mission Street Exit from Interstate 5, Salem
Weekday lunches, 11-2; dinners, 5-10; closed Sunday
Reservations: 585-4454
Moderate
Credit Cards: BA, MC
Full Bar

Dunes International Marion Motel Bar

Presumably, you wouldn't be in Salem unless you had some political motivation. Here then is the watering hole most favored by legislators, lobbyists, and the press. You're better off drinking than eating, and that rule extends to the complimentary meatball canapes during the happy hour. Drinks are large and reasonable.

200 Commercial SE, Salem
Bar hours: 11-2:30 a.m.
363-4123
Credit Cards: AE, BA, MC

Bush House

Bush House, built in 1877 as a typically lovely home of the period, has been nicely refurnished. It now reposes in the middle of a large park that makes a nice family visit for a Sunday afternoon: there's a small children's playground, picnic tables, and even a small formal rose garden. The barn has been turned into an art center where you can view exhibits and purchase works by local artists and craftspeople.

600 Mission Street S.E., Salem
Summer, Tuesday-Saturday, noon-5; Sunday, 2-5 p.m.; Winter, Tuesday-
    Saturday, 2-5
Admission Fee

EUGENE

The Country Inn ☆ ☆

The old frame farmhouse, surrounded by a high wooden fence, is located off a country road five miles north of Eugene. Inside is a honeycomb of small rooms and hallways crammed with wall hangings, draperies, paintings, antiques, furniture, and collectibles well worth browsing among. Dinner is consumed in a small, two-level room with only four tables, each reserved long in advance for the one sitting per night. Dining in such agreeable surroundings is a good way to form friendships, and by the end of the evening in this dramatic restaurant, most guests are talking animatedly to each other.

Two men have owned and staffed this restaurant for twenty-six years: Neil Koch, the opinionated, amusing, imperious waiter and host; and Jimmy Harper, the charming chef who regularly emerges after dinner to play the large organ in the dining room. Dinner and wine come from a no-choice menu that is often unchanged for months. If you inquire about this, Koch is likely to say that he has no time for haggling about wines since it would "interfere with the perfection of the food." Be that as it may, the dinner will consist of (to chose a typical recent menu): a champagne cocktail, a clear broth of garden vegetables, a family-style salad served surrounded by fresh flowers, a steak in a mustard sauce with potatoes and sauteed cabbage, and then homemade ice cream with a sauce made from Oregon wild berries. The food is quite good, as it should be for the going price of $27.50 a person.

Properly appreciative guests (those who enthuse about the broth, for instance) will be rewarded with some dessert wines or a showing of the owners' private collection of porcelain.

> 4100 County Farm Road, Coburg
> Reservations at least one month in advance: 345-7344
> Dinner only, 7 p.m.; closed Sunday, Monday
> Expensive
> No credit cards
> Wine

The Oasis

Half a block from campus you can enjoy a luncheon kebab or stuffed Arabian bread sandwiches in this inexpensive Middle-Eastern restaurant. We particularly recommend the soups, made fresh daily from lamb or beef stocks. For dinner a best bet is the kebab plate of lamb, beef, chicken, and kufta. On Friday and Saturday nights the crowd, mostly students, is treated to bellydancing.

> 875 East 13th, Eugene
> Daily, 8 a.m.-9 p.m.; closed Sunday
> 342-3122
> Inexpensive
> No credit cards
> No liquor

New Oregon Motel ☆

You may not like to practice your sidestroke in full view of the diners at the adjacent Sambo's, but this motel is adequate, reasonably priced, just across the street from the OU campus, decorated in motelier modern, and a favorite place for students who are putting up their parents. Just thought you might like to know.

> 1655 Franklin Boulevard, Eugene
> 345-8731
> Moderate
> Credit Cards: AE, BA, CB, DC, MC

McKenzie River Highway ☆ ☆

This is probably the most varied and beautiful crossing of the Cascades. From Eugene, following Route 126, you pass farm country alongside the green water of the river. If you follow 126, you will see dazzling water falls and the amazingly transparent Clear Lake. But a far more spectacular route is Route 242 (closed winters) from Belknap Springs—a narrow, twisting route that brushes past waterfalls, berries, vast, lunar-like lava fields at the pass, and awesome viewpoints. There are no tourist facilities on this thirty-six mile stretch, so you might plan to have lunch at Holiday Farm near McKenzie Bridge, an old stagecoach stop with antiques, a bar, and good plain food (open all day, April to November; 822-3715).

The McKenzie is also famous for its trout fishing and riverruns, made in boats with upturned bows and superb guides.

COTTAGE GROVE

Village Green ☆ ☆

It may be located right along the freeway, but this resort motel has many nice touches. The ninety-six rooms are spacious, many of them shielded from the highway and facing the golf course or the pool. Beds are turned down while you are out for dinner, and when you return you will find candy kisses on the pillow along with a sweet note from the management.

The dining room must be approached with great caution. It is a most comfortable place, with a large stone fireplace, armchairs at the tables, and an adjacent poolside patio that is a grand place for drinks or a summertime lunch. But the food exceeds the kitchen's grasp. Chicken livers can come mushy and over-sauced; the prime rib can be tough and over-cooked; vegetables are mostly frozen and tepid. It is a place requiring simple ordering, such as the lightly dressed plate of shrimp and avocado for a first course. The wine list is extensive and pompously presented.

The resort is aimed at conventioneers, but it is also well-suited for families. One nice family excursion leaves from the area: a summer weekend trip on an old train drawn by a 1914 steam engine. The thirty-seven-mile round trip winds through the Row River Valley and ends up at a large railroad museum at the Village Green station. There are also bus tours of the nearby gold-mining country, where both deserted and working mines are on view.

> Interstate 5 at Cottage Grove exit
> Restaurant hours, 6-10 p.m.; Sunday, 4-9 p.m.
> 942-2491
> Expensive
> Credit Cards: AE, BA, CB, DC, MC
> Full Bar

ROSEBURG

Wildlife Safari ☆

The statewide billboard campaign may induce suspicion, but this is not a roadside ripoff. It is a large, 600-acre, drive-through wildlife preserve in lovely, rolling country. The natural habitats are well arranged, with predators discreetly fenced from their prey. A taped tour, clear and informative, is given each car; you can stop the tape at any point that particularly fascinates you, such as when the ostriches converge on the car and peck on the windshield. Afterward there's a snack shop and a care center for baby animals, some of whom are available for petting by children. The adult fare is $3.50, and it's worth it.

> Oregon 99, four miles west of I-5, five miles south of Roseburg
> June-August, 9-6; September-May, 10-4:30
> 679-6761

GRANTS PASS

R. Haus

The restaurant is in an old lodge that has been renovated, filled up with antiques, and given some Bicentennial touches and an old-fashioned parlor upstairs with music machines. The gimmickry extends to the size of the portions, which is colossal. Still, the dining room overlooking the Rogue River is pleasant enough, and the food is fairly well cooked. There is a cream of lentil soup that is unusual and tasty, and if the thought of a 22-ounce steak turns your stomach, you can have roasted chicken or some stroganoff. On some nights the chef will use fresh vegetables. Sunday mornings they do a decent brunch.

> Rogue River Highway, 2 miles east of Grants Pass
> Every night, 6-10 p.m.; Sunday 11-3
> Reservations: 476-4287
> Moderate
> Credit Cards: BA, MC
> Full Bar

Riverside Motel ☆

The Rogue River is one of Oregon's most beautiful, chiseled into the coastal mountains and inhabited by splendid fighting trout. This motel allows you to stay right on the Rogue, in modern rooms with balconies overhanging the river. The rooms are attractive, and the motel's amenities include two heated pools.

From the motel you can catch a two-hour jetboat excursion on the river into a deep canyon called Hellgate. The finest trip is by the specially made, three-person Rogue River boats down the 120 miles of the fast-flowing river to the ocean. The trip takes about four days, leaving lots of time for fishing, swimming, and camping. Boat operators are listed by the Chamber of Commerce Box 970; 476-7717.

> 971 Southeast Sixth Street, Grants Pass
> 476-6873
> Moderate
> Credit Cards: AE, BA, CB, DC, MC
> Pets limited

MEDFORD

Red Lion Motel ☆

This is an adequate motel, smack in the middle of Motel Row and smack in the middle of the price range. The slight advantage of this one is the location, farther from the freeway exits. New units overlook a small creek, which in turn overlooks the freeway; so we prefer rooms facing the small inner courtyard with a garden and pool.

> 200 North Riverside, Medford
> 779-5811
> Moderate
> Pets allowed
> Credit Cards: AE, BA, CB, DC, MC

Harry and David Orchards ☆

Out of this famous orchard country come comice, bartlett, winter nellis, bosc, and d'anjou pears, as well as superb peaches and apples. Harry and David's fruit-of-the-month club has spread these pears all over the country to everybody's uncles and aunts. The orchards are not easy to see, but the firm started in the mid thirties by the late Harry and David Holmes gives tours of the processing and packing plant and will sell you just about any combination of excellent fruit that you or your relatives may desire. They pack peaches in September, pears and apples for the three months following.

> Bear Creek Orchards, on Route 99, just south of Medford
> Tours, August 15-December 15, 8-11 a.m.; 1-4 p.m.
> 779-2121

JACKSONVILLE

Jacksonville ☆

This little town five miles west of Medford was first settled in 1852 when the gold rush spilled north from California. Today, after a fifty-year decline, almost the entire town has been tastefully restored. The main street is a nice place for a stroll or a ride in a mule-drawn stagecoach; the side streets feature well-kept-up nineteenth century frame houses with fenced front yards.

Jacksonville Museum—is situated in the 1883 county court house. The excellent collection is poorly displayed, but you can look at fine Indian artifacts and pictures, a nineteenth-century drawing room, and pioneer children's furniture. The most impressive display consists of the equipment, paintings, and photographs of Peter Britt, a Swiss settler who came to town in 1852 seeking gold. (Daily, 9-5; Sunday, noon-5; closed Mondays off season.)

That Store—is a good delicatessen in the old Bella Union Saloon. You can get fresh bagels, sandwiches, salads, and beer; out back is a small dining room and an outdoor beer garden. The wooden addition to the building, incidentally, seems so authentic because it was built in 1970 as a movie set for "The Great Northfield Minnesota Raid." (170 West California Street. Daily 10-9 in summer, 11-7 in winter.)

ASHLAND

Chateaulin ☆

We count this the best place for dinner before walking around the corner to the Shakespearean Festival. The room has many nice touches like blue-and-white check tablecloths, fresh flowers, and large, dark, wooden chairs. The menu is small, but excellently prepared. Both seafood and vegetables will be fresh during the proper seasons. The entrees, which are augmented by daily specials such as sweetbreads, sea bass, or a rack of lamb, are accompanied by the unusual touch of delicious pommes dauphine. Chef Bernard Pradel is particularly good at sauces and pastry. The only flaws are likely to be minor things like a cool soup, slightly stale bread, and the small wine list.

50 East Main Street, Ashland
Daily, 5-9 p.m.; closed October and November
Reservations: 482-2264
Moderate
Credit Card: BA
Wine

Mum's Cottage Cafe ☆

Tiny—four tables and a counter—and extremely informal (the waitress will be barefoot if it's a warm day), this is an excellent vegetarian restaurant. The day's menu and prices depend on the whims of the owner, Englishman Keith Simmonds. There are wok dishes, East Indian dinners ranging in cost up to $3.90, big salads, omelets, and occasional international adventures into things like Mexican food.

A typical night might offer meatless lasagne with three cheeses, mushroom stroganoff, asparagus from a wok, and quiche Lorraine. Whole-grain breads are baked on the premises. Dessert might be a splendid pie from a whole-grain crust, home-cranked ice cream, or plain old chocolate mousse. Even the yoghurt is homemade (and delicious). There are many teas and coffees but no wine or booze; and you are asked not to smoke.

2425 Siskiyou Boulevard, Ashland
Noon-9 p.m.; closed Sundays
482-4767
Inexpensive
No credit cards
No liquor

Oregon Shakespearean Festival ☆ ☆

Summer evenings in Ashland mean Shakespeare mounted on an open-air stage resembling a 1599 London theater, the Fortune. The acting is good, the production values are very high, and the youngish company is likely to mount a comedy that will make a splendid evening of theater. Afternoons, and during the spring season from March on, you can also attend plays in the excellent small playhouse, where modern American classics join the Elizabethan fare. The festival, set in a lovely park, has forty years of experience behind it, making it the nation's most consistent Shakespearean festival.

There are some sour notes, too. The company is not an equity one, so it does not bring in major stars or directors; accordingly the mature Shakespeare of the tragedies is not going to be all that memorable. Tourists can bring out the ham in some of the actors. The undistinguished town of Ashland still has not caught up with the possibilities of its major industry. But if you are passing through, you would be foolish not to try to get tickets for an evening performance.

Lithia Park, Box 27, Ashland
March-May, indoors, evenings at 8, Saturday, Sunday at 2; closed Monday; mid-June to mid-September, daily at 2 and 8 p.m.
482-4331

Oregon Caves Chateau ☆

Your visit to the Oregon Caves is made much more pleasant by this fine old wooden lodge. The lobby is full of comfortable chairs in front of the big marble fireplace, and the cheerful dining room has a mountain stream babbling through. The view from the agreeable rooms is of a virgin forest and the ravine into which the structure is built.

The caves themselves display intriguing formations of marble, with a higher proportion of fine effects to dreary corridors than is the norm. The guides are just as corny as cave guides always are.

Children under six cannot enter the caves, but a baby-sitting service is provided at the chateau.

Route 46, 20 miles east of Cave Junction
Open: May 30-September 10
Telephone: Oregon Caves toll station 1
Moderate
Credit Cards: AE, BA, MC

Eastern Oregon

Eastside Cafe ☆

This large establishment has been here twenty-eight years, serving up American food to the locals, but specializing in Chinese and Japanese food for the Asian population that also farms in the area. Much of the food is served family style, in a curious progression from fried chicken and other down-home specialties to some extraordinarily good Chinese items at the end of the meal. Or you can simply order the oriental fare and skip the standards.

The Japanese menu is limited mostly to some nice tempura prawns, but the Cantonese chef excells in Chinese dishes. One of the best is Mandarin chicken—batter-fried cubes of chicken in a pineapple and tomato sauce. With a day's advance notice, the kitchen can do more exotic specialties. The decor may be unexceptional, but the cooking at this restaurant is exceptional for this remote part of the country.

105 Southeast Second Street, Ontario
Daily, 11:45-2:30 a.m.
Weekday reservations only: 889-9944
Moderate
Credit Card: BA
Full Bar

VALE

Starlight Cafe

You might be in this region on your way to the spectacular Owyhee Dam and Lake to the south. If so, drop into this twenty-four-hour cafe for a single simple reason: Audrey Burns is one fine pie-cook. Her finest achievement is an oatmeal pie, a rarity that tastes something like a pecan pie and just as good. The rest of the menu is what you'd expect in this deserted country: chicken-fried steaks, hot sandwiches, and breaded veal.

> A Street, Vale
> Every day, 24 hours
> 473-2500
> Inexpensive
> Credit Card: BA
> No alcohol

BAKER

Blue and White Cafe ☆

Mrs. Iva Jean Bremer is in charge here, supervising the two booths and fourteen stools of the cafe and assuring that the food turned out remains delicious and incredibly inexpensive. She bakes her own breads and pies—the cream pies are best—and puts up a daily special: ham hocks on Monday, swiss steak on Tuesday, chicken and noodles on Wednesday, meat loaf on Thursday, round steak on Friday, and fried chicken on Saturday. The most expensive meal you can order is a large, delicious, tender ground round steak for $2. The ambience is that of the classic, gossipy western cafe, from breakfast on through dinners, which end at farmer's hours—8 p.m. The food exceeds even the marvelous atmosphere.

1617 Dewey Street, Baker
Daily, 6 a.m.-8 p.m.; closed Sunday
No reservations: 523-6792
Inexpensive
No Credit Cards
No alcohol

Tourism in Baker ☆ ☆

Baker is a gold rush town born in the 1850s, one of the few that didn't go away when the gold petered out. The town is very pretty, with a park reminiscent of a New England commons, and numerous streets with well-maintained Victorian homes and mature trees. From the town there are several very interesting trips.

Gold Ghost Towns. Head west from Baker and visit towns that have vanished into rust and weeds, places like Whitney, Bonanza (with ruins of an immense stamping mill), Greenhorn, Granite, and Bourne.

Hells Canyon. You drive east from Baker, through the pastoral valley of the Powder River, and suddenly come upon the truly satanic landscape of the Snake River, coiled in eternal shadow thousands of feet below in an awful trench incised through somber lava walls. The best way to see the gorge is to cross at Oxbow Dam and drive north to Hells Canyon Dam; there you can board a jetboat and shoot the rapids below the dam, where the sheer, melancholy walls are the most awesome. (Arrangements through Jim Zanelli, Box 145, Oxbow, Oregon.)

When at Baker, the best place to stay is the new Sun Ridge Inn, faced in Oregon pine and offering modern rooms and large beds.

City Center Exit from Route 30, Baker
523-6444
Moderate
Credit Cards: AE, BA, CB, DC, MC

COVE

Red's Horse Ranch ☆ ☆ ☆

The Minam River Valley, in the Eagle Cap Wilderness Area, is the last major river valley in the state without any roads. It could hardly happen to a more lovely area, full of elk and deer and fish, dotted with lakes and waterfalls and snowfields. There is also an excellent ranch from which to organize your explorations of this fabled realm of the Wallowas, the land whence Chief Joseph was driven in the epic Indian story of futile courage.

Red's Horse Ranch has been operated by the Hawkins family since 1945. You can get here only by a short plane ride from either Enterprise or La Grande, or else by a three-hour pack trip on horse. The ranch has enough cabins for four or five families at a time — comfortable log cabins with fireplaces in the bedrooms, modern baths, a view of the Minam, and enough spacing between each of them so that you will feel utterly alone in the deep piney woods. Meals are served family-style in the lodge, and Carol Hawkins has fresh milk from the cows and splendid hams and bacon from her smokehouse, along with other delicious food.

During the summer there is fishing for trout, hiking, and horseback riding: each guest gets a horse included in the price of $35 a day for adults, which also covers all meals. Fall is the time for hunting: deer in early October, and elk in early November. The price of $100 a day includes the flight in, meals, and hunting guides. Be sure to book well ahead: Burt Lancaster might be bringing in his friends again that week.

Mailing address: Cove
Closed Thanksgiving to Memorial Day
568-4818
Expensive
No Credit Cards

BURNS

Pine Room Cafe ☆

The town of Burns, once the center of impressive cattle
kingdoms ruled by legendary figures like Pete French and William
Hanley, is a welcome oasis to one driving over this desolate, lava-
torn landscape. The land has been formed by ten million years of
volcanic activity and then branded on the American subconscious
in a few decades by the thousands of western movies filmed in the
area.

The best spot for dinner is the Pine Room Cafe, pleasantly but
incongruously decorated in Mediterranean motif and serving
moderately ambitious fare. The food, almost entirely prepared
from scratch, starts with hearty soups and sturdy breads,
progresses to steaks, prime rib, and chicken, and tops out with
lobster, grilled oysters, and frog legs. Margie Kinder has been
managing the place for the past twenty-six years, and she runs a
cheerful, competent operation.

Next door is the Ponderosa Motel, a moderately priced and
agreeable small motel (577 West Monroe, 573-2047, AE, BA, DC,
MC). The most rewarding sidetrip is thirty-two miles south, where
the Malheur National Wildlife Refuge hosts stopovers from 230
different species of birds, including trumpeter swans.

Route 20 and 395, Burns
Dinners only, 5-11 p.m.; closed Sunday
Reservations: 573-6631
Moderate
Credit Card: BA
Full Bar

PENDLETON

Cimmiyotti's ☆

It's just what you'd like to find in a rodeo town. The decor is homey and unpretentious. The local folks favor it regularly. It's small enough so the service is friendly. The food is not very ambitious; just excellent steaks from $6.85 up served with a loaf of bread, a baked potato, and salad. For dessert: chocolate sundae. It may not sound like much, but when a small city steakhouse learns how to do this cooking well, you would be mistaken trying to outdo it at the fancier places.

> 137 South Main Street, Pendleton
> Dinners only, 6-12; Sunday, 6-10
> Reservations: 276-9830
> Moderate
> Credit Cards: AE, BA, MC
> Full Bar

Bar-M Guest Ranch ☆

The Bar-M is a dude ranch that is also a working ranch, so if you want to help with the cattle, the hogs, the fence-mending, or tending the vegetable gardens, you can. The accommodations are quite plain, but they are historic. The lodge, with eight rooms and three shared baths, dates back to 1864 when it was built as a stage stop. The hand-hewn logs are still in good shape, and the rooms are furnished with the oval dressers of the period. In addition, there are four apartments in an annex of recent vintage, and two large cabins. One of the best things about the ranch is the food, fresh from the vegetable gardens and the raspberry patch. The meat is raised on the ranch, and the trout come right out of the Umatilla River which the ranch borders. Rates are about $185 per person for a week: meals, lodging, and horse included.

> Route 1, Adams, 31 miles east of Pendleton
> June 1-September 30
> 566-3381
> Moderate
> No Credit Cards

Hamley Saddlery ☆ ☆

Pendleton is the official center of the Wild West of your imagination, particularly during the Roundup each early September, the best and most traditional rodeo in the land. Appropriately, there is a first-rate outfitting store here, an institution since 1905 and a kind of L.L. Bean and Abercrombie and Fitch of the West. Hamley's is particularly strong in Pendleton woolens, from the nearby Pendleton Mills. (The Mills can be toured on weekdays, and its retail shop offers savings if you are buying yardage; otherwise you should stick with Hamley's.) There are complete lines of western clothes for men and women, notable for their high quality but not great variety. Plus of course boots, hats, blankets, riding gear, leather outerwear, gifts — and saddles, made on the premises.

30 Southeast Court Street, Pendleton
Daily, 8:30-5:30; closed Sunday
276-2321

BEND

The Tumalo Emporium ☆ ☆

"We've tried chefs," reports manager Dave Rasmussen, "but we found we preferred cooks." The reason is this is a very home-spun restaurant, cherishing family recipes and putting a premium on honest home-cooking.

The Emporium is a very attractive spot with some of the rooms, like the Victorian Room, cozily decorated with antiques and others brimming with flowers. The menu features carefully prepared steaks and salmon, as well as composed dishes like shrimp creole and canneloni. What distinguishes these dishes is the insistence on preparation from scratch: the canneloni, for instance, has a superb filling made from ham and spinach ground each day. The main attraction is the buffet, an enormous spread of roasts, salads, casseroles, home-made breads, beans, vegetables, and baked goods. The food is ample, inexpensive — $5 for dinner, $2.25 for the lunch version — and all derived from exacting family recipes.

Highway 20, six miles west of Bend
Daily, 11:30-10 p.m.
Reservations: 382-2202
Moderate
No Credit Cards
Full Bar

Black Forest Inn ☆

Axel Hoch is a German chef who bought this place a year ago and fixed it up nicely with a Bavarian motif, natural wood, steins, and posters. So far he hasn't found any strolling musicians, so the rather small restaurant is a fine spot for enjoying the chef's careful menu. There are several German items, such as a sauerbraten or a chicken in wine sauce with shrimp, mushrooms, and asparagus. Some good German wine can also be had.

The bulk of the menu reflects the chef's experience in France and Switzerland. He stuffs some huge Salem mushrooms with chicken and onions and a cream sauce, for instance. Another nice touch is a seafood Wellington of lobster, prawns, and scallops in a sauce Nantua and encased in a puff-pastry shell. This top-of-the-menu item costs only $7.25 on a complete dinner, an indication of the reasonable prices that go with this cosmopolitan place.

Century Drive, just southwest of Bend
Daily, 5:30-10; Sunday, 5-9; closed Monday, Tuesday
No reservations: 389-3138
Moderate
Credit Card: BA
Full Bar

Sunriver Lodge ☆ ☆ ☆

Sunriver is another resort by John Gray, the developer of Salishan, and it displays his same sure touch. The lodges are small buildings with several units in each, decorated with subdued Northwest colors and natural wood and stone. The most desirable rooms at this heavily-booked resort are in the 100 series, those closest to the main lodge and having views of the golf course and the mountains; rooms with numbers from 1-40 are most likely to have the best views. Like a proper Northwest residence, the rooms have patios, balconies with views of the splendid pine-and-meadow landscape, and large fireplaces. If you wish more seclusion or space, you can rent one of the 145 homes in the development that are available for rent: rents range from $57 to $77 a night, with a two-night minimum imposed. The public rooms at the George-Rockrise-designed main lodge, attractive to conventioneers, are just as smashing, although the conventional steaks and roasts in the dining room do not equal the resort's high standards.

Outside is a range of activities that no Northwest resort can surpass: tennis (eight courts), superb bicycling, downhill skiing at Mount Bachelor (thirty-eight miles away), cross-country skiing under peerless conditions, terrific gliding, golf on an adequate course, fishing in the Deschutes River (eight miles of which flows through the 5,500 acre resort-cum-land-development), riding, hiking, swimming, or just plain sunning. Things may seem a bit too arranged at this graphics-coordinated, $40-million resort planned to the last pious ecological sign, but it makes the finest family vacation at a full-facility resort that the Northwest can offer.

Route 97, 15 miles south of Bend
593-1221
Expensive
Credit Cards: AE, BA, MC
Dining Room Hours: 6-10 p.m.

Rock Springs Guest Ranch ☆ ☆

The setting is a lovely valley, Ponderosa pine giving way to open meadows. What makes the ranch even more attractive is its small, quality-conscious, secluded feeling. The dining room, featuring fine home-cooking, is in a lodge that displays gallery-quality western art and is not open to the general public. The cottages are comfortable, knotty-pine buildings with fireplaces, kitchens and most amenities. In addition to riding, hiking, and fishing, you can play tennis on two courts on the grounds. Summer rates are American plan and run to about $40 per person per day. In the winter, the cottages are rented to skiers.

> 64201 Tyler Road, 6 miles northwest of Bend
> 382-1957
> Expensive
> No Credit Cards

Inn of the Seventh Mountain ☆ ☆

This resort, fifteen miles from the skiing at Mount Bachelor and hence much closer than Sunriver, consists of 208 condominiums in handsome lodges on the edge of a bluff. The rooms are all furnished with a Murphy bed, a kitchen, fireplace and private deck. Rooms in building 15 have the nicest view of the mountains, and those in buildings 4, 5, and 6 overlook a pretty lake. Although the condominiums are privately owned, the decor is standardized, but stylish. The inn is a half-mile off the highway in splendid country. A small convention center, the ice-skating rink, two tennis courts, and an Olympic-size pool keep the place busy. The lodge will make arrangements for the many activities in the surrounding area: fishing, climbing, float trips and so forth. The dining room is as attractive as everything else in this landscape-cherishing resort, but the food is nothing special.

> Century Drive, 7 miles west of Bend
> 382-8711
> Expensive
> Credit Cards: BA, MC
> Pets Allowed

SISTERS

Black Butte Ranch ☆ ☆ ☆

Less well known than the famous ones, this condominium resort is probably the finest. The homes are built in dramatic angles with natural wood, and they nestle around a lodge, a heated pool, seven tennis courts and a superior golf course. You are well up into the aspen-bright mountain landscape. There are no conventions. The food at the lodge, dominantly steaks, is far better than that at the more famous resorts close to Bend. For your accommodations, you can have a sleeping room for about $25, a single room with a fireplace and a view for a few dollars more; the cabins and condominiums, where you will have complete facilities, including kitchens, go for about $40 a night in season. There is a general feeling of uncrowdedness and space, since the lovely old ranch, in its five years as a development, has developed only 250 homes, 100 of which are made available for transient rental. One has the feeling the homes have been dropped into place by helicopter, the landscaping seems so untouched. Hoodoo Bowl for skiing amid awesome scenery is twenty minutes away, and there is good fly fishing handy. One encouraging touch: fishing on the ranch is with barbless hooks only, and the trout must be thrown back.

Route 22, eight miles north of Sisters
595-6211
Expensive
Credit Cards: AE, BA, MC

WARM SPRINGS

Kah-Nee-Ta Resort ☆ ☆

This curious resort has grown up around the hot springs (92 degrees) nearby, where there is a large pool and a village of tepees on concrete pads that you can rent for a night of simulated Indian experience. The new part of the resort is a modern arrowhead-shaped motel of glass and wood looking out over the river. The resort, owned by confederated Indian tribes and partially managed by them, is aimed primarily at the convention business. The dining room offers an ambitious continental menu, with Caesar salads, peaches in champagne, live lobster, and an apricot-stuffed game hen baked in a clay pot, mixed in with the usual convention-goer fare. The rooms have balconies with nice views of the mountains, and also an electronically controlled liquor dispenser that puts forth two-ounce bottles and automatically records the transaction on your bill. Golf, fishing, biking, and Saturday night Indian dances are offered. Horses are available for rides away from the tourists and into the juniper hills.

11 miles north of Warm Springs
553-1112
Expensive
Credit Cards: AE, BA, MC

CRATER LAKE

Crater Lake ☆☆

The spectacle of this collapsed volcano, a deep blue lake set in a vast geological wonderland, is stunning. Since the accommodations at the lodge are quite poor, it makes sense to camp at Rim Village campground, where naturalists give summertime campfire talks. The two-hour launch tours from Cleetwood Cove provide the best way to see the incredible volcanic displays and to get a short course in geology. Then explore the surrounding meadows and mountains. Unfortunately this national park is small and usually jammed in the summer; winter visits are restricted to the south shore, but then the crowds have gone and the blue of the lake is even more brilliant against the snow.

THE DALLES

The Portage Inn ☆

The handsome, sand-tinted, modern structure looks fine as you approach it, and after you get over the view of the weed-choked site on which it is built, you will find some passably tasteful rooms inside. There are some other attractions: the view of the Dalles Dam from some windows (don't ask for the mountain views, since you get mostly asphalt parking lots in the foreground), some remnants of an 1891 Shaker Church on the historic grounds, and an ornate back bar in the lounge. On the other hand, you are fairly close to the freeways, the Inn attracts conventions, and the restaurant is nothing special.

Highways 80N and 197, The Dalles
298-5502
Moderate
Credit Cards: AE, BA, MC

The Dalles Tourism ☆

Here the Oregon Trail ended. Here was Celilo Falls, where Indians fished for salmon for generations until the dam submerged the falls. Here was Fort Dalles, built in a peculiarly ornate style by an interesting American architect, Andrew Jackson Downing, whose 1850 surgeon's house still remains as a museum (Fifteenth and Garrison). There are other good, small museums here as well: Carpenter's (Fourth and Union), with old tools; Nichols (Union and Fifth) for geological finds; and Winquatt (one mile east on Route 197), with Indian artifacts.

The nicest way to crown an afternoon of this reverie is to picnic at Sorossis Park, a large, shady park that is the highest overlook on the Scenic Drive through the Gorge. The Dalles Natural Foods and Dry Goods Store (314 Court Street) is the best place for getting picnic ingredients: organic produce, natural fruit juices, kefir drinks, homemade breads for sandwiches with cheeses or cashew butter, and fine fruits.

Best motel is the Tapadera (Southwest Second and Liberty, 296-9107, moderate).

HOOD RIVER

Hood River Inn ☆

It's too close to the highway, but otherwise the Inn has several advantages. Half the sixty-four rooms overlook the river and some have private balconies; the dining room and bar open out onto a deck right on the river during the summer; and the design of the building and the rooms is in a tasteful if rather incongruous Spanish motif. Food in the dining room is unexceptional, but the room is decorated with flair. You can get better food at the Red Carpet Inn along the freeway just west of town: good soup, a nice loaf of bread, decent steak, frozen seafood, poor coffee, and dreadful decor with shag carpet even climbing the walls — but at least this roadhouse is a local hangout uninfected by tourists.

> Route 35, Hood River
> 386-2200
> Moderate
> Credit Cards: AE, BA, MC
> Pets Allowed

CASCADE LOCKS

Scandian Motor Lodge ☆ ☆

Here is a rare delight: a good motel that is genuinely different. The striking architecture is beachhouse-bleak on the outside, with periscopic windows peering from the roof. Inside is a splash of color and bold Scandinavian design: brightly printed bedspreads, Norwegian wall decorations, tiled bathrooms done in authentic Scandinavian styles, and natural wood furniture. The rooms have Norwegian-style telephone showers and, for $2 extra, one room has a beautifully decorated small sauna. This is not just a motif: the owners, Jay and Gunnvor Tveidt, are as Norwegian as their names. The prices are extremely good—$16.50 for a double—and the views of the river and the Gorge, just east of the Bridge of the Gods, are quite splendid, particularly if you have a room on the second floor.

Highway 80N, Cascade Locks
374-8417
Moderate
Credit Cards: AE, BA, MC

Columbia River Gorge ☆ ☆

The landmarks are so famous they scarcely need mentioning: Multnomah Falls, the second highest in the country with a 620 foot plume in a forested glen; or Crown Point, with its sublime landscape of the serried mountains cut by the river. Here are two tips. The first is to be sure to take the 22-mile segment of the old highway, high above the modern freeway; it runs from Troutdale, outside Portland, to Cascade Locks. A second tip, if you want to see a waterfall without throngs of Kodak-snapping tourists: Oneonta Gorge is a dramatic, slippery half-mile walk in a stream bed beneath sheer, high walls, at the end of which is a secluded waterfall.

Index

THE BEST PLACES REPORT FORM

To the Editor, **The Best Places**
8 West Roy Street
Seattle, Washington 98109

_____ I Approve
_____ I Disapprove } for listing the following establishment:
_____ I Nominate

_____
_____
_____

In the space below, please describe your experience at the place:

Date of visit _____ Cost of meal/lodging: _____

I am not connected directly or indirectly with the management or
ownership of this establishment.

Signed _____